SUCH UNFORTUNATES

BY

ANDREW MANN

SUCH UNFORTUNATES

Kindle Books
A Division of Amazon, Inc.

ISBN: 9781070417912

DEDICATION

I WOULD LIKE to dedicate this book to all of those who are suffering with addiction. Those people include family members, friends, and lovers of addicts. I would also like to dedicate this book to the good people of this world that are someone's Angel and probably don't even know it. Those people, including strangers, judges, police officers, nurses, doctors, gang members, counselors, teachers, and other people who helped to save my life. I would also like to dedicate this book to all the people who harmed, hurt, abused, or hated me and whom without there probably would not be a book to write in the first place. Lastly, I would like to dedicate this book to Karen and if you finish reading this book you will know why.

CONTENTS

Dedication	v
The Crux	1
Hell	5
A "Normal" Childhood	16
Haddon Heights	19
My Mother	21
My Father	27
My Brother	30
Problems	32
Moorestown	41
Long Beach Island & Moorestown	45
Valley Forge Military Academy	49
The LSD Incident	54
Klonopin	57
High School/Girls/Cars/More Problems	59
My DUI Arrest	61
John	71
The Jen Incident	74
Mary	76
Caroline	79
Kates	82
Anxiety/Heart Attack	84
Doctors	87
Somehow, I Graduated High School	91
College	94
Kate 2/Thanksgiving Break-Up	96
Leaving College/Mike	99
The Doug Incident	106
First Cocaine USe	110

Back To College 113

Kicked Out of College 115

Atlantic City & Gambling 118

Opiates Enter The Picture 121

Working for the DEA 129

The Kate Situation 135

Breaking My Hand on Purpose 138

Valerie Returns 142

Paradise with Valerie Goes Down Hill Fast 144

First Street Buy 148

DEA Bust in Philly 153

Being Many Different People Everyday 162

Things Come to a Head 164

My First Detox 169

Hazelden 174

First "Relapse" 180

Kicked Out Again 182

Saving the Drowning Lady 184

Going to Live with My Uncle 188

Heading to California 192

Pathways/Florida 195

Alexis 196

September 11, 2001 199

Pathways Part 2/Scott 210

Second Major Relapse 213

My Brother's Wedding 215

Everything Falls Apart Again 217

Shawna 219

Back in the Saddle Again 223

Methadone 226

Megan 229

Subs & The Return of my Old Frien-emy, Klonopin 235

Inheritance/Stock Market/Engaged 237

Watching My Father Slowly Kill Himself 239

Hello, Ohio 242

Letter to Mom/Arrested 247

Coming Home After The Letter 256
Back in Rehab 260
Heroin 262
Shooting 264
Maureen 268
The Maureen Aftermath 280
North Carolina 286
Relapse in NC 288
Giving Up 292
Camden/Hell on Earth 293
Getting My Car Back 303
Driving Boosters 305
Israel 309
Speedballing 313
Losing My Car Again 315
Really Homeless 318
Drug Addict's Dream 320
North Camden 322
Where to Sleep In Camden 326
Gettig Robbed and Almost Killed 328
Paradise to Hell 332
Jail 334
Assault on a Police Officer 338
Abando 341
Giving a Girl Narcan 343
Ojas 345
The Truck 347
Terrible Winter 349
Dead Bodies/I Almost Become One 353
Gloucester County Jail 357
Overdose 364
Back To CCG 367
Hurricane Sandy 370
Sam 371
Kentucky 375
Back in CMD 379

Chris/Bear Mace Story 381

My Dad Dies While I Am in Jail 384

Paul, John, Joe Ripa, Patty the Nurse & Other Angels 387

Philadelphia Anarchists 392

Camdem Comes to an End 396

Straight & Narrow 399

Integrity House 402

Karen: My Final Angel 408

Nightmare Mike 414

Karen My Angel Continued 417

A New Life Begins 424

Afterthoughts 429

Acknowledgments 431

About the Author 433

THE CRUX

IN THE SUPPORT group known as Alcoholics Anonymous (AA), they refer to certain people as "Such Unfortunates." The AA Big Book, which is like their Bible, states: "Rarely have we seen a person fail who has thoroughly followed our path. Those who do not recover are people who cannot or will not completely give themselves to this simple program, usually men and women who are constitutionally incapable of being honest with themselves. There are such unfortunates. They are not at fault; they seem to have been born that way. They are naturally incapable of grasping and developing a way of life which demands rigorous honesty. Their chances are less than average." This paragraph basically summed me up. My chances of getting sober and surviving my addiction to heroin were, unfortunately, less than average–to put it mildly.

Whenever I would attend an AA meeting, they would always read this paragraph. It always made me think of myself and I knew that I was probably not going to make it. Strangely enough, I related more to that single paragraph than other things I had read or heard in their meetings.

The one part that they and 99.9% of the doctors, therapists, addiction specialists, and everyone else are wrong about is why I was that way and what causes people to become addicts in the first place. Their assertion that "they seem to have been born this way" is just complete nonsense. How you were born has nothing to do with why a person chooses to destroy themselves with a mood altering chemical. Heroin addiction—and any other addiction for that matter—never starts with heroin, cocaine, marijuana, alcohol, or any other drug. There are no "gateway drugs." It does not begin with some dealer coming up to you saying, "Try this! It will make you feel good." It also does not start with peers explaining, "Try this! Everybody is doing it." It does not even begin with some doctor prescribing you an addictive drug. There is no government conspiracy to make people addicts. It is not something you are born with, it doesn't run in your genes, and it is most certainly not a family disease. It has nothing to do with your age, race, sex, height, weight, or where you come from. You cannot outsmart it or be too naive to avoid it.

There is only one thing that 99% of drug addicts have in common. That one reason addicts do what they do stems from severe childhood abuse or trauma!

This abuse can be sexual, physical, emotional, or a combination of childhood trauma. I would say that most addicts have suffered from sexual abuse, which involves a lot of unimaginable incestual abuse. I am not saying that everyone who has suffered childhood abuse will become an addict, however, almost every addict I have met had this one thing – and only this one thing – in common. Every single one experienced horrible childhood trauma and most were sexually abused.

Sadly, the people that were supposed to be their protectors became their predators. They took advantage of these children for their own sexual gratification. When they do this, they kill a child's soul and innocence. In a flash it is gone forever. The child must now deal with feelings no child should ever have to endure. They will feel disgusting and unloved, and these feelings will never go away. The child no longer feels safe or protected. The child will feel as though what happened is their fault and will begin to hate themselves. This will lead to a future saturated with pain, anxiety, depression, and eventually addiction.

A Child who has been sexually abused will experience a whole host of other problems. Their lives will become a living hell, which puts them on the fast track to becoming an addict. As this child suffers in silence because they are unable to tell anyone, dishonesty becomes their most important survival mechanism as the truth is too painful. The lie becomes their truth.

The abuse also causes the child's brain to develop improperly. Compared to the brain of a non-abused child, the abused child's brain produces improper levels of serotonin, dopamine, norepinephrine, and endorphins. As a result, the child will suffer from learning disabilities, extreme boredom, depression, ADHD, anxiety, and a lack of vigor and lust for life. This child will not have the drive that pushes people to get out of bed in the morning, which makes accomplishing anything in this child's life ten times harder than it will be for everyone else.

For these young victims, normal things like school or playing sports will take an incredible amount of effort. They will also not experience enjoyment like others do when participating in these activities. They will instead start to daydream and create fantasy worlds in order to make their nightmare more bearable. The child will likely start getting into trouble by becoming a class clown, getting failing grades, quitting sports, and experimenting with drugs, alcohol, and smoking cigarettes.

They will become sexually active and lose their virginity at a very early age because they do not feel as though their body is something to be valued. They will also exhibit deep admiration for celebrities and believe that someone will love them if only they too could become famous or do something amazing.

No matter how hard they try, the abused child can only watch as everyone around them accomplishes things that they cannot. This makes them even more depressed. Soon, they are trapped within a vicious cycle of disappointment and despair.

Because their boundaries have been so violated, it will make them vulnerable to being taken advantage of by bullies and manipulators who find them to be easy targets. As a result, the abused child will fail at creating healthy relationships and secure boundaries with their peers because they simply do not know how.

Their intimate relationships will not be healthy ones because they feel revulsion with themselves. The abused child grows up disbelieving how or why another person could love them. They will practice dishonesty and their lies will inflict even more damage on these relationships that are based around jealousy and "all or nothing" terms.

These situations will happen and the child will not understand why. They will start to think they are just bad, a mistake, evil, gross, unloved, and a failure, then begin hating themselves even more as a result.

I know this because that child was me. I experienced all of these horrible things. I was engulfed in this nightmare before I had a chance to understand and dealt with it the best I could, which created the ideal environment for my drug addiction to manifest.

During childhood, I thought my life was bad and could not get much worse, but I was in for a big surprise. I was about to go to hell and back and live to tell about it!

HELL

I AM SEARCHING the floor of an abandoned house in Camden, NJ. Camden is one of the poorest, most crime ridden cities in the United States, if not the worst.

In Camden, there are drug dealers on every corner and it has the highest murder rate in the country. Rapes, robberies, and physical assaults are commonplace. Most of the city's residents are down-and-out and everywhere they look, abandoned homes and buildings stare back at them. Most people in the surrounding neighborhoods lock their car doors when traveling through Camden, or just try to avoid it altogether.

My search is for a usable needle among all the broken ones, which are everywhere I look in this "abando," as they are commonly referred to in Camden. "Abando" is slang for an abandoned home. Drug addicts use these to get high or seek shelter, and sometimes for both.

I need to find a needle, so I can inject the heroin I just bought. This is my only way of getting one as I am flat broke. I am currently in heroin withdrawal and need to inject heroin as soon as possible. I am in a panicked state not because I want to get high, but because I am feeling sick. At this point, I am just trying to get well! The withdrawal from heroin is something that every heroin addict fears. Words barely give it the justice it truly deserves.

Drugs such as heroin and other opiates are naturally derived from opium poppy alkaloids or created synthetically, and either process can be accomplished legally or illegally. Heroin, codeine, morphine, oxycodone, and fentanyl erase pain and produce feelings of euphoria. That euphoria is what keeps addicts coming back for more.

After repeated use of heroin or other opiates like heroin, your body becomes dependent on them. When you abruptly stop using them, your body goes into withdrawal.

Your body will adapt to the opiates by shutting down all your natural feel-good chemicals like dopamine. The more you use and the longer you use, the more addicted your body becomes. When you attempt to suddenly stop—all hell breaks loose. You will experience an awful mind-body illness like nothing you have ever experienced before.

At first, the withdrawal creeps up on you in the form of severe agitation and restlessness. Then a wave of panic engulfs you. Suddenly, you are in a dark ocean and a great white shark is chasing you. The shark is the withdrawal, and your brain is convinced that you must get high in order to swim to safety.

Depression then starts to accompany the fear. It is so bad that it feels as if all your loved ones are dying on the same day. You can start crying at the dumbest commercial on TV. If one of those homeless animal commercials comes on while you are in withdrawal, you will dissolve into a complete mess.

Time starts to slow as everything becomes boring and joyless. Life feels blander than ever. It is as if you are sitting in a movie theater for twenty-four hours straight watching the stalest black-and-white film to ever be produced.

You are now in a world completely devoid of joy where hopelessness, severe depression, overwhelming fear, anxiety, and suicidal thoughts creep into your mind. This is only the mental part of the withdrawal, which is just the beginning.

Now, not only do you have to deal with a mental anguish the likes of which you have never known or could have imagined, you also have the physical horrors to look forward to. Horrors that are going to affect every area of your body in awful ways; ways that most people have only experienced in movies.

To put this into perspective, I met a woman in rehab who had brain, breast, and liver cancer. She endured horrible chemo and radiation treatments and recalled how awful they were, but said they were nothing compared to what she experienced when she decided to kick a bad opiate habit cold turkey.

The first thing that happens is you start yawning uncontrollably and your eyes water profusely. Then, everything in your body starts to ache in awful pain; even your hair hurts. Your nose runs like a waterfall. Your back throbs and your head feels as though you have a 106-degree fever. Your legs cramp and ache, like you just ran a marathon. Your pupils become so dilated that any light feels blinding like a flashlight shining directly into your eyes. Every sound is like nails on a chalkboard. Your heart pounds loudly against your chest, making breathing difficult. You sweat profusely while feeling like you are freezing cold. Your skin is crawling and covered in goosebumps. Your stomach is on fire. You have cramps, uncontrollable diarrhea, dry heaving, constant nausea, acid in your throat, and projectile vomiting. Your muscles twitch non-stop with spasms throughout your entire body and you get the worst restless leg syndrome you can imagine. You can't eat, drink, or sleep, and getting into a comfortable position is out of the question.

It is, bar none, the worst feeling you can imagine multiplied by a thousand and it is assaulting your entire body. I have heard people compare it to a really bad flu and I laugh because, to me, they are comparing a paper airplane to a military fighter jet.

The only way to make this hellish nightmare stop quickly is to use heroin or which ever opiate you are addicted to. The other option is to wait it out until it gets better. This could take anywhere from three days to three months depending on the amount and length of your addiction.

To give you an idea of what waiting it out feels like... imagine starving yourself for three days. Get to the point where you are so hungry that you just can't take it anymore. Now, take a collection of your favorite foods and place them in front of you; the catch is you can't eat any of them. That is exactly what the craving feels like when you try to wait it out. Now, imagine that feeling for three months straight, twenty-four hours a day, seven days a week.

So, let's say you made it through a week of suffering, and you use heroin one time to get some relief. One slip up and you are right back to where you started. You must either start using again regularly or begin the withdrawal all over from the beginning. By giving into the drug, that week of unbelievable suffering and incredible will power meant very little and you accomplished nothing. It is akin to self-torture.

I don't care how tough a person you think you are or how strong-minded you are, if you take that robust craving and add in the horrible sickness, then try to endure this for hours, let alone months, there is little chance anyone will succeed at beating their addiction. There needs to be either a jail or rehab type of setting to even have a chance at accomplishing this.

Once you feel this awful sickness, nothing else matters except getting well! I could care less that these needles I found may be contaminated with terrible diseases like AIDS, hep C, or whatever. I can worry about that later. For example, all those people that jumped to their deaths on 9/11… To the people on the ground, this appeared to be a completely irrational act, but to the people with the fire at their backs, it was their only option. Right now, I have a fire on my back.

The abandoned house I am in has no windows and is completely stripped of anything of value. The inside looks like a bomb hit. It is very dark, smells awful, and trash is everywhere. There is writing all over the walls. Things like, "God help me" and "Why me?" and "How the fuck did I end up like this?" Pretty much everything I and every addict who has stared at these same walls is thinking!

I can see the tools of drug addicts everywhere I look. There are milk crates set up as chairs, a makeshift table topped with burnt candles, aluminum cans with burn marks, little metal cookers provided by the needle exchange, used cotton balls(which addicts use as a filter to suck the heroin into a needle), and cigarette butts. Most importantly, there are hundreds of used needles, many of which are broken or bent beyond usability.

I sift through the needles sticking myself as I try to find a usable one. Finally, I find a workable needle and try to rinse out the blood. I am not doing this because I'm worried about what terrible thing could be in the blood; I am doing this because something much worse could happen… It could clog the needle and ruin my shot!

I grab a can and try to hold its bottom still. This is hard because I am shaking so badly. I open the two bags of heroin I just bought around the corner and empty the contents into the can's bottom. I also pour in one bag of cocaine, which by itself you would never use while in withdrawal, but the heroin will counteract the cocaine's intensity in about five seconds. The heroin alone is just not enough for me anymore. I need the rush of cocaine, too.

I have drawn up 30cc of water into the needle, which I spray into the can's bottom. Next, I pull the plunger from the back of the needle and use it to mix everything together until it all becomes a liquid. Putting the plunger back into the needle, I then rip a piece of cotton from a used cigarette butt and work it into a small ball. I drop that ball into the mixture and use it as a filter between the liquid and the needle's tip. I draw back on the plunger and notice that the mixture has grown to 40cc, which tells me that the cocaine is very good quality.

My stomach becomes a storm of fluttering butterflies as my whole body is screaming out for me to inject this mixture and to do it– right now! My tongue is stuck to the roof of my mouth because it is like a scorched desert. My heart is literally beating out of my chest. I am now ready for liftoff.

Desperately, I search for a vein in my arm, which are bulging because the belt I was wearing is now fastened around my bicep. I push the needle into a vein. It enters painfully ripping my skin because the needle's tip is dull from multiple uses. After I feel it is in, I pull back on the plunger to be sure red blood comes back in letting me know that I am in the vein and clear to inject. I watch the red blood fill the needle, then slowly and steadily push the plunger in. The mixture exits the needle and enters my bloodstream.

Immediately, I taste the cocaine in my tongue. The taste is unlike anything else in this world; a sickly-sweet chemical taste that lets me know the rush is about to begin. The cocaine rush starts to hit me as it quickly builds to a climax. I feel as if I am on a rollercoaster doing a freefall. Dopamine floods my brain a thousand times faster than any natural way ever could. My ears begin ringing as if I am in a tunnel with a freight train coming straight at me. I feel as though my heart is about to explode, which is almost too much to handle, but thankfully at that very moment the heroin takes over in the form of a warm, calming wave of pure euphoria. Suddenly, everything slows down. I have reached the end of the roller coaster and am now on a different, but even more pleasurable ride.

The euphoria of heroin is so much better than any natural feeling your brain can produce. It is like an endless orgasm, but much more intense. The whole world immediately becomes a rose-colored happy place. All the bad things have their volume turned down or their murmur flat out disappears. You feel so good, it's like you just won the lottery, threw the winning touchdown in the Super Bowl, and married the girl of your dreams all at the same time.

Any pain or ache is gone, all insecurities have vanished, depression has been vanquished, and you do not feel sick anymore. Your whole world is now perfect and you are feeling completely content. Within thirty seconds, you have gone from rock bottom to being on top of the world.

I pull the needle out of my vein and release a deep breath. I just dodged a bullet; the same bullet I have dodged a thousand times already. Blood comes trickling down my arm from the needle wound and I wipe it away with my shirt. Having done this hundreds of times, my shirt has completely changed colors.

My clothes have not been washed or changed in weeks. My pants are covered in blood stains and holes. My shoes have holes in them and are falling apart. I have not showered in months and smell horrible. If you were standing next to me, you would probably get sick.

I am so skinny that you can see my rib cage; just like the people in the Holocaust pictures. My arms are covered in track marks and abscesses. My left foot is broken in three places and I have no idea how this happened. I have a urinary tract infection that is a lot more painful than my broken foot. In addition, my nose is broken, and I have six staples in the back of my head. I also have no money, no ID, no phone, no car, no family, and nowhere to live.

I have been sleeping in the basement of an abandoned house where two people were murdered. Rats run over me all night as I sleep, and gunshots have become such a regular occurrence that they don't bother me anymore.

My own "family" has completely given up on me. I use the word family loosely. Still, there is no one to turn to. My life is worse than I could have ever imagined in my worst nightmare, but as I sit high on heroin, none of that matters.

I am content being high and not having anyone bothering me. My only concern is where I am going to get more drugs when this wears off. I glance at the wall of this abandoned house and notice a name written on the wall. That name is Ferra, which sticks out to me.

The reason it is significant is because Ferra looks like Ferrari. I have always loved Ferraris ever since I was a young kid. It comes to mind that less than three years prior I had been behind the wheel of a convertible Ferrari in beautiful South Florida. I had a place to live, a girlfriend, money in the bank, friends, family and all the things most people take for granted in their daily lives.

I never really appreciated things like that before. Once they were taken from me, I never took them for granted again. That is one of the gifts you receive from addiction. You get this ability to appreciate every little thing you have, no matter how small. Things like waking up and not being drug sick, having food to eat, a place to sleep, or even heat are blessings, but most people never think twice about them.

For a moment, I think about how far down my life has gone since Florida. Now that I have heroin in my system, my appetite has also come back. I imagine being able to go to McDonald's and buy whatever food I want. Every penny I get goes toward drugs. The only food I eat now is from a church that gives out food every day to the homeless. I think about all the times my parents wanted me to go out to dinner with them and I said no. I think about all the times I threw food out. I start to think about what life will be like if I can ever beat this addiction.

Thinking this way is not helpful to me in my present situation. I have been told that I am a "hopeless case" who will "never beat this addiction" and that I will "die from drugs" so many times that it does not even phase me anymore. I believe it. I just hope it happens before I suffer much more. I decide to take a couple of minutes to enjoy the high before I must get back to work.

The "work" I am referring to is finding a way to make money by whatever means necessary, like stealing, begging, panhandling, selling needles, and walking people to buy drugs and other things. I need at least ten dollars to buy a bag of heroin plus five dollars to buy a small bag of cocaine. I am living my life fifteen dollars at a time.

When I finally get fifteen dollars, I run to North Camden to buy drugs and get high. Then, I get back to "work" and the cycle begins again–repeating itself over and over and over again. It never ends. Your body never stops getting sick and there are no time-outs or breaks. You become a prisoner in your own body constantly racing against the sickness. Catching the next high to keep the monster at bay is always on your mind–twenty-four hours a day.

I am stuck on a nightmarish merry-go-round pulling me further into a downward spiral: Avoid the sickness… score drugs potent enough to feel high for a few minutes… forget how awful my present situation is… rinse and repeat.

Homeless addicts in Camden support their habit in four main ways. Besides prostitution, which is mainly a female's way of making money in Camden, the most common way to make money is to boost. Boosting is when addicts rob stores outside of Camden, then bring the products back to sell to the bodegas, or corner stores, in

Camden. They mainly steal Prilosec, Zyrtec, Rogaine, and Mach 3 razor blades. I tried this and was very unsuccessful. The first time I tried, I was arrested.

Other addicts will scrap metal and sell it to scrap yards. However, there are two major problems with scraping. First, you must steal the metal because not many people have valuable metals just laying around in their trash. Second, you or someone you know must have access to a truck to transport the metal to and from the scrap yards. Most homeless drug addicts in Camden do not have vehicles, so they need someone with a truck to make real money. I tried scraping and was also arrested.

The third way is to beg. This is the most embarrassing and degrading way to make money and there are several ways you can go about it. One way is to walk around the Transportation Center asking people for money as they are waiting for a bus. Another method is to stand in front of McDonald's or Dunkin Donuts and ask people for their change. Or you can make a sign stating you are homeless, then stand at a light on a highway off ramp. I tried each of the schemes, too, and as you can probably guess, I was arrested.

The fourth way is to sell needles from the Needle Exchange. The Needle Exchange would give out hundreds of needles once a week. Addicts would stock up on them, then stand at the entrance to North Camden and sell the needles for two or three dollars apiece to people going to buy drugs. Surely, if I had attempted this method, too, I would have ended up in jail.

Once arrested, you will get to visit a place no addict—or any human being for that matter—wants to go to: Camden County Jail.

This is one of three ends to drug addiction. The other two involve institutions and death. I have experienced all three and the worst of them, in my opinion, is jail. It is such an awful ordeal being crammed into a cage with men inches from you twenty hours a day with no privacy. I believe death might be a better option, especially for those with a life sentence.

At this point, you are probably wondering why anyone in their right mind would choose to live this way.

The answer is very simple, they don't! No one wants to live this way. It is a direct result of an abusive childhood or severe trauma. Before I judge someone, I try to put myself in their shoes. So, now I will try to give you an idea of what living in my shoes was like.

A "NORMAL" CHILDHOOD

I WAS BORN in Woodbury, New Jersey at Underwood Hospital. I was raised in a town called Haddon Heights until age ten, then we moved to the upscale town of Moorestown. This is where I spent the remainder of my childhood and attended high school.

My mother and father were named Ellen and George. They met in college and married a few years later. I also had an older brother named Adam who was two and a half years older than me.

My father George was the Vice President of a local hospital. In the fifties, his parents had come to the United States from England. They lived in West Islip, New York on a lagoon. His father worked for AT&T while his mother was a homemaker. My grandfather Basil was a sweet man with a very kind and gentle personality. Later in life he developed Alzheimer's disease and passed away, which was very sad to watch.

My grandmother Rita was a very pretty woman, even in her old age. For some reason she was always very angry and had a terrible temper. She raised my father by screaming and yelling at him. He had a sister that she was very hard on as well. My aunt was not pretty like her mother and my grandmother let her know this. She even made her feel as if this was her fault. She would tell her to lose weight, change her hairstyle, dress better, and things like that. She did it out of anger and not out of love and concern.

My father hated the way his mother treated him and his sister. Instead of learning from her mistakes and doing the opposite of his mother, my father became just like her and raised us with non-stop anger. I believe he even had a much worse temper, which is hard to believe if you met my grandmother. This is an old woman who was kicked out of a DMV and the workers pleaded with us to never bring her back. She was that difficult to deal with.

At times, my father would have the sweet side of his father, but these instances were few and far between. Anger and rage dominated my father's personality. This led him to have a miserable life for the most part as did those around him. Happy family times were always accompanied by my father's angry outbursts. We lived in constant fear of my father's temper, which caused us to walk on eggshells our entire lives.

My mother worked for an outplacement firm that found people jobs. Her parents were named George and Gwen. She had two brothers, both of whom were strange because of the abuse they suffered from my grandfather.

My grandfather was an engineer for Campbell Soup Company. He had his own company, which Campbell Soup ended up acquiring. They then hired him to run it for them. His company grew mushrooms, and he had a hand in developing Penicillin and making it available for many people.

My grandfather was a multi-millionaire. His father had been a patent attorney who collected money from about sixty patents he held for different inventions. He owned a lot of land in Gettysburg,

Pennsylvania, which included a large section of a mountain, some land with a beautiful stream that he eventually sold, and another small plot of land that had a home, which later burnt down after it was struck by lightning.

While he was very rich, he was also a very cheap man. He was extremely anal about everyone turning off lights when they left a room, drove an old beat up car, and basically wore the same three suits for years.

He never flaunted his money and was very humble. He was involved with the church, but he never really settled on one religion. He went from Catholic to Protestant and on his deathbed, he said he wished he had become Jewish. Even with all his admirable traits, my grandfather was a very sick and disturbed man.

He was very much into young girls and always had them around. He was always taking pictures of them which bothered my mother and uncles when they were growing up. I am convinced beyond a shadow of a doubt that he molested my mother and her two brothers, which indirectly led to my drug addiction.

My grandmother was a sweet half-Jewish woman. I think she knew what was happening in her family but lacked the power to stop it. This made her depression and other mental illnesses much worse.

The combination of having a mentally ill mother and a sick, predatory father was what created my mother. This is the part that makes me feel bad for my mother, but the fact that she could not recognize and break the cycle is something I will never understand.

HADDON HEIGHTS

HADDON HEIGHTS IS where things first started to go wrong. Being so young, I had no idea what was going on and why certain things were happening, which just confuses a child's mind and makes childhood even more difficult than it already is.

Haddon Heights was a Norman Rockwell type of town. It was basically an all-white, middle class, crime-free, safe place to live. It was not a large town, with around 12,000 people. It had three elementary schools and one high school. The local swim club was named Haddon Glen and played a big part in the town.

The Haddon Glen swim club was in a huge area with three large pools. One pool was very deep and had a high dive while the others were easier to swim in because they were only a few feet deep. You had to pass certain requirements and receive particular bands before you were allowed to swim in each pool.

It was an extremely fun place and enjoyed by many families. One of the greatest parts of childhood was becoming a member of the swim team where you learned all the different strokes. We had practices and participated in swim meets against other swim clubs, so not only did you learn to swim, but you also learned about competition. They had different age groups so everyone could swim in races regardless of age or ability.

Swimming in the swim club was one of my only fond memories of childhood. It was a blast hanging out with everyone at the swim meets where we would compete against another town's swim club. It made you feel a part of something. Plus, I really enjoyed competing and it was nice just being around friends.

I also played baseball for the little league teams and was one of the best players in my age group for our whole town. I became a pitcher, which meant the game was in my hands. After we won an all-star game against another town, a lot of pressure was put on me for the upcoming year.

Most of my childhood up to this point seemed normal from the outside. Behind closed doors, things were different. One of my earliest memories was when I was in first grade. I kept dropping my pencil under the table to look up the teacher's skirt and was doing this obsessively. At a young age I was thinking about sex and older women. Strange things also started to happen with my mother.

MY MOTHER

MY MOTHER WAS a very sick and disturbed woman, but when you are eight years old, there is no way to comprehend this. I just knew that I felt strange and disgusted by my own mother and I wasn't sure why. I was convinced there must be something wrong with me.

As was the case with my father, my mother also had traits from her father and mother. Sadly, she took almost all the worst parts from her father and her mother except for her mother's giving nature.

My mother suffered from severe depression just like her mother had and there were times when she would be bedridden for days. She would cry out to my brother and me for help because my father was not around or at work. I hated to see my mother like this and tried to avoid her as much as possible. I was told that as a baby I was very close to my mother, but as time went on, I gravitated toward my father and never swayed.

Later I came to understand that my mother was probably molested by her father. This killed her ability to really show love, even to her own child. As a baby, you can sense in the same way an animal can if someone really loves you. Eventually, I think I was able to sense that my mother was incapable of showing me real love and looked to my father for the love I desired and needed in order to flourish.

My mother viewed me as a tool for her sexual gratification and to appease her. The more I shied away from her as most children would, the more resentment she developed toward me and started demonstrating favoritism toward my older brother.

My older brother went in the complete opposite direction as me. He started to have an unhealthy love for my mother. This led him to hate me and resent my father. He wanted our mother all to himself.

When we were very young, he would become insanely jealous, hateful, and hurtful toward me. So much so that he was more like my worst enemy than my brother. I do not blame him completely. The sexual abuse my brother also faced from my mother led him to be incapable of feeling normal emotions and brotherly love. Most brothers will fight with each other, but deep down they truly do love one another and have each other's backs. My brother never "had my back." In fact, he kicked it more than anyone else.

While I can still remember some of the sexual abuse my brother and I suffered, some memories exist as broken pieces while others are foggy and unclear. It is as though my brain is protecting me by allowing me to remember everything that happened in vivid detail except for the abuse, like a curse word edited from movie dialogue; a defense mechanism that blocks a person from remembering something that is too awful to think about.

I can remember bits and pieces. For example, my mother would take a bath with my brother and show us how to insert a tampon while she was naked.

She would grab our penises and other things mothers should not do with children. I would tell her to stop and my brother would say she needed to do this so we could go to the bathroom. I remember her pushing her vagina in my face and it disgusted me so badly that it caused me to have problems with women for many years afterward.

While growing up, I would have the most horrible ear infections. It got to the point where I was crying from the excruciating pain, so the doctor put tubes in my ears. Years later I found out that forcing a child to perform oral sex on a woman can cause this. I am not sure if that is what caused it, but my ear infections left me in agonizing pain as a child and they continued for an unusually long time.

My mother would only be protective of us if a girl was around. Her jealousy and possessiveness made her hate these types of situations. I can remember one such incident when a little girl in the neighborhood pulled her pants down in front of us. When my mother found out, she got so furious that she pulled us into the car and said if we wanted to see a naked girl, she was going to show us herself.

As I think back, my mother's inappropriate actions went back as far as I can remember, and they occurred almost daily. She would wear shirts with no underwear and would purposely bend over right in front of me. When I would move or look away, she would glare at me in disgust.

Sadly, my mother never seemed to grasp that what she was doing was wrong and causing damage to her children. I truly believe she felt it was her right to do these things to us because the same things were done to her by her father.

Instead of taking responsibility for her own actions, she claimed that she was a victim every chance she got and became a professional at it. This became her defense mechanism and rationality for all her inappropriate actions.

She would tell anyone who would listen about how bad she had it. First with my father when we were young, she said how hard it was on her because he was so angry all the time. Then she wanted people to feel pity for her because of how bad of a child she said I was. After my father lost his job, she told everyone how horrible it was for her to have a husband who lost his job. She even claimed to be a victim of my brother's when he moved away from her. She told everyone that he had deserted her. Above all, her worst demonstration of victimhood was how she handled my drug addiction because, in her mind, she was the one and only true victim.

She would lie to her friends and say she simply could not understand why I would use drugs when I had such a loving mother who did so much for me. She knew damn well what her part was in all of it, but completely left out these important details.

Whenever I did anything wrong, she would announce it to every one of her friends. Almost all of which would show concern for me instead of anger, and that upset her. She wanted reassurance that she was being badly done, too.

When she finally found a woman that would agree with her, it completely backfired on her. After all, no mother would tell another mother to desert her son unless that person was not a great person to begin with. A mother's love is supposed to be the strongest bond there is.

The woman my mom befriended willingly told my mom that she was right and agreed that she had an awful son and a horrible family. It should have come as no surprise when this "friend" left her in her time of need and let her own son rob my parents' home after Hurricane Sandy. When questioned by police, she said, "Well, her son is a drug addict. He probably did it!"

Her son also falsely claimed that I had broken into all the houses in our neighborhood. He said this to throw police off his trail because it sounded believable to say that a drug addict was responsible. It was a complete lie, but the police were thrown off by it. The only house I ever "broke" into was my own. Luckily Tom, one of our neighbors, stuck up for me and explained to the police that I never broke into anyone's house.

The part my mother didn't understand was how this woman could turn against her. She couldn't see that the only reason this lady sided with her was because she herself was not a good person. When you trash your family, not only is that a reflection on you, but if someone agrees with you, they probably are not the kind of friend you want around. My parents had taken this woman out on their boat and invited her over for the holidays because she had no one. I remember one of our other neighbors had said how unattractive she was, but he wasn't speaking about her looks he was talking about her personality. He said what an ugly woman she is – inside and out. Her son, the same one who robbed our home, eventually ended up in his bathroom trying to commit suicide that summer. But my mother, by trashing her family, had put this lady in a position to take advantage of her which she did.

By trashing her family to this woman, my mother inadvertently put this "friend" in the perfect position to take advantage of her. In fact, one of my mother's friends asked her, "Why in God's name would you tell a person like this all these bad things about your family?" My mother also couldn't believe that this woman's children had problems, too, and she had never said a bad word about them to her. She felt betrayed, but when you find someone low enough to agree that you should desert your family, what else would you expect, I thought.

Moorestown, which is a very wealthy town and home to some very successful people, gives outsiders the impression that they must be incredibly stuck up, but most of them were good people who showed concern for me. Although, being around people with money, and money in general for that matter, has always been a blessing and a curse for me.

The only way my mother ever showed any love was through her

checkbook, but that came with strings. If she ever bought you something, you were reminded of it for life. There were no free rides. Things were never bought because of "love." She always looked at it as though that money could have gone to her. This was another of the bad traits she picked up from her father.

Living with a mother like mine was a nightmare at best. I don't think she really grasped the devastation her actions caused me. Most people who are sexually abused are victimized by a friend or relative, but they still have a loving parent at home to guide them. For me, there was none of that. For example, while most incestual abuse is done by a father, the child still has a loving mother to turn to and lean on.

The only person I could turn to was an angry father who unleashed fits of rage, and the only thing worse than dealing with my mother was having to deal with my mother and father together.

MY FATHER

MY FATHER WAS not so much of a bad man as he was a flawed man. He never sexually abused us, but he would often dish out emotional abuse and had repeated anger out-bursts daily. His temper had a hair trigger, and everything had to be his way. We had to be quiet and obey his every command or he would flip out. His anger would ebb and flow, but it was always there.

I remember how he would take a nap as soon as he came home from work. If we made any noise or woke him up, there was hell to pay. Looking back at family videos, five minutes can't go by without hearing him yelling or screaming. Often telling me angrily, "Get over here!" or, "Do this now!" and, "Andrew, now, damn it!"

My whole family lived in constant fear of my father and his heated outbursts. My father also exaggerated a lot. I was never taught the value of honesty from neither him nor my mother. My father and my mother's actions taught me the value of lying from as young of an age as I can remember.

My father lived as unhealthy a life as possible. There was a point where my father smoked five packs of cigarettes a day. He couldn't make it through a shower without smoking. As soon as his alarm clock went off in the morning, he would light a cigarette first before turning it off. Eventually, this led to him having a heart attack and being forced to quit. In fact, he blamed his heart attack on me. Not his smoking five packs a day or being overweight and not exercising.

He once took us on a canoe trip to the Pine Barrens in New Jersey. As usual, it was turning into a "family nightmare." He was yelling from the minute we got there to the minute we left. "Get in this damn canoe," and, "Paddle right! Paddle left! Stop!" As an eight-year-old, I didn't know what to do. Three months later when he had a heart attack, he blamed it on me for not paddling correctly during the canoe trip and the anger it caused him. Sadly, I believed him and blamed myself for almost killing my father.

Anywhere we went with my father, he would get angry just like he did during the canoe trip. I hated doing anything with him. The crazy part was that he could be completely normal around other people for short periods of time. I couldn't understand why he was able to stop himself from going crazy whenever a friend or someone else was around, but he couldn't do that with us.

I developed many phobias because of the sexual abuse. Two of which were public restrooms and peeing in front of others. These phobias would haunt me for life.

There were so many things in life that were more difficult than they should have been, or I simply could not do them because I was unable to pee in public. I could not pee for employment drug tests, during school or in the military, on planes or buses, or any public place for that matter unless I was completely alone. Later in life, I even went to a hypnotist that boasted a ninety-five percent success rate curing people with what they called a "shy bladder." That also failed.

My "shy bladder" was the most extreme case the doctor had ever seen. It was nothing for me to drink two gallons of water and not be able to pee if people were watching me. I remember in the army processing station being the only person who could not pee with hundreds of people around me. They thought I was trying to hide something, but it was just impossible for me to go.

My father would get so angry when I couldn't pee, he would just start screaming and hitting the steering wheel. He would yell, "Just go, god damn it! Go! You have five minutes to pee, Gooooooo!!!" During most vacations and any other time I was away from home, it was not uncommon for me to painfully hold in a pee for up to eight hours or longer.

My dad's anger was also an embarrassment to us. I remember going to a Philadelphia Phillies game with him. My dad hated curse words and a man behind us kept saying, "Fuck the Philly Phanatic," so my father challenged him to a fight. Things became so heated that they threw us all out of the stadium.

On the way home, he almost hit someone in the street, so the guy called him an "asshole." My dad immediately stopped the car in anticipation of fighting him, which caused my brother and I to burst out laughing. When we got home, he pulled us out of the car, then hit us. He didn't hit us that hard, but it was still another great "family nightmare" fun night!

My father never showed love in normal ways. He never once said, "I love you." Throughout my whole life, neither my mother nor my father ever told us that they loved us, not once. I still believe my dad loved us in his own way, but he was simply not a good father in the way he should have been.

MY BROTHER

My brother Adam was probably the worst brother a kid could hope for. While I was more athletic, better looking, and had many more friends, he was more concerned with being a good student and pleasing my parents.

Even though we suffered similar abuse, his experiences were not to the same extent as mine. I believe that he either completely blacked most of it out or became fond of it. Like I said before, he became obsessed with my mother and craved her attention. He never viewed me as a brother, but more of an obstacle; something that was in his way.

He had such a disease of jealousy that I think it stemmed from the abuse as well as family genetics because my mother's brother was the same way. Instead of wanting me to do well, my brother wanted to see me fail. He enjoyed causing me pain, especially emotional pain. He would literally spend his time thinking up ways to harass me.

When I was about six years old, he started telling me I was fat. He would literally follow me around day and night calling me everything from "fat boy" to "lard butt" to "whale." Even though I was as skinny as a rail, when you are told nonstop that you are fat, you start to believe it. He didn't do it in a playful way either. My brother was sinister and calculated.

He would get so much joy when he saw me crying. It got to the point where no matter what I ate, he would say, "Fat boy shouldn't eat." No matter what I wore, he would tell me, "You look fat in those clothes." If I was wearing a bathing suit, he would announce that I looked fat in it. I can remember one instance when he got our entire group of friends to chant, "There's a whale in the pool!" Granted, the whole time I was skinnier than him and most of our friends.

This was one of the first disorders I developed. For many years after, no matter how thin I was, I always thought I was fat. Even at six years old, I was making myself throw up after eating.

I could never wrap my head around why my brother treated me this way when I never showed jealousy toward him or would say mean things to him. I never called him fat or any other derogatory words, and I never laughed at him or encouraged others to do this. I just wanted him to be my brother. However, no matter how nice I was to him, it never made a difference. Things kept going from bad to worse.

My brother became my worst enemy. He even convinced kids in the town to hate me. When I was being bullied by older kids, he couldn't care less about protecting his younger brother and would join in.

PROBLEMS

THE FIRST REAL sign that there was something wrong with me was when I was held back in kindergarten for what they deemed a "learning disability." Another common denominator of children who have been sexually abused is being held back in kindergarten and/or being diagnosed with one or more learning disabilities.

When you are abused, it can manifest as a learning disability or Attention Deficit/Hyperactivity Disorder (ADHD). In fact, I strongly believe a lot of learning disabilities are a direct result of some sort of abuse or trauma. Essentially, the abuse manifests itself in ways that resemble learning disabilities. While other kids are interested in learning, the abused child is busy trying to peek under the teacher's skirt, daydreaming about being someone else, and so forth.

For example, if I broke someone's legs and they tried to run, but were unable to, some people would say he has a running disability. While they are not wrong, the real problem isn't that he can't run because his legs aren't working like others do; the problem is his legs were broken by me. This is the issue that needs addressing rather than just saying this person has a running disability. Someone broke his legs, which is what truly needs to be addressed and fixed.

Then came the brick throwing incident. One day I was in my back-yard with my brother and our friend Kevin. My brother got Kevin to chant that I was an "adopted fat pig-beast that no one loved." He kept repeating this over and over, and over again. Eventually, I picked up a brick and threw it at Kevin, hitting him square in the head.

He had to get stitches and was left with a scar across his forehead. I still remember my brother smiling about how mad I had made my parents. To make matters worse, he told them that he and Kevin were just minding their own business playing in the backyard when, out of nowhere, I came up and clocked Kevin with the brick. My mom of course believed him and said what an embarrassment I was to her as Kevin's mom was her best friend. Things like this continued throughout childhood.

One night, there was a bad thunderstorm. At this point, I had de-veloped extreme anxiety about sleeping alone in my room with the lights out and the door closed. The darkness scared the hell out of me.

My father had gone away somewhere, which left my brother and I alone with my mom. This situation put me in a very bad position because it meant that I could either be sexually abused by my moth-er or my brother would be endlessly harassing me.

I'm not sure why this event sticks out to me, but I remember it as clearly as if it happened last night. As usual, I wanted to leave my door open while I slept because the dark scared me. My brother knew this and purposely closed it, then told my mom to make sure it stayed closed, so she came and told me it was staying closed no matter what. I guess the combination of the thunderstorm and the pitch-black room caused me to be extra terrified. As soon as they closed that door, I panicked and started screaming with fear.

My mother and brother were in my mom's room and I could hear them laughing together hysterically. The louder I screamed, the harder they laughed. This continued for what seemed like forever. It is still hard to imagine a mother laughing at her panic-stricken child while they are screaming with terror. This was the first time I seriously considered suicide. I remember looking out the window wondering if I would die if I jumped out.

The next big problem that developed was when all my friends turned against me. There was a local girl named Valerie and all the boys I knew thought she was the prettiest girl my age. One day at the swim club, she asked me if I would go on a date with her.

I was nine years old and this was a big deal to all the boys my age. Up to this point, I had been friends with everyone in town. I had about twenty friends over before the date and they all wanted to know if I was going to kiss her and things like that. I could see my brother inside pacing furiously. He hated the fact Valerie asked me out and it enraged him that I had friends over.

There was a kid named Luigi who lived on the opposite side of town who was infatuated with Valerie, but she said that he creeped her out because he was always following her around. He became so jealous that she asked me out that he told people he wanted to fight me. I really didn't know him very well at that point and some kids were frightened of him, but I was a tough kid and fighting didn't scare me. Although, he became friends with my friend Jess, and Jess' family was close with my family. His brother Drew and my brother were friends and our parents would get together on birthdays, New Year's, and other such events.

The night I went on a date with Valerie, we attended a Phillies game. Soon, everyone started calling us boyfriend and girlfriend, but this is when my friendships started to change.

A friend told me that Luigi was very jealous and was trying to turn kids against me. He said my brother had told him all these horrible things about me and even told the other kids that I had some contagious disease he had just created out of thin air. I really didn't understand what this whole thing was about, but when I found out my brother was part of it, I became extremely worried.

My fears became a reality when he came home one day and said, "You think you're so cool because Valerie asked you out. Well, all the kids are starting to hate you and siding with Luigi. Luigi told everyone he can beat you up and I know he can."

To which I replied, "What the hell are you talking about? I don't even know Luigi. Why are you people even sitting around talking about me?" He laughed, "Just wait till you see everyone again. They all hate you!"

I found it hard to believe that everyone would hate me and believe I had some horrible disease, but quickly found out that my brother was speaking the truth. I can remember the following day at the swim club and some kids said something like, "There goes the freak with that contagious disease," and some girls said, "Stay away from him."

I remember the next time we all played football together, no one wanted to be on my team. I was usually always the first person picked and now my so-called friends didn't even want to be on my team. Since my brother told them all that I was a liar with a catchy disease, kids from across town that I didn't even know well kept saying, "Don't throw the ball to 'sick boy.'" It felt so awkward having all these kids–especially the ones I considered to be my friends–treating me as though I should be confined to a leper colony.

Things also changed for me at school. Word got around and everyone started treating me different too. The kids in my school stayed away from me, so I started eating alone except for one friend.

My brother had found the perfect weapon in Luigi because he was a kid who would hate me and get everyone else to turn against me. I never saw my brother so happy all my life as I went from being one of the most popular kids in town to being one of the most hated. I couldn't believe how mean kids could be when they followed the pack. They left me out of everything. I wasn't invited to parties and no one called me. I started to hate being at school and going to the swim club, or anywhere else for that matter. Eventually I lost Valerie, too.

So, with me being an overly emotional kid already, I had no idea how to handle this situation. I lost all my friends except for two, the whole town seemed to hate me because of this girl, and now she was gone. It was like, what the hell else could go wrong?

After the Valerie fiasco, my mother's abuse combined with my brother's relentless attacks combined with my father's anger and the whole town hating me... I had completely stopped smiling. There are no pictures of me smiling after this point. I had nowhere to hide, so I had nothing to be happy about.

At school, if I was not being made fun of, I was being ignored. At the swim club and around town, I was being bullied and reminded of how everyone hated me. My friend Kevin told me he asked the kids why everyone hated me, and their answer was because Luigi and my brother told them to.

Meanwhile at home, from the minute I walked in the door, my brother would constantly tell me how everyone hated me and that I should do the world a favor by killing myself. Later in life, my own mother even encouraged me to commit suicide.

Although I could get away from my brother's attacks, I still had to face my mother's rage or her sexual advances. Having to deal with sexual stuff from my own mother was probably the worst of all the terrible things I had happen during my childhood.

If I was able to avoid school, the town, the swim club, my brother, and my mother, the only option left was to be around my father who was angry and yelling all the time. If I had had a normal life with a normal family, being around someone like my father, who couldn't go five minutes without yelling at me, would have been unbearable. Unfortunately, unbearable was better than every other available alternative.

I used to be able to escape by going to school, but now school was a nightmare. There was nowhere for me to hide, nowhere for me to feel safe or happy and I was only ten years old! I have read books about people who suffered abuse, but they always had a safe place to turn, somewhere they found happiness, or at least someone that they felt okay around. Every option was a bad one and I had no one to turn to. I had to deal with this all on my own.

Another bad situation was that my family and everyone else in the town still expected me to pitch winning all-star games for them. Since I had been the pitcher who won the big game for Haddon Heights during their all-star series, everyone wanted me to play baseball—except me.

When all the kids on the team hate you, there is nothing fun about playing. During my last year at Haddon Heights, I didn't want to play on the baseball team, but my parents forced me.

All the local parents would tell me that I couldn't let them down. So, even though I put forth my weakest effort, I still made the all-star team. The coach was a complete asshole, too. In fact, his kid was one of the ones picking on me.

Earlier in the season, a new kid named Blaine, who grew up to become a pro-baseball pitcher and he won the World Series, moved to our town. He never joined in with the other kids who were picking on me and was more concerned with sports. I got the sense he was being used by the town, too.

Blaine was on this coach's team, which was playing against the team I was on during the first big game of the season. Blaine could throw the ball lightning fast and the coach was so excited because he thought his team was going to be undefeated that year. I squashed his dream by pitching a no hitter and in the final inning, hit off Blaine and started a rally. We beat the supposedly unbeatable team and the coach was furious.

Fast forward to the all-star team. This same coach became the coach of the all-star team and kept telling me how they were depending on me to win. Although he saw all the kids picking on me and did nothing to stop it.

I could beat up any of those kids one-on-one and probably even two at once (I was a very good fighter and always have been), but I guess I simply lost the willpower to stick up for myself at this point. The second day of practice was approaching, and I was trying to figure out how to avoid going. Meanwhile, my brother had two of his friends over and he kept saying, "My brother can't take a punch on his 'little pitching arm.'" As a result, they took turns holding me down on the ground and punching me so badly that my whole arm was black, blue, green, and purple. The next day at practice, my arm was extremely sore, so I couldn't throw the ball hard at all.

Even though I showed the coach my arm, he just kept yelling at me to throw harder, so all the kids started to laugh. By the time practice was over, I'd made up my mind that I wasn't going back. When I got home, my mom came into my room with nothing but a t-shirt on to tell me I needed a back scratch. I had had enough of everyone and everything. The next day, I decided to run away. I planned to ride my bike as far as I could get and talked my friend Kevin into coming with me.

We left early in the morning and rode our pedal bikes all the way to Long Beach Island, which was about sixty-five miles from where I lived. I didn't have a plan for once I got there, so I decided on the fly to go to our neighbor's shore house. Not too much time had passed before I gave up and had no choice but to call my parents.

It had taken us about seven hours to ride all the way there and we were exhausted. When I called home, I told my mom that I was at the Troy's house and needed a ride. At first, she didn't understand. The Troy family had a house two doors down from ours in Haddon Heights, but also had a summer home in L.B.I., so when my mom heard me say "the Troy's house," she thought I was at the house in our neighborhood. As soon as I said "in LBI" she started screaming and questioning how I could do this to her, then she just hung the phone up.

Kevin's mother ended up driving all the way down to get us. When I got home, my Dad was worried about my safety because the Pine Barrens were dangerous. My mom said I embarrassed her and let the town down by not going to baseball practice. She said I was to immediately ride my bike over to the coach's house and beg him not to kick me off the team. This was the last thing in the world I wanted to do, but if I didn't, I would have everything taken from me and be grounded indefinitely. So, I rode my bike over to his house.

After I knocked on the coach's door, he came outside and slammed me against a tree, then told me that I let the whole town down. He also told me that from now on I would practice, but I had to sit on the bench during all the games and watch as everyone else played.

That was about all I could take of Haddon Heights! I had become so miserable that it was impossible to hide how I felt. So much so that our neighbor who was a nice old Jewish lady told my parents she thought I should see a doctor because I was so depressed, but they didn't listen to her.

My parents did not want Adam and me to go to Haddon Heights High School. They wanted to move to Moorestown, New Jersey because it was a very wealthy town with better schools. Plus, word had gotten out about an all-black town nearby called Lawnside and the school board had decided to bus the students from there to Haddon Heights, which went over like a lead balloon. Most of the parents in Haddon Heights did not like this one bit, so they all sent their kids to other schools, like Catholic schools.

The strange thing for me was that I had had one experience with a black kid, and it wasn't bad. In fact, it was the exact opposite, so I didn't see what all the fuss was about.
This kid had come to our elementary school and played a football game with us. The thing is, he was the only black kid in an all-white town. Once the game started, it was obvious to him that the other kids were picking on me, but instead of jumping in with them, he stayed by me and played on my side against the majority of kids.

To this day, I have never forgotten him or what he did for me. This kid who knew no one and had a different skin color in an all-white town could have easily joined the herd of kids taunting me, but he didn't. He took the high road by doing the complete opposite and repeatedly told them to leave me alone. Still to this day, it is one of the kindest and bravest things I have ever seen and from a child for that matter. I really wish I knew his name and could thank him.

Not long after we moved from Haddon Heights to Moorestown, New Jersey, my brother made a big deal about how it was all my fault that he had to move and leave all his friends because no one liked me. He told me his friends threw a going away party for him and everyone there was sad to see him go, but happy I was leaving. My mother also told me how awful it was that she had to leave her best friend and that it was all my fault.

Haddon Heights was supposed to be this loving, caring small town, but for me it was hell! It really left an impression on me about how mean kids could be to each other.

MOORESTOWN

MOORESTOWN IS A very wealthy town in southern New Jersey. It was declared to be the nicest place to live in America by *Money Magazine* in 2006, I was not excited to move there. I was never excited about anything. I just wanted to get through life with the least amount of pain possible. In Moorestown, many more problems surfaced for me.

My anxiety first reared its ugly head whenever I had to pee in public, then I started developing fears of large, wide open spaces. This eventually got so bad that I felt as though I was going to fall into the sky.

My depression also started to surface daily, but it was nothing like my mom's as hers was more of a severe depression that lasted a few weeks at a time and made it impossible for her to leave her bed. My depression was milder, yet constant and difficult to gauge since I had never truly known happiness. It wasn't until later in life when I was able to feel happiness that I was able to see how depressed I really was. To put it into perspective, if you were always sad from as far back as you could remember, you wouldn't realize it any differently. Feeling sad becomes your normal.

Anytime I thought of Haddon Heights, I would get a sick feeling in my stomach. I didn't know what to expect in Moorestown, but an interaction with a kid at school on my first day was a bad one, so things were not looking promising. At first, I thought, "Oh, no! Here we go again."

On my first day of 7th grade, I sat down at a table. Within minutes, this kid named Mikey who eventually became my friend walked up and said, "Don't sit here!" After that, things got better. I did whatever I could to fit in with the "cool kids" who were getting into trouble and doing things like smoking cigarettes. I also started to smoke cigarettes, but not so much to fit in as it allowed me to get away from myself. The short buzz from nicotine made me feel different from how I usually felt and, to me, this was a good thing.

I was having trouble sleeping so I started stealing my dad's beer and drinking some to make myself go to sleep. My mother also started giving me her Valium to sleep. She noticed I wasn't sleeping, so she would just break out one of her pill bottles and say, "Take this."

One day at school, someone said we could get a buzz from drinking cough syrup, so I started to drink it. I would lay in my bed buzzed on cough syrup and pretend I was someone else.

I also started making myself pass out, so I could catch a buzz. We played this pass out game where someone would hold onto your neck while you took deep breaths until you passed out. When you came to, you would have this really cool feeling come over you since your brain had been deprived of oxygen, so for a few moments you didn't feel like yourself. When I got home, I would lay in my bed and make myself pass out over and over again.

I would literally do anything that would stop me from feeling like myself. I remember shooting the basketball in my driveway for hours because it allowed me to pretend I was someone else.

One day while I was trying to get away from myself, I ended up meeting a kid named Joey who became my closest friend. Through him I became friends with everyone else. By the end of seventh grade, I was in with the most popular kids and started to get interest from girls. In fact, I hooked up with the prettiest girl in my school and her name was Lindsay.

Lindsay was the girl in my grade who I thought was the most beautiful. I really liked her but had no idea she even knew who I was. Late one night, she and a girlfriend called my phone. She told me that she liked me and wanted to get together the next day, which we did. I really started to like her–and Moorestown.

The problem with me and girls was that I was attracted to them, but I was at an age when everyone started exploring sex and when you have been abused, normal sexual experiences can be awkward at best, especially when sober.

That summer was the first time I got really drunk. A friend we called "Shorty" had a sister who bought us all forty-ounce bottles of beer. We drank them in the woods while we made a fire and burned poison ivy. We peed on it to douse the flames. The next day, my penis and testicles were covered with poison ivy because of the smoke from the burned plants. This should have been an omen of things to come with mind altering substances.

The most amazing part of that night for me was not totally because I was having a great time being drunk for the first time with friends; it was amazing because I realized I had peed in front of people for the first time without a problem. So long as I was drunk, my shy bladder that had plagued me for years was cured. This taught me that being under the influence of alcohol helped ease my anxieties. I truly enjoyed the way I felt when I was drunk. I absolutely loved it!

That summer, my parents bought a beach house in Long Beach Island, New Jersey and they told us we were going to spend the summer there. At first, I didn't want to go because I had hooked up with Lindsay and having fun in Moorestown was all I could think about. Looking back now, LBI was probably when I had any good times in my childhood, mainly because I was drunk most of the time.

While sober, I could feel my anxiety problem getting worse and worse. I started to get anxious about everything. I never ate lunch at school because I was too nervous to eat in front of the other kids.

I also started to believe something was wrong with my heart. When I would lay on my side, I would start having heart palpitations and breathing would become difficult. I even went to a doctor to have it checked out and he said my heart was fine, but I didn't believe him. It still felt like something was wrong.

LONG BEACH ISLAND & MOORESTOWN

I STARTED SPENDING the summers down in Long Beach Island and the rest of the year in Moorestown. In high school, I played football and was good at it, but I never really put in the effort I should have because I didn't want to give up half the summer for double session practice when I could have been drinking.

I remember we would have Friday night calls at our houses to make sure we were in bed, so we would be well rested for the game the next day. I would wait until I got the call, then go out drinking with my non-football playing friends.

Getting drunk and partying became as necessary for me as getting sleep was to other kids. It gave me relief from my anxiety, shame, and depression. Given the choice, I would have stayed drunk constantly.

Girls became a part of my life, but not in a normal way. The only part about a relationship that I focused on was the sexual one, but because of what I had gone through, the sexual part of a relationship was far from easy.

If I started becoming intimate with a girl while sober, I would have flashbacks of past abuse, then immediately become disgusted and wanted nothing to do with her. As I'm sure you can imagine, that didn't make for too many healthy relationships. The only way I could be with a girl was to drink just enough so I was still coherent, but numb enough that my memories of abuse wouldn't resurface.

Things at home were as bad as ever, but the older I got, the less I was expected to be there, so I tried to spend the least amount of time around my family as possible.

Meanwhile, my dad lost his job. When I say this, I mean he got fired. My father's habits did not win him many friends in the corporate world, so once new management took over the hospital, he left and started working for a company called MedQuist. They were a medical transcription company in Marlton, New Jersey. The CEO of this company was a man named Dick (of course, his name would be Dick). He was a real ass to say the least. He was tall and skinny and kind of acted like the evil boss on "The Simpsons."

My father was very bright, almost a genius and a great businessman except he was no good at playing politics. Especially when it came to someone like Dick. Dick was very cruel toward my father and after firing him, I was left with a father who was always home and a whole lot angrier. Getting treated badly at work and then fired destroyed my father's confidence. He never went back to work.

My mother berated him for losing his job. The most twisted part of the whole situation was that the things my father had implemented at MedQuist had helped it become a very successful company and Dick was eventually replaced as CEO.

My dad's job loss meant more problems for me. I would now come home from school to a mother and father who were always there. As you can imagine, this wasn't a good thing and made it so I didn't want to be home ever.

My mother would constantly tell my brother and I how hard she had it having a husband who was out of work. Of course, my brother agreed with her and would say things like, "You should get a divorce." The problem was that we were wealthy.

My Grandfather paid for our college educations, but now that he no longer had his wits about him, my mother had control over his millions. During this time, my parents owned two homes and did not need the money. I think my dad figured that the only reason he needed to work was to leave extra money to my brother and I. As his parents didn't really leave him much, I guess he decided it was fine to just forget about working and stay home. Although, quitting work twenty years before retirement age is usually not good for anyone–especially my father.

It was extremely difficult for me to watch his downward spiral because I felt bad for my father. Even though he was angry and raged all the time, I could still tell that he at least cared about me. Yet, my dad did not have a supportive family behind him, and this did not help the situation one bit.

It didn't feel right to me that my mother was talking badly about my father to us kids, but that's what my mom was like. She had no loyalty toward her family in any way. If we did something she didn't like, she would complain to anyone who would listen including but not limited to friends, neighbors, and even strangers.

For example, when I ran away and rode my bike all the way to the shore, she told several people what a bad son she had for putting her through so much worry. One of the things that escaped her was that I was gone for eight hours and she didn't even know I was missing. When she found out I was in LBI, she realized that I hadn't gone to all-star practice and that's what upset her. She wasn't concerned about my well-being. She was worried about how it looked to the other parents that the all-star pitcher wasn't at practice. While my mother enjoyed gossiping about how horrible her family was, she conveniently left out the part about how she was sexually abusing her own flesh and blood. I seriously doubt they would have felt the same sympathy for her had she revealed this deep, dark truth.

The truth was completely lost on my mother. The crazy part was that she could go to church and act holier than thou while knowing she was abusing her boys, which is about the most unholy thing I can imagine a person doing. I still have no idea why it never bothered her. At least it never seemed like it did.

VALLEY FORGE MILITARY ACADEMY

AROUND THIS TIME, I almost got sent to Valley Forge Military Academy in Valley Forge, Pennsylvania. While the abuse happened less often in my teenage years, it managed to manifest itself in ways that were more creepy than anything else.

One day, I was at home in my room and my mother started yelling for me to come to her room like there was an emergency. When I opened the door, she was laying naked on her bed while talking on the phone. She said nothing to me and kept talking as though nothing was wrong.

Immediately following this strangeness, I went to school upset. It had been a few months since my mother had done anything like this, so I was caught off guard. When I got to school, the first thing I did was ask a kid for a cigarette and went into the bathroom to smoke it. No sooner than I had taken a couple of drags, I was caught by the vice principal and suspended for two days.

When my parents found out, my mother started screaming, "How could you do this to me?" then told my father to "get rid of this embarrassment." She told me to leave home and that I was not allowed back.

My older brother started scolding me, too, saying how my friends were dirtbags and that our parents shouldn't let me hang out with them. He hated that I had friends now, so this was his way of trying to get me to lose them. The only problem is, by this point I was friends with pretty much everyone in my grade, so if my parents stopped me from hanging out with my "dirtball" friends, they would have to stop me from going to school, which they actually tried to do by taking me to Valley Forge Military Academy as an attempt to scare me.

Most kids were frightened of Valley Forge Military Academy because it had a reputation for being a very tough place. The kids who went there were supposedly as tough as nails and enjoyed fighting. It was also rumored to be a very strict place. Most kids were scared but it had the opposite effect on me. As soon as my dad took me there, I wanted to stay because it was an opportunity to get away from my family. My dad couldn't believe it.

My dad never knew that my mom was abusing me. Later in life, he found out through a letter I wrote, but he didn't believe me. It was just something he couldn't accept, but he was also unbelievably smart, so the fact that I wanted to stay at Valley Forge Military Academy should've tipped him off that something was very wrong.

For most kids, attending Valley Forge Military Academy was a fate worse than death, so they fought it with everything they had. Yet, here I was begging my father to enroll me. Even the colonel overseeing the school admitted, "This is a first!"

My parents never went through with sending me there. My dad even said he took me there in an effort to scare me straight, so I would do my best to avoid trouble, but it was not long after that I found myself in trouble again.

When I showed up at school after my suspension, my friend Mike told me that a group of my friends saw that one of Joey's neighbors had a quad, so our friend Matt was going to pay him to steal it.

We all went out that Friday night and brought along a dog we'd found and named Banjo. I can't remember where we found him, but he loved hanging around with us kids. When we got to Joey's, we went through his back field to get into his neighbor's barn, then stole their quad. We drove it back to Joey's and rode it around for a while, then abandoned it in his backyard.

The next day, all the guys except me met at Joey's house and were riding it in plain view of the house they'd stolen it from. The quad's owners, who turned out to be the parents of a girl who went to our high school, saw this and immediately went over to get it back. When they showed up, apparently Matt–the "mastermind" behind the whole thing–blamed it on me because I wasn't there, and everyone went along with him.

Joey called me later saying he felt terrible and that it was all Matt's idea to put the blame on me. He also added that Matt said that nothing was going to happen to me. While I wasn't completely innocent, the whole thing got started because of Matt, which would have been like Adolf Hitler blaming his generals for the war. Yes, I was there, which made it my fault as much as anyone else's, but to blame it solely on me was wrong. If I had learned to stick up for myself, I would have said something, but after Haddon Heights, I just stayed quiet. Matt was the whole reason that this thing started and now he was blaming it on me.

I also experienced my first anti-Jewish talk from friends when they had no idea that I was a quarter Jewish. They said, "He did the slimy Jew thing and blamed it all on you," and, "Only a Jew would shift the blame after causing this whole thing." After that incident, I never told people I was a quarter Jewish.

The girl's parents called the police to report their quad stolen. When they called to tell them they had it back and did not want to press charges, a local cop named Detective Henry who was way too over-zealous decided he was going to press charges anyway.

I understand what we did was wrong, but at most we should have been charged with joy riding. Instead, he filed charges of grand theft auto. Not long after, Matt and his parents paid a visit to my home.

Matt's father was a physiatrist and kind of a wormy-looking person with a condescending attitude. Matt fed his parents the same bullshit story and conveniently left out the part about him offering to pay Mike, which was the catalyst that got the whole thing rolling. I could tell Matt felt a little bad because he couldn't look me in the eye, but I couldn't believe what happened next.

Matt's parents sat in our home and lectured me on how I was never going to see their son again and, basically, how it was all my fault. For some reason, I didn't get up and start screaming the truth to everyone. It was as though my will to stick up for myself was broken. As soon as they left and my parents shut the door behind them, my mother turned to me with this look of absolute hatred on her face and started crying. She began screaming about what I was putting her through.

Not long after, my father came up to me and said, "I am never going to let adults come into our home and yell at you ever again." That sounded great, but he should have said something when they were berating me. Even if Matt's parents believed his bullshit story about me asking them to steal the quad, they were still acting like Matt was just an innocent bystander when in reality he was just as guilty as me. I wanted to ask them, even if I had suggested stealing the quad, "Am I in charge of Matt? Am I that powerful that I could make him and the others do whatever?" The fact that his father was supposed to be this smart doctor who counseled people but was still able to place one hundred percent of the blame on me was beyond comprehension.

After telling Joey and the other guys what Matt's parents did, two of them apologized to me and said they never thought it would get that far. They also asked why I did not speak up with the truth.

THE LSD INCIDENT

DURING MY SOPHOMORE year in high school, friends from my football team drove over to pick me up. We rode in my friend Todd's jeep. Todd was one of the most popular kids in our school and a lot of girls seemed to be in love with him. Sadly, later in life he committed suicide.

As soon as I got into Todd's jeep, they informed me that we were going to a party, but first we were going to have a party of our own. We were all going to drop LSD. I had a huge fear of LSD because I'd heard that people had lost their minds on it and, for some reason, I was sure this would happen to me. But they were so persistent that I eventually gave in and took it under my tongue.

We drove to the party and the LSD kicked in as soon as we got there. It wasn't like I had imagined. I wasn't in some fantasy world with pink elephants and rainbows, but I definitely felt strange and uneasy. During the party, I drank a lot to chase away my fear of the LSD. That night when I came home and was all alone in a dark house, this strange terror hit me like a sledgehammer. I was having my first panic attack, but didn't know what was happening, so I started to think I was losing my mind.

Suddenly, this sense of impending doom washed over me. I felt as if I was falling and going to die. I remembered when I was a kid on a swing set staring at the sky and thinking how scary it would be if I fell into the sky, which frightened me. Now it felt like this was going to happen.

I hated the fear of falling because of the complete lack of control that accompanied it. I also hated heights. Considering these elements, the terror created by my imagination and picturing myself falling into the sky was about as scary as it gets. The sky is something you can never get away from. It is always there. For me, it was as if I was looking over the edge of a tall building whenever I was outside.

The next day, I stayed in my room scared to death. How was I going to avoid going to school? I didn't know what I was going to do. To a normal person who understands gravity, my fear sounds completely irrational, but to me in my state of panic, the possibility of it felt so real. I was just waiting to plunge into the sky.

On the way to school, I tried my best to keep my eyes closed. When I got there, people kept asking me if everything was okay. Some said that I looked "white as a ghost." By second period, I was in the boys' locker room so absolutely petrified that I burst into tears. I went to see the guidance counselor, Mr. Boris, and told him I needed help.

I was so scared to tell him that I had taken acid and explain what was wrong, but I had no choice. When I finally did, to my amazement he was caring and understanding, not judgmental and angry. This was on the level of something I had never experienced with anyone before, especially not in my family.

I was shocked when he took me for a walk outside and told me he had heard of this before. I told him I thought I was losing my mind. He gave me a pass to leave school early and I walked home with my arms out waiting to fall into the sky, imagining how it would kill me. When I got home, I was covered in sweat and tears.

That night, my dad and I went to dinner. When we sat down, I took a look out the window and broke out in a panic. Crying, I told my dad I had to leave. Reluctantly, he agreed, but when we got back to the car my dad's anger had dissolved into concern as he could see how scared I was. I told him honestly what had happened, which was very rare for me.

The next day he took me to a psychiatrist named Dr. Klein. Dr. Klein was a super nice man. He saw right away that I was having a severe anxiety attack. I told him what happened and said I was sure I was losing my mind.

He replied, "So, let's fix it then." The confidence he exuded made me feel much better. I could tell he truly believed me and that he really gave a damn. He told me that he was going to write me two prescriptions. One was for the anxiety. This was the Klonopin, which is like Xanax. The other was Zoloft, which is an antidepressant like Prozac, but he told me it was going to block the acid flashbacks. That was a very smart thing to say to me.

I told him that I was afraid I was stuck on a permanent acid trip. Had he told me he was giving me an antidepressant, I probably would not have taken it thinking it was not going to help me anyway. Since he told me it was going to block the "acid flashback," I was willing to take it on a daily basis, which is a very important thing when it comes to taking antidepressants.

KLONOPIN

When I took the Klonopin, about a half hour would go by before it took effect and the anxiety went away. I felt some peace for the first time in as long as I could remember. It was like a miracle. A lot of people say I should not have been put on a drug like Klonopin that young because it is extremely addictive and has horrible side effects. But at this point, I needed something that strong because nothing else would have given me peace. Without it, I probably would have killed myself by drinking alcohol nonstop to keep from losing my mind and been unable to leave my house.

The problem was that I was only fourteen and began taking a dosage eight times greater than a normal adult dose. Instead, I should have been trying to figure out what the root cause of the anxiety was rather than trying to manage the symptoms with more drugs. In this respect, a doctor is no different than a drug dealer. My parents were really the ones who should have been monitoring this situation and asking questions.

Klonopin numbs you to the world, which was completely fine with me. It also stunts your brain's growth because it causes your natural chemicals to be obstructed. You get side effects such as constipation and it decreases your motivation, hinders your memory, affects your ability to learn, decreases your sex drive, and even slows your breathing. It can cause you to produce less testosterone, less growth hormone, and other important biological chemicals essential for normal child development.

It is also dangerous because its effects are enhanced when it's mixed with alcohol and other drugs. Alcohol had especially become a huge part of my life by the age of fourteen. With everything that was already going on with me, the last thing I needed was something that would help things get worse.

HIGH SCHOOL/GIRLS/CARS/MORE PROBLEMS

I JUST BARELY got by in high school. I was smart enough to get decent grades, but I never had any motivation or reason to want them as badly as others did. I did not think about my future. I was just hoping to get through each day as best as possible.

I made some close friends in high school, but long-term healthy relationships with females was not in the cards for me. I had hooked up with a lot of girls while I was drunk. I lost my virginity on a beach while completely wasted, which was the only way sex was possible for me.

When I turned seventeen, my parents bought me a new Mustang GT convertible. Having a car brought more girls into the picture. My mother said she hoped it would inspire me to behave and get good grades.

My father helped talk her into it because he wanted a convertible and that was one of the stipulations for me getting the car. I had been through this before with a dirt bike. If I wanted something and asked them for it, I would only get it if it benefited my father in some way. He literally bought me a dirt bike for my birthday that only my brother and him could ride because it was street legal and I was only fifteen, two years away from being able to ride it. This meant I could never ride it without him or, God forbid, my brother. They were the ones who got to enjoy my birthday present.

Now when it came to the Mustang, I didn't want a convertible car. There was something about convertibles that I hated, but my dad had one when he was young, so I ended up getting a convertible. My dad got to drive the car whenever he wanted and my mom constantly reminded me that it was not my car, but theirs.

It was dark green with a tan top—and very fast. It had a 5.0-liter engine and was decked out with all leather interior. It even had fancy rims, which were rare for cars to have back in those days. Not long after getting the car, I got into an accident and received my first DUI.

MY DUI ARREST

My parents were gone for the weekend, so I decided to invite a few friends over for a party at our house in Moorestown. The next morning, I woke up to my friend Shane calling me to say that the waves were huge on Long Beach Island. I was a surfer and would go down to the shore in the winter on weekends to surf if the waves were decent enough. I had a wetsuit that made this possible with the cold water.

After Shane told me about the waves, I decided to drive to the beach. Shane lived in a town near mine called Medford, but his family had a shore house in LBI, too. Shane and I were both lifeguards in Long Beach Island and had met in L.I.T., which stands for 'Lifeguard in Training.'

My friend John also drove down to the shore with us. John was from a town called Woodcliff Lake in North Jersey. John's family had many houses in LBI as his dad was the CEO of a large circulation company, of which he owned forty percent of the company. John and I met after I ended up fighting someone for him indirectly, but I will get into that later.

We all met up at John's house, then went to check the waves. When we got to the beach there were no waves at all. Shane had called the surf report, but it was wrong. This unfortunate turn of events led us to come up with the idea of drinking beer. It was eight o'clock on a Sunday morning and this seemed like a great idea to me.

John's house had these soda machines that were filled with cans of beer instead of soda. We drank under the sun on his back deck all morning long. We even were doing beer funnels, which is when you take a funnel that has a tube attached to it and someone holds it up while pouring beer into it. The beer flies down your throat in seconds. It was not quite noon yet and I had already downed more than twenty cans of beer. I was very drunk by this point.

I can remember at around noon, I decided to go back to my house and sleep off the buzz before driving back to Moorestown. Shane said he was going to leave, too. He said I should just follow him because his dad knew all the state troopers and if we got pulled over, we would be fine. For some crazy reason, I agreed.

Trying to get into our cars was difficult since we could barely walk. I had a hard time starting my car, let alone driving it. Going down the road, Shane was in front of me driving a black Nissan Pathfinder and I was following in my Mustang. We made it about a mile on the main boulevard when Shane slammed on his breaks at a light and I smashed right into the back of him. My car wedged completely underneath his, and then there was a loud bang followed by an explosion as my airbags went off and sliced up my arms.

The first thing I noticed through the smoke from the airbags was a guy yelling in my window asking me if I was alright. The horn was permanently sounding, and I could do nothing to stop it. It was so loud that I could barely hear anything else.

Shane got out of his car and said, "Holy shit! What do we do?" We stared at each other and decided at the same time to get the hell out of there. I told the guy who was concerned about my well-being that we were fine and didn't need his help as I saw other people starting to gather around.

My car was still running. Shane started his car, then put it in four-wheel drive and drove it off my car to reveal its mangled front end. With all things considered, it was amazing that I could see perfectly fine out of the windshield even though it was broken.

I immediately turned off the main road and onto a small back road with a twenty-five mile per hour speed limit. I started driving very fast in the direction of my beach house, which was on the beach side while John's was on the bay side, but they were only a couple of streets apart.

I remember all these people out for a peaceful Sunday walk on this beautiful day and here comes this smashed up Mustang doing a hundred miles an hour with the horn blaring, airbags out, and smoke pouring from the windows. I can only imagine what they were thinking.

I pulled into my driveway and tried to get the horn to stop any way I could. Eventually, I had to use a pair of pliers to rip off the battery cables, so the horn would shut off. Then, I went inside my house and started freaking out, "What in the hell was I going to do?" We didn't have cell phones, so I had no idea what happened to Shane. John had left after us, so I wasn't sure about what happened to him or even if he knew what had happened to us. The only thing racing through my mind was how in the hell I was going to explain this to my parents.

After about twenty minutes, I started hearing car doors shutting and brakes squealing in front of my house. I looked out the window and saw that my house was surrounded by police. They got a phone call alerting them to a bad accident and when they showed up, there were no cars. They went searching and found my car fitting the description, just sitting in my driveway. I was so drunk I did not think to put it into the garage. I may have gotten away, but I doubt for long as someone must have gotten our license plates because they caught Shane at his house in Medford. He made it all the way home.

So, I walked out with my back to them and lit up a cigarette. I was trying to act like I didn't know anything was wrong. The first police officer to approach me smacked the cigarette out of my hand, then slapped handcuffs on me, which immediately put me on the defensive. I decided in that moment that I wasn't going to say two words to these police officers.

They took me down to the station and asked me all these questions. I refused to answer any of them. They became angry and started being complete assholes because I was keeping quiet. I was bleeding from both arms, and they didn't even offer me medical help or even a napkin.

Eventually, a cop told me that if I didn't blow into the breathalyzer, he would immediately revoke my license, so I decided to take it. I blew a .19. This was about two hours after they found me and about three hours since my last drink. I bet while I was driving, I was easily over a .23 or higher, which is off-the-charts drunk considering .08 is when the law says a person is legally impaired. After I blew into the breathalyzer, the cop said, "We got you now and we are going to charge you with everything."

My parents and my brother showed up about an hour later. The first thing my father said to me was, "Are you ok?" All my mother said was, "I'm disgusted by you," and would not look at me. My brother smiled and shook his head.

As soon as they saw my parents, the police completely changed their attitude toward me. They finally asked if I needed medical attention and said because I was under eighteen, they would release me to my parents right away. They charged me with driving under the influence, hit and run, leaving the scene of an accident, reckless driving, and obstruction of justice.

During the ride home, not one word was spoken. When I got home the "three" of my parents meaning my mom, dad and brother informed me that not only would I never get the car back, but I was grounded indefinitely. My mother and brother decided they wanted me out of the house. My mother told me how she had spent all this money on the car and now her insurance was going up, and this, that, and the other, on and on. She told me that she was going to the lawyer's office in the morning to have my name stricken from the will.

My brother informed me that I had three days to find a residence and move all my things out. He said he had met a girlfriend at college who was going to use my room as her own when she came to visit. He also made up a list of things I was and wasn't allowed to take with me when I left.

This is when a miracle showed up in the form of a family friend named Frank. He and his wife had been very nice to me. They owned a business and I'd worked for them at one point. They were just all-around great people. When he heard about the accident, they were worried and wanted to see if I was okay, so they came right over.

I think Frank was completely amazed by what my brother was saying to me and told him to "to shut the hell up." Then, he told my parents to "stop talking about money and the goddamn car and focus on your son." He couldn't believe that they were discussing the will. He could not believe my brother was involved at all.

He then came to me and said, "Andrew, this is not good, but your parents will get over it. The important part is that you are okay." He told me that if I needed something, he would be there and asked if I was okay.

I lied and told him I was fine, but I had never had anyone truly care about my well-being like that and it meant so much to me. Because he jumped in, my mother had to ease up while he was there and feign concern. She told him she was "just angry and not thinking." Frank was a great man who had nothing to gain by sticking up for me. He did it because it was the right thing to do. I thought about how different my life would have been if someone like him was around all the time.

As soon as he left, it was back to reality. The only problem was that I was seventeen, so legally she could not kick me out yet. The next day, my mother said she and my brother had gone to a lawyer and removed me from the will. I thought that was a funny thing to say to me since my brother was the only one concerned about the will. It was all he talked about after my mother started discussing finances with him at age ten. I couldn't care less about the will, but I think my mother thought it was a good way to hurt me.

My mother had disclosed all the family's financial details to my brother at a very young age. Ever since, he had been figuring out what his cut would be with me and without me before he even turned eleven years old. He used to say he was going to be a millionaire when he turned eighteen. I found it hypocritical how he would trash our dad for living off my grandfather yet couldn't care less about doing the same thing himself.

The following week, my dad came and told me that I was going to be meeting with Igor, his attorney, about the accident. I went to see Igor at his office and the first thing he said to me was that he didn't want to hear anything about the accident. He told me he was just going to try to postpone the court date as much as possible, I would be able to drive to college for the first few months while I got to know people. That way I could hitch a ride with them to and from school while my license was suspended. This would make my life a lot easier.

That summer, the strangest coincidence happened. I was given a new lifeguard partner named Donnie. Donnie and I became friends instantly and on our first day working together, we realized he was the guy who had run up to my car asking me if I was alright. He was also the one who had told the police that I was probably drunk because he could smell the alcohol. Donnie was the only real evidence the cops had except for two other girls who were on the scene and apparently said the same thing as he did to the police.

For all they knew, I hit someone I knew and exchanged information with him before leaving the scene, which was completely legal. Then when I got home, I was so upset about my car being hit that I started drinking. Of course, this wasn't likely, but as I learned from watching TV, it isn't what you know, it's what you can prove in a court of law.

Donnie apologized vigorously to me and told me that he would recant his statement or say whatever I wanted him to when we went to court. I told him that I appreciated it, but it wouldn't matter since there were two girls who had seen the accident, too, and were likely to testify. I also told him that my lawyer was postponing it.

Shane received a ticket from the New Jersey State Police for leaving the scene of an accident, but not for driving under the influence since he was given the ticket the next day, so they had no way of knowing if he had been drinking or not, and I for damn sure was not going to tell them. They didn't even bother asking me about Shane, not once.

Then, from out of nowhere on the day before my birthday in August, I received a call from Igor. He told me that there was a visiting judge who was a good friend of his and that we were going to go to court. He said we had the best chance of beating the case with this particular judge. So, the day after my birthday, I went to Long Beach Township Municipal Court to face the charges.

The prosecutor started out by making her case against me. She called a police officer to the stand and asked him how he knew that I was drinking and driving if they had arrested me at home. He said I told him that I was drinking at my house, then started driving to the store when I hit a car. I then took off because I was drunk and scared. The rest of the stuff he said I didn't answer.

The officer was lying through his teeth. I wasn't drinking at my house, I wasn't on my way to the store, and I knew the person I hit. The police were still not aware of this fact. I think they just figured the person I hit must have had a warrant or something and I just got lucky that he decided to run, too. As they say in AA, assuming will make an ASS out of U and ME.

I couldn't believe how bad this police officer was lying and pointed this out to Igor. Igor was smart and picked up on it right away. During his cross examination, he asked him if I divulge any information about my age, weight, eye color, etcetera, to which he answered that I would not.

Igor continued by asking, "So, the only thing he would tell you is the one thing that would incriminate him in this case?" He also asked him why he thought it was easy for me to answer the most damning questions, but not the ones that involved basic information. The officer had no answers and sat there looking guilty as hell. After that, everyone in the courtroom could tell he was lying, especially the judge.

Next, the prosecutor called Donnie with complete confidence that he was on her side and the key to nailing me. The first thing she asked him was, "When you approached the defendant's car, did you smell alcohol, or did he look intoxicated?" Donnie replied, "Absolutely not," and added, "he looked and acted completely sober." She got more flustered than I've ever seen anyone get, then she angrily asked why his signed statement said he smelled alcohol and that I looked drunk. He said, "I didn't sign willingly. They forced me to sign something without letting me read it."

I had to stare at the ground by this point because it was hard for me to keep a straight face while this was going on. Then, she snapped back, "Why would the police force you to do anything?" He said he didn't know, but that was what they did. When she heard this, I thought she was going to explode. She then started arguing with the judge.

Now, before the trial began, the visiting judge saw my lawyer Igor and made a big thing about it. Apparently during law school, he did not have money or anywhere to stay, so Igor let him live with him for free. He made it a point to say what a great man Igor was and how he would always be indebted to him.

The prosecutor already knew she was at a disadvantage, but still thought she had an open and shut case. The first witness she called was the cop and it was so obvious that he was lying. She calls Donnie and he basically says that corrupt cops are trying to frame me. It was quickly turning into a circus.

The judge said something like, "Do you dare call the next witness or do you want to drop the charges?" The last witnesses left were the two girls. They were around my age and you could tell they didn't want any part of this. I was with eight guys their age and the last thing they wanted to do was get us into trouble. Seeing what was happening, one of the girls spoke to the prosecutor and said she didn't want to testify against me and asked if she was free to leave.

The prosecutor was not happy with this turn of events, especially when the judge said that she didn't have to testify because this case already had enough problems, then stated that he was inclined to put a stop to this debacle. Had the prosecutor not been such a bitch, she probably would have succeeded at having me found guilty of some of the charges, but she snapped at the judge by saying something like, "Well, I disagree with your handling of this whole thing!" Upon hearing this, the judge declared that all charges were dropped.

I still remember the looks on the faces of the policemen who had arrested me. They were so angry that I thought the rest of my life was going to be plagued with speeding tickets and harassment. For some reason, that never happened. It was the exact opposite. They would drive by my house and see my friends and I drinking on my deck. They knew we were under twenty-one, but never bothered us. Go figure.

JOHN

JOHN WAS THE other friend I was drinking with that day. We met after I got into a fight. One night, a group of us were partying on the beach. It's strange, but my brother was there. He had only one close friend in LBI named Chris. I was close friends with about twenty people that lived on the five streets surrounding our house. We were always throwing beach parties.

None of my friends knew my brother well, but for some reason he was with us that night. I guess I always figured that if I was nice to my brother, he would want to behave like a true brother to me. So, I think I invited him that night.

As usual, I was drinking heavily. By the time I decided to pee in the dunes, I was drunk. As I was walking back, I saw that a group of guys had approached my friends and outnumbered them by at least four to one. I got closer and saw one of them was yelling into my brother and my friend Greg's faces about how he was going to beat up John.

Since most of the kids on the beach were John's friends, this guy just assumed we all knew him and that made us guilty by association. I guess he wanted to make a point to John or scare him by threatening us. Either way, I didn't care because I was drunk and knew how to fight. Even though there were times I should have stuck up for myself by using my mouth, when it came down to fighting, I never had a problem..

I rushed up and got between this guy and my brother, then pushed him with force. It turned out that the guy's name was Paco. He came back at me and I shoved him again, then it was on. I was punching with everything I had, but he was strong, and he soon took me to the ground. Suffice to say, he was sober, and I was a drunken mess, so he had the upper hand within a few minutes.

At this point, I had never lost a fight in my life. Paco started hitting my face and making contact more times than I was making with him. He was definitely going for the win when, out of nowhere, came my friend Greg and I heard him yell, "Get the fuck off of him," as he tackled him to the ground.

The crazy part was that none of Paco's friends jumped in. As it turns out, they were just a group of guys who went around starting fights, but Paco was the only one who would fight. People were indeed scared of him. The rest of the guys dressed tough and talked tough, but they couldn't fight. I think they were also thrown off by one of us being so eager to fight after being outnumbered, so they simply decided not to get involved.
A girl we were with said I hit him a lot and she thought I was winning until we went to the ground. Later I found out that Paco was at least three years older than me. He was on the wrestling team and was very good at it. He also did all kinds of martial arts. People were proud of me for fighting an older guy that had a reputation for being so tough. Word later got around to John about me fighting Paco. Some people told John that I fought for him. When John and I met, we sort of became instant friends.

Greg was the geeky kid that "popular kids" would not hang out with in high school, but I liked him and even invited him to come to my house during my Senior Prom. I had all my friends over for an after-prom party. Greg didn't go to his prom, but at least he got to hang out at our prom party. My friends from high school were nice to him as a favor to me.

I always respected Greg for jumping into that fight. The worst part about it was when word of the fight got around to people's parents. I'm sure they were wondering why my older brother didn't do anything to stop me from getting pummeled.

Although, he did do something; it just wasn't anything honorable. Adam made up a story about him jumping into the fight instead of Greg. Not only did he do the cowardly thing by just standing there, but taking credit for something he never did was just so low. I should have ripped into him when he told my parents about his "bravery" for jumping in to protect me from Paco. My mom kept going on and on to her friends about his "bravery" for sticking up for his brother. Yet again, I bit my tongue and said nothing.

Everyone who was there knows the truth, most of all Greg. I never said anything to anyone until now. It feels quite therapeutic to clear the air with this book. I have been bearing the weight of other people's dishonesty for too long. I am the one who got hurt the most by them. But as I found out in life, the truth always comes out in the end!

THE JEN INCIDENT

I MET A girl named Jen my first summer at the shore. She and her brother Paul were some of the first people I met in LBI. Jen was a super pretty blonde girl that everyone liked. We ended up dating shortly after we met.

One night, we all went swimming in the ocean and Jen and I kissed. After that we became inseparable. She would sunbathe while I would surf. My older brother never surfed. He would just lay on the beach and stare at Jen. I am sure he hated that I had such a pretty girlfriend.

One night, I invited my brother to Jen's house for a party after my father asked me to because Adam was driving. Jen and I had been dating for a few months by this point. Since Adam had started driving, it made it easier to get to and from Jen's house. Even though I invited him to the party, I was surprised when he said he wanted to come.

After getting drunk at Jen's house, we all decided to go eat at a diner. Adam drove. On the way home, he went out of his way to drop me off before Jen. He even told me that my parents said I had to be home at a particular time. Now, my parents never cared what time I came home, but with him driving, I didn't have much choice.

The next day Jen came to me crying. She told me that my brother had taken her home last, then basically forced himself on her. I liked Jen and cared about her, so I had never attempted much with her. My brother had taken advantage of her while she was drunk out of her mind and they did everything but have sex.

I told her that I appreciated her honesty but our relationship was over. I knew deep down in my heart that what my brother did was horribly wrong, but Jen played a part as well and I remembered her clearly agreeing with my brother that I should go home early. My brother was an older guy with a car and young girls were enamored by things like that, so she wasn't completely innocent.

I then went home and started beating up my brother. I had braces and he grabbed my lips, so I was bleeding everywhere. When my mother heard the commotion, she came running. When she saw me covered in blood, she became furious with me. Of course, my brother was crying saying I beat him up.

When I told my mom what he had done, she turned and slapped me across the face, then started tending to my brother. He was crying, but I was the one covered in blood. She started telling my older brother that everything was going to be alright. She wasn't going to let me hurt him anymore. She turned to me as she walked away and said, "I wish you would just disappear!"

A similar thing happened on New Year's Eve. My brother and I were smoking out of his bedroom window when my mother came charging into the room and hit me square in the face even though Adam was the one holding the cigarette.

When Jen hooked up with my brother, it really made me start to wonder how trustworthy girls were, but another experience I had made me really doubt women and their motives even more.

MARY

During my senior year of high school, my friends and I all got fake drivers licenses. One night a group of us decided to go to a place called JJ Grottos in Philadelphia, Pennsylvania because we knew they would take our fake IDs with no problem.

While getting drunk at JJ Grottos, we noticed a man at the bar drinking alone. That man turned out to be none other than Bob Weir of the Grateful Dead. This is one of the two reasons why this night will always stick out to me.

He was in fact a very friendly guy and signed autographs for us with no problem. At this point in time, I had no idea who the hell Bob Weir was, but he definitely did not act like some rude celebrity.

Before that night, there was a girl named Mary who went to my high school and girls I was friends with said had a small crush on me. It's not that I didn't find her attractive, we just hung out in different circles, so we never got the chance to hook up before.

That night, we left JJ Grotto's together. My friend Joey drove us home while Mary and I kissed in the back seat. After Joey dropped us off at my house, we went into the basement where we started making out and were getting close to having sex.

I was drunk earlier, but I started to sober up during the ride home. We started performing oral sex on each other, which caused me to flashback to a time when I was being abused. I was immediately turned off and didn't want anything more to do with her.

I told her I was going to take her home without explaining why I had stopped. I could see she was upset by this, which I understood, but I could not explain to her why I had stopped so abruptly. My feelings of disgust were so profound that I couldn't wait to get rid of her. I can remember dropping her off at her house and how even giving her a kiss goodbye was difficult.

For the next few days, she called me nonstop. I mean, literally, about ninety times asking when we were going to get together again. I ignored her enough that she eventually got the hint and gave up after about a week. I even tried my best to avoid her at school.

The problem was I couldn't tell her why I was so turned off by her and this really offended her. This wasn't the first time something like this happened to me nor would it be the last time, and the consequences of which were going to be awful.

Two weeks had passed when I ran into my friend Jessica. She was always very close to me and was one of the first girls in Moorestown who I liked and dated. She also always stuck by me later in life and is a person that has always meant a lot to me. At this moment, Jessica told me that she had something she needed to talk to me about.

I knew Mary had talked to her, but I couldn't believe what came out of her mouth. She told me that Mary told her that I had tried to have sex with her, and she said no! She said I also kicked her out of my car and made her walk home because she had rejected me.

I was completely blown away by what I heard. I told Jesse that she should look at my caller ID and see the ninety calls in a row from Mary or talk to Joey about how she was basically begging me to have sex with her in the back of his car. After that, Jesse said she knew Mary was lying. She knew me well and that was not how I acted at all. If anything, I was passive when it came to sex.

At this point, I should have confronted Mary and told everyone the truth to clear my name. I could have simply showed them my caller ID and let them hear the messages from her. If what she said had indeed happened, why the hell was she calling me forty times a day begging me to take her out? But at that time, I didn't have it in me to do that. I just avoided her and the situation at all costs.

People say only a guilty person gets all upset and yells when some-one accuses them of something. But not doing anything doesn't help your case either. I know beyond a shadow of a doubt that this incident hurt my reputation in Moorestown. Another sad outcome was that it made me think badly of women and not trust them at all, which was just another thing that was going to make my life even harder, as if I needed that!

Shortly after the incident with Mary, another situation happened that was similar. This time it was with a girl named Caroline who I liked a lot.

CAROLINE

I WANTED A long-term girlfriend like the other guys I knew. Something permanent, but every time I was being intimate, I would get so turned off that having a normal relationship was becoming impossible.

Caroline was perfect in my eyes. She was pretty and she had an amazing personality. The first night we hung out together, everything clicked. It was one of those nights when you do everything right and everything goes your way.

I could tell very quickly that Caroline was falling for me. It was as if everything she learned about me caused her to like me even more. We ended up kissing one night and it was perfect. My feelings for her were very strong.

The second night we spent together, we drank beer and went back to my house. We had the whole house to ourselves and I knew we were going to be intimate, so I started drinking as heavily as I could.

When we finally got to the bed and started rounding the bases, I just wasn't drunk enough and started having sexual abuse flashbacks. I immediately became so grossed out that I wanted nothing to do with her anymore.

I told her that we had to stop and that I needed to go to sleep. It was such an uncomfortable situation. She was wondering if she had done something wrong, but I just wanted to get away from her as fast as possible. I felt so awful after she left. I remember looking in the mirror and just feeling this terrible hatred for myself.

Here was this girl who I would have loved to have had a relationship with and now I was just disgusted by her. I couldn't even be around her or hear her voice without feeling ill.

It was like mind torture. Like the devil himself was flaunting this girl in front of me just to jerk her away at the last minute. Just thinking about it made me depressed, so after she left I started drinking heavily until I finally passed out.

The next day she came by my house and I told her that I couldn't hang out. I wouldn't answer her phone calls either. Two days later at around two o'clock in the morning, she showed up at my house with a friend and she was drunk out of her mind.

When I went out to see her, she asked, "Why don't you like me? What did I do wrong?" I said that she did nothing wrong at all to which she replied, "Well, can I come in and stay the night with you?" I told her 'no' and that I had to go to sleep. That is when she became furious and started yelling that she hated me.

She yelled "I hate you" at the top of her lungs. She kept screaming it over and over until her friend dragged her back to the car crying. I felt lower than I had felt in a long time. I wanted to tell her that I agreed that she should hate me. Still to this day, I always wonder about her and maybe if she reads this book, she will know that there was nothing wrong with her and that the exact opposite was true.

There were a couple of girls that I was able to have semi-normal relationships with, like Jessica who stuck up for me against Mary. I also dated a girl named Kate for a little while. I had another Kate in my life, too, but that went sour, to say the least.

KATES

THE TWO KATES were in my life before and during high school. One was from my town who I dated, while the other was from Long Beach Island, which I hooked up with, but never dated. The first night I met 'LBI Kate' was during a party at her house. The first and last time we ever spoke were very similar in many ways.

Kate was a girl who lived in our LBI neighborhood about five streets away on the bay side. Her father was a lawyer who was also head of the Republican party in Pennsylvania. Her mother was a very beautiful woman who my friends and I called a M.I.L.F., which is short for Mother I'd Like to Fuck. She also had a brother that no one liked because he acted like a stuck up rich kid but was the biggest wimp I met in my life.

This night, I went to Kate's party with guy named Anthony who lived down the street. At this point, I didn't know Kate or anyone else at the party except for Anthony. I had seen Kate before when one of my friends said he thought she was pretty, but we were never introduced. The first time we spoke, she started accusing me of stealing a CD from her house.

I was sitting down on a couch in her house and she came up to me all upset. She said that I was the only person there she didn't know, so I must have stolen her CD. She said she wanted me out of her house immediately. I told her she was crazy, and I angrily agreed to leave.

As I was walking out, Anthony came walking in with her CD and said he was listening to it in someone's car. I said something like, "You see, bitch? I didn't steal anything from you!" She immediately said how sorry she was and that I should stay. I told her to fuck off and started walking home.

I heard footsteps behind me and turned around to see she was following me. She started telling me to stop and I just kept saying, "fuck you," and, "leave me alone," but she wouldn't. She followed me all the way to my house, but I walked inside and went to my room.

The next thing I know, this girl is following me into my house and right into my room. I couldn't believe that this girl whom I didn't even know had the balls to do that. I started yelling, then she started yelling, then out of nowhere we just started kissing, and I'm still not sure how exactly this happened. Only a moment before, I hated this girl and now I was kissing her. No sooner than it had started, it was over, and she left.

In the morning when I woke up, I found her name and number written on a piece of paper. I think I liked her from that moment on, even though she ended up hating me, which I will get to later in this book.

ANXIETY/HEART ATTACK

THE FIRST TIME I truly believed I was having a heart attack was in a Wawa one night with my friend Shane, the same guy whose car I slammed into while drunk. We were in line to purchase something when I started feeling as though I was having a heart attack and started thinking I was about to die. Normally by nine o'clock at night, I would have already been drunk, but for some reason I was still sober.

This intense feeling of panic overcame me. I could feel my heart racing and I started to sweat, then pain began shooting down my left arm. I had to get out of the Wawa immediately. I could see the walls closing in on me as if I was in a movie.

I went outside and Shane followed me to see what was wrong with me. I told him that I was having a heart attack and needed to go to the hospital right away. Shane drove me to the hospital while I clutched my chest. I was expecting my heart to stop at any moment and was especially fearful because of a nightmare-daydream I had during the blizzard of 1996.

In my messed-up mind, I imagined that when we die, the devil puts us in a giant pizza oven and turns the heat up all the way. We can never die and are left to suffer the scorching pain forever. I am claustrophobic and the idea of a hell like that was extremely frightening to me. I was a very deep thinker and would imagine this intensely painful heat that was not going to stop for millions of years. I was sure that as soon as my heart stopped, I would get thrown into an oven. It was just too much to comprehend.

When we reached the emergency room, I told them about the symptoms I was having, and they brought me back right away. The doctors hooked me up to an EKG and ran some blood tests.

After about two hours of waiting, the doctor told me that my heart was fine. I was just having an anxiety attack and he offered me some Valium and said to follow up with a psychiatrist. I was so scared that I was going to die that I refused to leave the ER for hours.

This was the first of many ER visits when my anxiety would become too overwhelming. Throughout the next four years, I would take myself to over forty-eight different emergency room visits in four different states.

Every day that passed, I started to become convinced that I was going to die. About half an hour after waking each morning, panic attacks and anxiety would start. My heart would start skipping beats and my breathing would become difficult. I would hold my chest and repeatedly check my pulse. Although, the more I checked, the worse it got. I would take Klonopin to make it better, but it would only help for about an hour or two, and then the anxiety would return.

I was a nervous wreck while driving because I was sure my heart was going to stop, and I didn't want to crash into a family and kill them. I would go to class and just sit there in a panic waiting for my heart to stop. From this point on, every day of my life I truly believed was my last until I discovered opiates. There was not one day that I did not spend most of my time thinking about death. Other people my age were busy planning their futures while I was planning my funeral.

When someone endures a bank robbery and the robber points a gun in their face, they believe in that moment that they might die. A situation like this can really scar someone emotionally and cause them a lifetime of problems. For me, every day became a life-threatening experience, which was very real to me. I have been in an armed robbery and would rather experience it all over again instead of dealing with how I felt during an anxiety attack. Seriously, any day of the week and twice on Sunday! It was like living with a gun pointed at my head twenty-four hours a day.

So, while other kids were thinking about their futures and eagerly anticipating college, girlfriends, learning new things, and getting a career, then settling down with marriage and kids, and all the other things one should be doing at my age, all I could think about was how much suffering I was going to face in Hell.

That horrible feeling of believing you are going to die every day starts to wear on you after a while. You will look for relief in anything. If someone told me that drinking cat pee would give me some relief, I probably would have tried it.

The only thing that offered any relief was the mind-altering substances. The ones that worked best were the ones being prescribed to me by doctors.

DOCTORS

THE FIRST PSYCH doctor I saw, the one who originally prescribed me the Klonopin and Zoloft, eventually died of a heart attack. He was a nice man that I liked and trusted. He was probably one of the most helpful of all the doctors I have seen.

Later, I started seeing Dr. Blum. Dr. Blum was a Harvard educated physician who came highly recommended by my mother's doctor. She said he would be the perfect fit for me.

My mother saw a psych doctor on a weekly basis. She was on antidepressants like Prozac, Paxil, and Zoloft. She was even given lithium, which is a super strong and dangerous antidepressant. She also took a whole host of benzodiazepines. She took Valium, Xanax, and Klonopin. She had Ativan to sleep and Temazepam if that didn't work. Her medicine cabinet resembled a pharmacy.

She even gave Valium to my girlfriend Kate from Moorestown. Kate was over at our house one day and told my mom that she got nervous when speaking in front of crowds. My mother automatically

seemed not only concerned, but also willing to help in any
way she could. This was a huge difference from the way she acted
toward me, which was uncomfortable to watch. I felt like she was
acting, but it was also amazing how quickly my mom went to push
drugs as a solution to a problem.

My mother and father could put on an act in front of other people,
so that they looked like they were the most caring parents in the
world. When Kate said she got nervous, my mother listened and
tried to help. She gave her Valium because she said she believed it
would help. She seemed genuinely concerned. Kate even said how
nice my mother was.

Later in life, my mother would claim that she had no idea how I
became a drug addict. With all the "love and support" she showered
on me, she couldn't have imagined in her wildest dreams why I
would ever take drugs. I truly believe that my mother believed this.
It was like she had a block preventing her from looking inward. For
some reason, her doctors were never able to get her to either. She
even went to see my doctor, Dr. Blum, one time.

I liked Dr. Blum. He was a very educated man. He was nice to talk
with and genuinely seemed to care about my well-being. It's sad to
say that the only people in my life who cared about my well-being
were being paid.

By this point, I had lied about almost everything in my life. I would
never tell anyone what was really going on in my family. It was too
shameful. If you are not completely honest with a psychiatrist, you
make their job incredibly difficult. To break through and help me,
Dr Blum would have had to have been a miracle worker because I
was holding back so much information.

I always wondered if my mother was scared that some doctor was
going to put two and two together. But as time passed, I realized that
my mother didn't think anyone would ever believe me and she was

right, for the most part.

We had money and looked like an all-American family. There was no way in hell anyone would believe there was sexual abuse in our family. I think she just planned to tell people I was born sick. No matter what anyone tells you, children are not born sick. If they are having a problem, there is a reason behind it. This doesn't mean their parents are at fault, but there is a reason.

I started having a weekly meeting with Dr. Blum to get my drugs. He prescribed me Klonopin and Zoloft just like Dr. Klein(nice doctor). By this point, I had found out that Zoloft was an antidepressant and not an "acid flashback blocker," so I stopped taking it regularly. I hated the way it made me feel and the benefits took months to kick in anyway, which I never really felt. Mixing it with alcohol and other drugs made feeling any of its benefits almost impossible.

Klonopin is a completely different story. Klonopin will make your body physically and mentally addicted. The longer you take it, the more tolerance your body builds. You must take more and more just to get the same effect. If you try to stop, not only will you go into withdrawal, but it also makes your anxiety problem ten times worse than before you started medicating.

I would drink almost every night because the Klonopin wasn't enough. I would take Klonopin during the day and drink at night. Alcohol is the worst thing you can do if you have an anxiety problem. It causes something called rebound anxiety.

Rebound anxiety is basically a by-product of drinking alcohol in excess. It causes your anxiety to get worse the next day. If your anxiety was at seven and you drank that night to get relief, the next day it would be at an eight. It becomes a vicious cycle. When I wasn't completely obliterated by alcohol, I experienced debilitating anxiety.

I told Dr. Blum about my problem with anxiety, but I never revealed exactly what was causing it. His training told him that I was depressed and that is what was causing my anxiety problems, so he thought that if he prescribed me Zoloft, it would eventually help ease my anxiety and I would not have to rely on the Klonopin anymore, or not as much anyway. That would make complete sense for another person and would probably work, but mine was a much more complicated case.

A female psychiatrist I saw before entering college specialized in knowing if children were ready for college or not. She was able to recognize how much of a problem I was having.

She told my parents I was an extremely sick child who needed a ton of help. The last thing they should be thinking about was sending me to college. She thought I needed to be put into an inpatient facility where I could get serious therapy.

My parents never told me that she said all of this until many years later. After she told my parents this, they told her that that wasn't what they wanted to hear. Apparently, the woman noticed the hypocrisy oozing from my parents and pointed it out to them.

She said that they had paid for her opinion, but what was the point of bringing me to see her if they would not accept her opinion? She wanted to speak to me after talking to them, but they would not let her.

I forget her name, but if she ever reads this, I want to say, "Thank you for being an honest person and telling the truth. Had my parents listened to you, I may have received the correct help."

Just as I am pointing out all the wrongs that were done to me, I also want to point out the good things and the occasional hero that popped into my life.

SOMEHOW, I GRADUATED HIGH SCHOOL

MY HIGH SCHOOL graduation meant nothing to me. I wasn't proud of myself and I was even surprised when my dad got me a graduation gift. As usual, the night turned into a family disaster, which I was blamed for.

My mother, father, and brother all came to my graduation. A friend of mine was having an after party that I planned to attend. During the ceremony, I saw my parents in the stands, but we had not discussed anything about doing something together afterward. Apparently, my father had brought me a shotgun as a graduation gift and wanted to surprise me with it.

Before the ceremony ended, my parents left. The room was crowded, and my father hated crowds because they made him furious. If we were in a movie theater and someone kicked his chair, he would go nuts. It always seemed to happen, too. It was as if his anger had become a self-fulfilling prophecy and the "kickers" would always sit behind him. I would get such anxiety just waiting for this to happen because it was embarrassing and unbearable to watch my father get so angry at these people.

My father and mother were waiting in the parking lot and told my brother to tell me to come home, so I could open my gift. He did come up to me, but he told me that, "Mom and Dad were angry that I didn't come see them in the stands". He said that they had left.

My father was very caught up in the idea that you will respect your parents no matter what. When I didn't come home after graduation, he took a lot of offense at this. When my brother said they were angry and left, I completely believed him because that was what normally happened. Therefore,I just went out with everyone else to the party after.

I remember looking around at all the parents hugging their kids and telling them how proud they were of them. Everyone was smiling, happy, hugging, and kissing their family members. I was the only kid there with no one and it felt so strange.

When I came home after the party, the three of them were sitting on the couch furious. The first thing I heard was, "What is wrong with you?" I became so angry upon hearing this that I told them what Adam had said, but my mother didn't believe me. They told me I was such a disappointment and that my brother was so nice for staying home with them and providing support, "Like a good child would do".

I couldn't believe my father didn't at least stick up for me, but he felt as though I was not respecting him for getting me this gift. I would have loved to have had a normal family gathering after graduation and gotten the gun. I couldn't believe that no one believed me and instead believed Adam. While I expected this from my mother, never did I think my father would believe my brother over me, especially with this situation.

For the rest of that summer before college, I tried to avoid my family at all costs. If they were in Moorestown, I would be in LBI and vice versa. If we were all at the same house, I would go out with my friends. The more I avoided them, the happier it made my brother and the angrier it made my mother and father.

COLLEGE

READY OR NOT, off to college I went. I remember the first time I drove my car down I-95 to Virginia. I was a ball of sweat thinking I was going to start falling down the highway or die of a heart attack.

I had to stop in Baltimore and take myself to the emergency room. In the ER, they did every test possible but could not find anything wrong. I was so scared that I didn't want to leave the hospital. In fact, I stayed in the ER for eight hours before finally leaving.

From there, it took me two hours to make it to Randolph-Macon College in Ashland, Virginia. As soon as I pulled into Ashland, I lit up a cigarette and again got this horrible chest pain. Again, I went to the nearest ER sure that I was having a heart attack. It literally took me over a day and a half, plus two ER visits just to make it to college.

I got lucky when the college overbooked freshman boys, so eight of us had to be put in an all girls' junior dorm, which was fine with me. My roommate was one of the only black guys on campus, but De Andre and I got along well.

In college, I did not have any focus or direction and could barely make it to class most days. I would find someone to drink with every night and even started snorting Ritalin.

Ritalin is an amphetamine type drug that people use to treat ADHD. It's basically methamphetamine in pill form. When you take it, your appetite goes away, you can't sleep, your heart races, and your brain gets flooded with dopamine. That is what attracted me to the feeling, but this was about the worst possible thing a person with an anxiety problem should take.

I believe the abuse I faced caused my brain's levels of dopamine to be about twenty percent of a normal person's range. My brain was basically always in a dopamine deficient state. When I snorted the Ritalin, for about ten minutes I would have this euphoric rush. My brain would always want more as soon the high wore off. During that short ten minutes, my anxiety wasn't even on my mind.

As soon as that initial high wore off, feelings of complete panic, intense anxiety, and craving would take over me. I would either end up in the ER or need to chug hard liquor as fast as possible until I passed out.

I hated the feeling it gave me once the high wore off. I was basically getting ten minutes of feeling good, then eight hours of feeling bad, but it was impossible for me to say 'No.' If it was available, I would do I everytime.

During my first major break from college, another bad thing happened. On Thanksgiving Day, Moorestown Kate whom I was dating and I broke-up.

KATE 2/THANKSGIVING BREAK-UP

MOORESTOWN KATE WAS one grade below me. I thought she was one of the two prettiest girls in her grade. When we first met, she had basically used me to make her ex-boyfriend jealous and I used her for a hookup. Eventually, we got together as boyfriend and girlfriend.

We met while I was having a party at my house. Meanwhile, about three streets over, a friend of mine named Sarah was also having a get-together. I had about eighty people at my house and Sarah had around twenty at hers.

Sarah called me to ask who all I had over, and I asked her who was at her house, and she mentioned Kate. I knew Kate had recently broken up with her boyfriend. I thought she was pretty, so I told Sarah that I was coming over.

When I got there, I went right up to Kate and introduced myself, and she said, "I know who you are." I then asked if she wanted to go to a party with me and she said 'yes.' So, we left and walked to my house.

I think she was surprised that I was having a party at my house and left while it was going on. We walked right in and I invited her up to my bedroom, so we could talk and hear each other. We ended up kissing that night and the next day, I invited her to my house for Thanksgiving and she seemed okay with it and agreed. When Thanksgiving Day came, she never showed up or called, which kind of shocked me.

A friend of hers told me that she had just used me to get back with her boyfriend. When he heard that she had hooked up with me, he was jealous and immediately wanted to get back together with her.

About a month later, Kate got back in touch with me. Things with her boyfriend still weren't working out and she wanted to know if I was still interested in seeing her. So, we started dating.

While Kate and I were dating, there was this girl named Zoey who I thought was really pretty that had become my study partner. She was two years younger than me, but she was smart, pretty, and a lot of fun. Later, she even became a doctor.

One night about a week after I crashed my car in LBI, Kate told me that she was too tired to come out with me. The week before, she said she had to stay home and babysit her little brother with one of her friends. Later, I found out that her friend had two guys over and this really made me stop trusting her. So, when she didn't want to come out with me, I figured she was cheating on me. I came home drunk around one o'clock in the morning and called Zoey to see if she wanted to come over.

As soon as Zoey arrived, we sat on my back deck and talked. I started taking shots of Vodka and 151 Bacardi, so that I could hook up with her. I offered it to her, but she declined to drink, which impressed me about her.

Eventually, when I was completely wasted, I just leaned over and started kissing her. I then asked her if she wanted to go up to my bedroom. She agreed and we started making out in my bed. For some reason with Zoey I wasn't grossed out even though we did everything but have sex. I could tell that besides kissing, everything else was a first time for her. Afterwards, I drove her home and we never hooked up again. Even though things were on the rocks, Kate and I were technically together, and I had just cheated on her with Zoey.

So, that first Thanksgiving home from college, Kate and I were supposed to spend the night together. Exactly like that first Thanksgiving, she never called or anything. I guess Thanksgiving was not a good day for us.

Somewhere in the back of my mind, I thought she may have found out about Zoey. Turns out she had. Either Zoey or someone else had told one of her friends and it eventually got back to Kate that I had cheated on her.

That night, she went out to a party and hooked up with two different guys, then made sure I found out to get revenge on me. It hurt and I felt bad, but I just did not care about myself or anyone else enough to want to be a good partner at that point in my life. I made important decisions completely wasted and these were some of the consequences. Years later, Zoey even apologized to me by saying, "I hope I didn't ruin your relationship with Kate". But it wasn't her fault. It was mine.

Like most of the bad things in my life, there always turned out to be a bright side. I was never happy with Kate and I know that she was never happy with me, so in the end, the sooner it was over, the better. I felt bad about cheating on her for a long time and tried to apologize to her a couple times which never went well.

LEAVING COLLEGE/MIKE

AFTER THE BREAKUP with Kate, I headed back to college and things just got worse. When I wasn't too anxious to go to class, I would be sitting in class taking my pulse while feeling like I couldn't breathe. Studying was the last thing on my mind. After my first year, my grades were so bad that I got put on academic probation.

At home, I had this friend Mike who everyone, parents and friends alike, told me to stay far away from. He never went to college, which was rare for a Moorestown kid. He would tell me how much fun it was at home. He would say how great he was doing by not going to college.

I still have my high school yearbook and all these kids signed it and included a warning about steering clear of Mike. They wrote things like, "Lose your excess baggage, Mike is the devil," and, "When are you going to smarten up and see that Mike is going to bring you down?"

During my senior year, Mike showed up at a party that was being held by a girl named Katie who was in my class that never had a party before. This was during the big blizzard of 1996 and we were all drinking heavily. Mike and another kid named Scott came in with a box of shotgun shells. They told everyone they were building something cool. Mike was telling everyone about this girl named Lynn who went to our school and how bad he hated her. He said he was going to make a huge firecracker and put it on her door to scare her. We should all have taken him more seriously considering what he had done about a month earlier in December.

There was a family who had these awesome Christmas decorations set up in their front yard that included life-sized reindeer and Santa's sleigh. One night, we were all driving to a party at our friend Shuvaro's house when they stopped by this house. There were three cars packed full of kids. I was in the back seat of my friend's Jeep Grand Cherokee squished between two people, so I could hardly see what was going on. I saw the first car pull over while the other two cars pulled behind him. I asked what was going on and Mike told us we were all in for a surprise, which made us all think, "Oh no!"

The next thing I see is Mike and my friend Ryan running out of the first car with gas cans. They doused the deer and Santa's sleigh with gas, then Mike ran back to the car. When we saw him again, he had a welding torch. What came next was funny at first, but then it turned very unfunny fast.

Mike ran up to the deer and lit them on fire. By the time he got to Santa, the whole thing went up like a bomb had hit it. It was engulfed in thirty-foot-high flames that touched the night sky. Mike ran back to the car and we all took off. Everyone was dying with laughter, but I felt terrible. Then, I got angry at myself for not trying to stop it.

At that point, I had no idea whose home it was. As we were driving away, I saw a bunch of fire trucks speeding by. It made me think that the prank could have caught the house on fire. When I was a kid, I remember our neighbor always telling my mom that I was an incredibly deep thinker. I imagined a family working hard to set this whole thing up and how I would feel if someone had done this to my family. That night and for many years after, I felt bad just for being there, especially after I found out whose house it was.

That should have made me see Mike as the person he was, but if I wanted drugs, I needed to be around people like Mike, which is the sad part. The good kids were not getting wasted every day and did not want to be around it all. I felt like a good person trapped by a demon in my brain. It was almost like I was two different people.

I would come to realize that there are two different types of drug users. The most prevalent type are the good people who need to take drugs to cope with horrible circumstances. They may commit crimes or lie to get drugs, but when you take the drugs away, they are good, honest, and very loyal people.

The second type is the truly bad people. Whether they use drugs or not, they will commit crimes. The drugs are just the icing on the cake. They are prevalent in the jails where people like them shine. They are the ones that use and abuse the system while making everything harder for the people who truly need help.

This incident should have convinced me to take Mike very seriously and realize that he was dangerous, but we were all partying nonstop during the week of the blizzard and were not thinking clearly. My parents and my brother were stuck at our beach house during that insane snowfall, so I got to be home all alone.

I wanted to have Kate over to my house, so I asked the guys to drop me off at home. On the ride back to my house, we stopped just like we did for the reindeer, but this time I wasn't having any part of it. I got out of the truck we were in and started walking home. After I jumped out of Scott's truck, Mike went and put the firework he made on Lynn's front door, lit it, and ran.

The thing never went off and no one thought too much about it except Lynn and her parents. They found the device and didn't think it was funny and called the police.

The police ended up reconstructing the bomb and realized it could have done some serious damage, so Mike was charged. Mike in turn told on the guys who helped him build it. I think Mike and three other people got in trouble.

Another crazy part was that Mike said his father was upset that he got the most serious charge. Mike had built the damn thing and Scott drove him to drop it off, but the other people in the truck had no idea what the hell was going on. The only people who should have been upset were the two guys besides Mike that ended up with charges, one of which was Shuvaro.

Shuvaro called me furious at Mike. As far as I am aware, he really should not have been charged with anything. On Mischief Night, people always threw fireworks at people's homes. In fact, it happened to our house in Haddon Heights. But Lynn's family was upset, and that Detective Henry wanted to prosecute.

All the guys talked about how Mike should have just taken the fall alone. Scott helped Mike build it and drove him there, so maybe he deserved some of the responsibility. Besides them, the other guys should never have been charged.

Any sane person would have seen this as a sign to stay away from Mike. To add insult to injury, another thing happened not too long after that and someone almost got killed because of Mike.

Mike met a girl named Melissa. She lived in Haddonfield, New Jersey, which is about a ten-minute drive from Moorestown. Melissa had a boyfriend when she met Mike and, naturally, he was upset that she was now hooking up with Mike. In fact, Mike filmed Melissa without her knowledge and showed it to everyone, including all the guys at her work and I think he found out. Eventually, he threatened

Mike, and Mike threatened him back. He had apparently shown up at Mike's work with five of his friends. When Mike saw him, he ran out the back. Mike looked big but would always run from people.

Then, I received a call from Mike saying he needed me to pick up our friend Eddie, then come to meet him. He explained that he needed friends who could fight because this guy had brought "a posse" with him.

Mike called the guy and told him that he had his friends on the way over to fight him. What Mike should have said was that he called his friends to fight for him, so he could put up a good front for Melissa, but he was too much of a wimp to fight anyone.

By this point in my life, I had bought an SKS, which is a semi-automatic version of an AK-47 assault rifle. I also had an AR-15, which is a semi-automatic version of an M16 assault rifle. Mike asked me to bring the guns. He told me that these guys might bring guns, too. Not fully considering the consequences of such an action, I brought them.

When Eddie and I showed up to the apartment building where Mike lived, we saw him standing outside with our friends Chris, Kevin, and Eric. We parked and started to walk toward them when, suddenly, I started to see shadows and figures moving all around us. Within ten seconds, about fifty guys had surrounded us. Mike took off running. I don't think I have ever seen anyone run so fast in my entire life. He could have won the Olympics with that speedy sprint. It was one of the most cowardly things I have ever seen in my life.

Chris, Kevin, and Eric followed shortly after, but much less cowardly than Mike who could have been in another state by now. This left Eddie and I, who were not really sure what the hell was going on until it was too late. We were like baby calves surrounded by a pack of wolves.

Someone was loudly asking, "Which one is it?" and, "Which one do you want me to shoot?" The next thing I know, one of them comes running through the crowd of guys and hits Eddie square in the face with "The Club", which is a security device used to prevent people from stealing a car. The swing was violent, and it connected so perfectly with Eddie's nose. The sound was horrifying, and blood splattered in all directions. Eddie dropped to the ground like a sack of potatoes.

A second later, I had about ten guys punching me and I was swinging in all directions. I would get one punch in only to get hit on both sides of my face and the back of my head every time. It was clearly impossible to fight this many people no matter how good of a fighter I was. I then got hit on the kneecap with The Club and it felt as though my kneecap had become dislocated. This dropped me to the ground. All I could do was cover my face and hope it ended soon. I remember saying, "It really takes ten of you with a 'bat'?" (I called The Club a bat for some reason) and one of them said, "That's your fault for not bringing one!"

I could hear Chris yelling from a second-floor window, "The cops are coming!" He was at least trying to help. I found out later that Mike was hiding upstairs. Chris's yelling got them to stop punching and kicking me, but one said I busted his lip, so his friend smashed my car's lights, then they finally ran away. To my immediate left, I saw Eddie lying a few feet away in a pool of blood.

After seeing Eddie, I scared myself with a thought that popped into my mind. Eddie has been a good friend to me and when you have had people be as awful to you as people have been to me, you appreciate the good people that much more. I was loyal to people like Eddie and promised myself that I would do everything in my power to prevent anyone from hurting them. I came so close to grabbing the SKS/AK-47 and firing shots at these guys that I could taste it. Had I grabbed it and started firing, I would have at the very least killed a few of them. Thankfully, that did not happen.

I grabbed Eddie in my arms, and he bled all over my shirt. His nose was completely smashed in, and he was crying and shaking. I felt so bad for him, and I was furious with Mike for running away.

The police showed up shortly thereafter and asked what happened. They were not very sympathetic towards us. We had just been assaulted with a deadly weapon and the first thing they said was, "We have a bunch of rich kids from Moorestown starting trouble."
We gave them the description of the car and they stopped it about ten minutes later in the next town over. They said they didn't find any guns, so they let them go and never charged them with anything. They just committed aggravated assault with a deadly weapon and the cops did nothing.

To make matters worse, Eddie needed to go to the hospital. His nose was broken, and he was in severe pain. Mike refused to go. He stayed with Melissa and smoked weed. I went with Eddie to the hospital and his dad met us there. Eddie's father could not believe Mike never came and neither could Eddie. Eddie never talked to Mike again after that, and he could not understand why I continued to be Mike's friend.

THE DOUG INCIDENT

THERE WAS ANOTHER fight that happened right after the Mike fight that still haunts me to this day. I feel I should have done more. I was always someone who would never back down from a fight. But this night while having a severe anxiety attack, I went to this party and froze. I had a friend named Doug who lived in LBI. He had an older sister named Lori and they were both at this party. A local kid named Brian showed up looking to start a fight.

Brian was kind of a local legend for fighting like Paco had been, only a little worse. When he was fourteen he had severely beaten up a grown man so badly that the man almost died. They said Brian could knock people out twice his size with one punch. Although, his uncle was the mayor, so he always got away with it. He was never prosecuted or even arrested.

Earlier that night, I started having a severe panic attack at home after a friend gave me a hit of marijuana. Marijuana made me so anxious, especially if I was sober. Immediately after smoking it, I tried to find a party to drink at as quickly as possible.

In LBI, finding a party was not difficult at all. It took me about ten minutes to find one about six blocks from my home. I showed up to the party and heard a bunch of yelling and screaming going on as soon as I walked in. I just wanted to find the hard liquor and start chugging and avoid whatever it was until I was drunk enough to stop my panic attack.

As soon as I got to the second floor of the house, I saw Doug's sister Lori had started yelling at Brian. The next thing I knew, a whole crowd gathered around me and started egging it on. Apparently, he hit her, but I never saw it because so many people were blocking my view. Doug stepped in to defend his sister and Brian punched him, too. He hit Doug so hard that his punch knocked Doug's teeth through the skin of his cheek.

It turned into an out of control circus as a crowd of people fell down the stairs, throwing punches. Right after everything cleared up, I saw Doug lying on the ground with blood pouring out of his face. I ran up to him and took him in my arms and just like with Eddie, Doug's blood got all over me. As if this wasn't bad enough, the situation was making my anxiety even worse and I started to feel like I was having a heart attack.

I could hear someone talking in the background, which turned out to be Brian taunting him, saying, "You want some more?" That normally would have been my cue to start fighting, no questions asked. I still wish I had gotten up right then and started fighting him, but I didn't because of the panic attack. I remember my lungs felt like they wouldn't take in air and I felt a sharp pain all along the left side of my body. I was sure that my heart was going to give out at that very moment because of all that was going on. In the state I was in, the last thing I could do was fight.

I remember thinking, "Just wait thirty minutes, Brian, and then it's on!" Like Popeye eating his spinach, I would drink my hard liquor. I went upstairs and started doing shots of hard liquor right out of the liquor cabinet in this house without asking. I did eleven shots in three minutes, then came down looking for Brian. He was gone. Everyone was starting to leave because someone said the police were on their way.

For the next few hours, I rode around on my bike for three hours looking for him. I almost fought some guys that had nothing to do with Brian because I thought I saw him.

I felt so awful for not fighting him when I had the chance. I was so mad at myself. It bothered me day in and day out for a while. Doug never said anything about it, and I think he was too out of it to realize that I had a chance to fight for him. Doug eventually had to see a plastic surgeon to get his face sewn back together. To add insult to injury, when I got home my mother noticed the blood all over me and looked shocked, but her shock quickly turned to anger.

She saw a hickey on my neck from a girl I was with the night before. She went nuts, calling me "disgusting" and said this would not go on in her home. She yelled at me to take my clothes off right there and get washed, then called me a "disgusting child." The whole time I was covered in blood and not once did she ask if I was hurt.

The next day, my dad came to the shore for a visit. I told him what happened to Doug. We also found out that Brian was in my brother's lifeguard patrol. My dad told my brother that he "better have a talk with this Brian kid who attacked one of your brother's friends." I didn't expect Adam to do anything, but he found a way to do worse than nothing.

He came home from his day of lifeguarding and said he talked to Brian and that I was a liar. He said, "Brian told me he wasn't even at a party last night and I believe him." My dad had gone back to Moorestown and my mom immediately yelled, "How dare you make something like that up and put the blame on that poor kid." She told me to apologize to my brother, which I did by extending my middle finger. My mother lost it when she saw that and said, "Someday you will be gone, and I pray it happens soon!" She then told Adam to apologize to Brian for me making up this story about him.

It was after that, that I really gave up on my brother for good. While this was nothing unusual, I knew at that point that my brother was my enemy and that he would never change. Later in life, my mother found out everything I had said about Brian was true. I am sure it never mattered to either of them one way or the other. My brother knew at the time damn well that Brian did everything I said he did, but since he hated me, he would not be on my side now, or ever. The irony of my brother and mother calling me a liar was just comical; it was like seeing Hitler calling one of his soldiers a Jew hater.

FIRST COCAINE USE

NOT SURPRISINGLY, MIKE was the first person to introduce me to cocaine. I had come back from college one weekend to see Mike. He was working at a restaurant and met a cook there who was from Camden, and could get cocaine. Camden would eventually become a big part of my life when I got deep into drugs.

The cook said he could get us an eight ball of cocaine for one hundred and fifty bucks. Mike told me that he had done it before and that it was a thousand times better than Ritalin. So, one night we decided to get high on cocaine.

I was having some people over during the college holiday break and we decided to get cocaine. We were nervous driving into Camden. We could be robbed, shot, or arrested. This was also part of the excitement and fun of it. We got off the exit to Camden and headed toward the place where we bought the drugs, which was less than a block away from the highway. This was as safe as you could get when going to buy drugs in Camden. It just wasn't smart to venture too far off the highway in a city like this.

We drove slowly down this dark street and pulled up at this row home that was falling apart. The next thing I knew, we had ten black guys around the car looking in. They started asking, "How much do you want?" The cook finally got in my car and pulled out the eight ball of cocaine. An eight ball is about the size of a ping-pong ball. He said he wanted to see us taste it to make sure we weren't cops.

I put my finger into the baggy and rubbed some onto my gums. I saw that in a movie. Mike did the same. The cook then said, "Okay, we good. Give me the money and the powder is all yours."

Nobody would ever confuse this guy with a rocket scientist, but it's just funny how him asking if we were cops and watching us rub it on our gums proved to him that we weren't cops. It just didn't make any sense to me. He must have seen it on a TV show and thought if dealers ask someone if they are a cop and they are, they have to admit it. This blew me away because it wasn't as though getting into a car with an eight ball was legal in the first place.

We bought cocaine and then drove back to Moorestown. Camden and Moorestown were close, but they might as well have been on two different planets. Moorestown was a mostly all-white town with a lot of huge beautiful homes. It was safe, sheltered, quiet, prosperous, well-manicured, and super clean.

Camden was the exact opposite. White people stuck out like a sore thumb. We used to joke that you could get a ticket in Camden for a "Code 3W", which stands for Walking While White. It was mainly a black and Hispanic area. There was a lot of crime, drugs, poverty, abandoned homes, and burned-out buildings while a guttural feeling of despair blanketed the entire city.

Relieved to be back at my house, we invited the friends who did cocaine to get high. Everyone in my basement getting high were people I had met through Mike, not one was from Moorestown. The Moorestown people were upstairs drinking.

The cocaine wasn't a thousand times more powerful than Ritalin; nowhere near it. The initial high was definitely more intense, and this was followed by paranoia, then a strong craving to do more. It does give you a dirty feeling, which is a common side effect of Ritalin and other amphetamines. I would get so anxious that I would have to drink massive amounts of hard liquor to make it go away, but that initial high kept me coming back for more. When we ran out, I felt like I was going out of my mind wanting more. If a dealer had been at my house, I would have kept using until I ran out of money or had a heart attack!

The next morning, I drove back to college feeling awful both physically and mentally. I felt like I had destroyed my body and made my heart so weak that it was definitely going to stop at any moment now after using cocaine.

BACK TO COLLEGE

BY THIS TIME, the only reason I was going back to college was because it was where I was supposed to be, not because I had aspirations, goals, or cared about getting good grades. I cannot remember one time saying to myself, "This would be great for my future career," or, "this is going to make my life easier."

When most people go to college, they are overcome with the freedom of being away from their parents. They are finally able to drink and party without Mom and Dad putting a wrench in the works. For me, this was already the story of my life since I was a young child. I spent months at a time without my parents since I was twelve. I had been drinking alcohol to excess almost every night throughout my high school years. I never had a curfew, or any other real rules imposed upon me.

While this may sound great to some kids, it's important to remember that I was also never given any direction in life. Neither my mother nor father ever sat down and said, "You need to do well in school, do your homework, think of a career, learn how to save money, or anything else that would have led to a good future. They basically set me up for a "life" where I needed to rely on them for everything.

It may also sound great to have parents that are rich and buy you a lot of things, but when that is the only way they show love, it's not that great and can be more of a problem than you would think.

When my parents got angry, they would say things like, "How could you get bad grades and misbehave when we bought you a new car that cost $28,000?" They would never say, "How could you get bad grades? We love you and taught you to do better than this." While I'll admit it can be fun at times, it also sets you up for a life of problems, disappointments, let downs, and low self-esteem.

When I went to college, they deposited money into my checking account and gave me a credit card. I had always had access to their credit card since I was twelve, but never used it. My brother, on the other hand, spent over $20,000 dollars in his first year at college. He had every color Polo and Brooks Brothers shirt on the planet. In his mind, half of my grandfather's money was his and the other half was my mother's. He left out my father, myself, and my mother's two brothers. In my brother's mind, none of them lived up to his expectations and, therefore, he deserved it more than they did.

In my sophomore year, I was failing and in jeopardy of being kicked out, so my parents sat me down and explained how much money they (meaning my grandfather) had already spent to send me there. We didn't talk about how to get better grades, if I was okay, or anything like that. In their minds, it was all about money and nothing else. To them, this should have been enough of a reason for me to do well.

KICKED OUT OF COLLEGE

AFTER MY SECOND year at Randolph-Macon College, the school sent a notice home saying that I did not meet their standards and was not welcome back. My mother went crazy.

She explained to me that this was the final straw. I was out of the house for good this time and had two weeks to find a job and a new place to live. She also explained that they were taking away their credit card and I would not receive any help from them from now on.

She said I was a huge disappointment to her and that my whole family knew I would fail out of college because I failed at everything. She said, "You couldn't even pass kindergarten, so why the hell did she think I could ever get through college?" She said, "You threw away $50,000 of my money that I could have spent on myself." She again told me that I was "disgusting." I guess hearing this insult again along with all the hypocrisy she was spouting made me snap back. I said, "You are the one who's disgusting!" She started yelling about being on her period and bleeding. This is when my dad stepped in and told her to stop saying that to me.

She used to leave her dirty underwear all over my room. I was just so sick of seeing her dirty underwear throughout my personal space that I yelled, "Why the hell do you leave your dirty underwear all over my room?" She completely lost it when she heard what I'd said and started screaming, "This is my house and I'll do anything I want in my house." How dare I challenge her about anything, "How dare you!"

She yelled at me saying that I had nothing because everything I had belonged to her because she was the one who had given it to me; nothing was mine. My clothes were all things she bought, the house, my car, everything was hers and not mine. Then, she yelled, "Get out and don't ever come back!" and, "I HATE YOU!!!" at the top of her lungs.

My father had never heard her say that she hated me, and it even caught him off guard. He yelled for her to stop and seemed genuinely worried that this was going to permanently damage me. My mother's actions said "I hate you" louder than her voice ever could, so I was used to it by now and it phased me not one bit. She might as well have been yelling about water being wet and the sky being a nice shade of blue. I knew she hated me, and I had stopped caring about that a long time ago.

This was another reason I should not have gone to college. I knew I could never depend on my parents. They never did anything without strings attached. If I wanted any type of security in life, I needed to do it on my own or I would always be at my mother's beck and call. I would have to agree that my father was terrible and that she was a victim. I would also have to deal with her sexual desires at all times without any complaint.

Before I was two years old, I was already rebelling against her, so I knew I had no one I could depend on. I also had no life skills, no savings, and no idea how to live on my own. My parents gave me everything, so I never learned the value of money. If my mother wanted to take it away, I would be screwed. Later, she used this same tactic to control my brother for many years.

Most parents want their kids to be successful. My mother did everything in her power to make sure we could not survive without her, which she later admitted. Although, every chance she got, she would throw in our faces about how other people's children were becoming successful. I imagined myself explaining to her that these parents did not abuse their children and raised them with love.

As of now, my main concern, besides not having my car, was that I had nothing whatsoever. I asked her, "Where am I supposed to live?" and, "What money am I supposed to use?" My mom mentioned Atlantic City.

I forgot to explain earlier that she did teach us one economic lesson, and that was how to gamble in Atlantic City with a fake ID.

ATLANTIC CITY & GAMBLING

WHEN I WAS seventeen, I got a fake ID. My mom even gave me money to buy it because she loved going to Atlantic City. She would play the slot machines and wanted us to come. She would play high dollar games and win quite a bit, quite often. She easily won over three thousand dollars a night at least ten times if not twenty. One time, she even won ten thousand on a slot machine.

The casino she played at was the smallest one in Atlantic City. They treated her and my dad like high rollers. The first time I went there I won over a thousand dollars, then accomplished this again many more times. One day, I even won thirty-three hundred bucks in less than an hour.

The problem was I never saved that money. I never saw a reason to because I never really understood why saving was important, the need for credit, or anything along those lines. If my mom wanted something, she just bought it. My brother and I learned to do the same.

Going to Atlantic City taught me to lie about my age and that was fine because I was doing it with my parents. It also taught me that there were much easier ways to get money rather than working for it. I made more money in one hour of gambling than I did working a summer job. It also showed me how to get alcohol for free. Basically, underage gambling teaches a child all the wrong life lessons.

I was kicked out of my parents' house and I hadn't even been home from college for two weeks. At first, I started staying with Melissa, who was the same girl that Mike had us beaten up over. Melissa had her own apartment. I also stayed at my friend Kevin's mom's house and my anxiety got overwhelmingly bad there. I think it was a combination of not having anywhere to live and feeling out of control of my life that caused it to ramp-up. But, most likely, it was because I ran out of Klonopin.

I didn't have the money to see Dr. Blum. I thought when my mom said she was cutting me off from everything that she wasn't going to pay for my medication either. What I didn't know is that Dr. Blum had called my mother and asked where I was because I failed to show up for my appointment. He explained to her that I couldn't just stop taking the Klonopin because doing this could cause me to have a seizure and I could even die. I am sure she thought if I died in this manner that it would look bad on her for kicking me out. She agreed to keep paying for Klonopin, but nothing else.

I tried to go without the Klonopin for as long as possible, but it got so overwhelming that I felt as if I was in a dream world. I even hallucinated that a train was coming through the wall of Kevin's room. That was when I had my first seizure from Klonopin withdrawal and was taken to the ER.

At the ER, they gave me Klonopin and told me to never abruptly stop taking it or I could die from the withdrawal. That night, I met up with everyone at a bar, but didn't drive because of the seizure. I left my car at Melissa's apartment. When I got back, my car was gone.

Someone had broken into Melissa's apartment, found my keys and stolen my car. I called the police, but they had already found my car abandoned on the side of a highway and had even notified my parents.

This led to me coming back home to live with them. I truly believed for the first time that my mother finally realized that her actions could result in my death. Although, I don't think it was so much my death that worried her. I think it was all about her actions causing my death. When I say, "her action," I mean her kicking me out of the house. Had I died, I think she thought people would have asked, "Why the hell did you kick him out over a fight?" My mom was mostly concerned with convincing her friends that she was the victim. She loved getting sympathy and being viewed as a loving mother who was done badly by her son and husband. It was like a drug to her.

Most of my mother's friends cared more about my well-being than she did. I even remember her friends crying when the DUI happened, but she didn't shed a tear. If she wasn't bashing me, she would tell them about her awful husband. As much as they sympathized with her, I doubt they respected her for trashing her own family. I am sure they must have thought, "If your husband is so terrible, why are you still with him?"

OPIATES ENTER THE PICTURE

OPIATES WERE BOTH a gift and a curse for me. At first, they were the answer to all my problems. Then they created a whole new set of problems for me and finally became the problem!

Now that I was home from college, I started spending more time with Mike and his group of friends. We started snorting Ritalin and cocaine, drinking alcohol, and smoking marijuana daily. Mike had introduced me to a small-time drug dealer who became the first real drug dealer I started buying drugs from. His name was Mike, too. Mike the dealer drove a black Camaro S.S. and talked like Rocky Balboa. He had a pretty blonde girlfriend, which was shocking because he was ugly and not too smart. Mike would be overly cautious about everything and tried to make himself out to be something like a modern-day Scarface. The problem was that he lived at home with his parents and was a complete idiot.

For us, he was the closest thing to a real big-time drug dealer and he sure played the part. He would claim that he had to drive around the block five times to throw off the helicopters chasing him. He would also tell us to talk quietly because the CIA was listening to him, which made absolutely no sense.

One time he even claimed that this old man walking a dog was a government agent hired to watch him and he claimed he had already seen him ten times that day with the same dog. When we finally bought the drugs, Mike drove away, but as soon as he got next to this old guy, he decided the best way not to be seen or have attention brought to him was to slam on the brakes and light up the tires. His car looked like it was in a NASCAR race as its back end started fishtailing all over the street with a cloud of grey smoke rising around it. I thought this poor old man was going to have a heart attack and the dog almost ripped his arm off trying to run away. The same dog Mike claimed was a government spy dog. This was the kind of thing that happened regularly around Mike.

One night, Shane called me and asked if I wanted to go to a Philadelphia Flyers hockey game. After the game, we were driving through South Philly when we both decided to get some cocaine from Mike. Mike told us to meet him at an apartment in South Philly not far from the game. When we entered, Mike, another guy, and three girls were all lying on the couch spaced out and smiling. They were surrounded by hundreds of pill bottles.

After we bought the cocaine, I asked him what was in the pill bottles and he said "Percs, my dog, Percs." I didn't know what a "perc" was. He offered each of us three of them for free, which was nice of him. As nice as a drug dealer gets, I guess.

He told us to take one when we were coming down off cocaine. Coming down off coke was something I always dreaded, especially with my anxiety problem. The only way I could deal with it was to drink hard liquor until I passed out. I really didn't have much faith that these little pills could do much of anything, especially since I needed half a bottle of vodka just to calm down after doing lines of coke. But that night, I gave it a try anyway.

I came back to my house shaking and anxious from the coke and took one Percocet, then went down to my basement and waited. After about twenty minutes, I was about to give up hope and start drinking when suddenly I started feeling warm all over and I knew something was happening.

The warm feeling started in my stomach and spread throughout my whole body. Almost instantly, the shaking and that horrible feeling of coming off cocaine disappeared. The warm feeling brought with it a strange, but enjoyable feeling of euphoria. At first, I wasn't sure if this was real, but slowly the euphoric feeling started to completely overtake my anxiety like nothing else had ever done before. I laid down on the couch and, for the first time in years, did not feel this horrible anxious monkey on my back. It was like God himself had healed me.

Amazing things started to happen. I started watching whatever was on TV and was not bored. I didn't want to smoke cigarettes. The idea of drinking alcohol now seemed unnecessary. My depression was also gone, and I felt truly happy. But, being free of the feeling that I was going to die was the best. I felt tears of joy for the first time in my entire life. I laid there on the couch that night and felt happy; the very definition of 'happy.' I remember thinking that if I could always feel like this, life would be great!

I realize now what was happening was my endorphin system had become normal from the opiates in the Percocet. Percocet is a combination of Tylenol and a manmade opiate called Oxycodone. Each pill contains five milligrams of Oxycodone. The Oxycodone was what was making me feel so great as it is very similar to heroin.

The abuse I suffered, combined with depression, anxiety, etcetera, had my natural endorphin system working at about ten percent of what it should have been, which is why being in my own skin or sitting still was very hard. It was also why going to class and doing homework, sports, or anything for that matter seemed totally boring. A life without enough endorphins is miserable and extremely difficult. If a normal person had their endorphin system scaled back to ten percent for even one day, this is how their day would be:

They would not sleep well and when they woke up, getting out of bed would be the hardest thing ever. Once they get out of bed, taking a shower or even brushing their teeth would seem extremely difficult. They would have no energy or excitement for the day ahead. Going to work would feel like climbing a mountain. When they got to work, it would be incredibly boring. Their day would move so slow that they would be staring at the clock all day. Finally, when the day is almost over, they will be counting the minutes down. When they got home, they would be so tired that they would not want to do anything and would just sit there thinking about the next miserable day ahead. Trying to fall asleep, they would be stressed out thinking about how life is a chore rather than a fun adventure.

That is what life is like without endorphins. Next time you judge someone for becoming a drug addict, I suggest you try to live a week in their shoes, then if you can honestly tell me you wouldn't be searching for something to make you feel outside of yourself, you must be a robot. Now, imagine severe anxiety and depression disorders to deal with on top of that feeling of nothingness. This is what every day of my life was like before I found opiates, and why I thanked God when I did find them.

Many people I know who have normal levels of endorphins will throw up after taking Percocet. They will not enjoy the feeling because their systems are normal, so adding more endorphins is too much for them. My high was their normal. I decided that night that this is how I wanted to feel and, if possible, stay feeling this way forever.

The next morning, the Percocet was still affecting me. I woke up happy, motivated, and did not feel anxious at all. I can't tell you how great it felt to not be facing my death. At this point, I had believed that death was imminent every day for years, which had really worn me down. To have relief from that fear was like being chased by a man-eating tiger for miles and finally making it to safety.

That next night I took another Percocet and stayed home watching a movie. I had gone out every night of my life for so long to get drunk that it was so nice not to have to do that. Also, I only took one Klonopin that day. I normally took eight pills every day. I had become so dependent on them that it was amazing to me that I didn't need them either.

The next night I took the last one and went to look in my parents' cabinet for some more. Luckily, they had multiple bottles of them, so I started to take one in the morning, too. I would take one like a person drinks a cup of coffee to get my day started, suddenly I felt motivated to go to work and make something of myself. Then, I started taking one in the morning, one in the afternoon, and one at night. Soon I ran out of my parents' Percocets and called Mike the drug dealer to see if he had any more for sale.

He answered, "Eh, yo'. Absolutely I do," and said they were five dollars apiece. He added, if I bought fifty at a time, he would let me have them for four a piece, or two hundred dollars for fifty pills. So that is what I did.

When you take opiates daily, you build a tolerance to them very quickly. In a short time, I was now taking two at a time, four times a day. So, a bottle of fifty from Mike would last me for about one week. Soon after that, the fifty would only last four days. Not too long after that, I was spending $400 a week on them. In my mind, there was nothing wrong with this. There was never a point where I thought I was doing anything wrong. In fact, I was beyond grateful for these pills. When I was on them, I was at peace for the first time in my life and that was worth a lot more than four hundred dollars a week.

Opiates put the world in a new light for me. All those horrible things didn't seem so awful anymore. Not only was my depression and anxiety gone, they chased away all the terrible feelings I had about being in my own skin. I could even stand being around my family for short periods of time, which was a small miracle in and of itself.

Doctors had given me pills most of my life, and so had my mom. I figured I was old enough to give them to myself now. If I could have pressed a magic button that would have kept me high forever, it would have been a dream come true. In my mind, what the hell could go wrong? I would later find out, a whole damn lot!

The first time I started to realize that these pills were not all rainbows and fluffy kittens was on New Year's Eve of that year. My friend Brian had invited me to go to a New Year's Eve party on Long Island in New York. Before going, I ran out of my supply of Percocets. I called Mike and asked to buy more, but he told me that he'd already left for the Poconos, so I would have to wait till tomorrow morning. I wasn't happy about that, but I was not worried about it either. I just figured that I'd go have fun at the party and I'd be fine until then.

What hadn't yet crossed my mind was that my body had become dependent on them. I had been taking these pills every day for the past four months, multiple times a day, and this was the first time I'd ever run out. I would start going into withdrawal if I did not get ahold of some soon.

The withdrawal started on the drive up to Long Island which began as chills all over my body. The ride started feeling like it was taking forever and my nose started running non-stop. Even though I was cold, I started sweating through my clothes. I also became super agitated at every little thing. By the time we got to the party, I was feeling overwhelmingly anxious and incredibly miserable. I tried to drink it away with alcohol, but that didn't work. It just made things worse. I felt like I had a combination of the flu, stomach poisoning, an anxiety attack, and bad depression hit me. I didn't feel like talking to anyone or being at a party. Finally, at three o'clock in the morning I decided I couldn't take feeling like this anymore and wanted to drive home.

When you are going through withdrawal, it is practically impossible to get drunk. The more you drink, the worse you feel because you can't get drunk, or even buzzed. I told Brian that I felt like the flu was coming on and had to leave. I drove all the way home and got there at about six thirty in the morning. Low and behold, there was a message on my machine from Mike saying that he came home early and to call him if I still wanted the Percocets. So, at six thirty in the morning I called and woke him up. I told him that I needed some. He was upset that I woke him up but told me to come over anyway as he could never turn down money. I quickly drove over to his place and made it there before 7am. As soon as he gave them to me, I popped them in my mouth. I told him about the horrible flu I had and was hoping the percs would help. He said, "Yeah, the Perc Flu." I had no idea what the hell he meant.

I was in complete agony by the time I got to Mike's, but about twenty minutes after taking the pills, I felt that familiar warm feeling in my stomach and creeping up through my whole body. Within five minutes, all the bad feelings I had disappeared. It felt like a miracle. In only a few minutes, I went from feeling like I had the bubonic plague to feeling like I was superman on top of the world. This semblance of healing is probably the closest anyone can get to experiencing both Heaven and Hell, and while they still have a pulse.

Once I understood that this "flu" was in fact withdrawal from not having Percocet, there was no doubt in my mind that this is when I and most opiate addicts started to realize that they are in serious trouble. There is no easy or painless way out now. I am now a prisoner in my own body. The only way to avoid the pain was to take more opiates. Taking more is not the greatest solution to this problem either. They become extremely expensive, they are gone before you know it, they are illegal, and the more you take, the worse the "flu" or withdrawal gets. Most importantly, if you have suffered a lot like I have, once you get that feeling of freedom opiates provide, the last thing you want to do is stop taking them.

I may have called the withdrawal the "flu," but it is so much worse than the flu. Calling opiate withdrawal the "flu" is like calling a nuclear bomb a firecracker. I have read books by other addicts and they all say the same thing: opiate withdrawal is by far the worst feeling imaginable on Earth, and I agree! People will do all sorts of crazy things to avoid withdrawal. They will burn themselves with scalding hot water, they will smash their hands with hammers, let their feet get run over by a car, and much worse. All to get an emergency room doctor to give them a prescription. Yes, I did those things, too.

The part I never understood about the ER is that someone could easily get a shot of an opiate by just coming in and complaining about back pain. I would come in with full opiate withdrawal, which is about a thousand times worse than any back pain, and the doctor would tell me, "Get the hell out, you junkie." Considering doctors were the ones who were providing the drugs that got so many in this predicament in the first place, I found it very hypocritical of them to be so judgmental of addicts once they developed a crucial need for the drugs they had prescribed.

I had no idea how powerful this addiction was or where it would take me. I was drawn to the fact that I felt amazing and life had become semi-bearable—as long as I was taking opiates regularly. Many of the addicts I have spoken to have said that they wish they could go back in time and prevent their former selves from taking that first opiate. But for me, I never saw it that way. While opiates did bring me into the depths of Hell, it wasn't like my life was going great to begin with, by any means. Even though my life was hellish before opiates and continued to be, the break they gave me from my reality was exactly what I needed at the time.

WORKING FOR THE DEA

Now THAT I had quit drinking and going out every night and had the opiates in my system, I was actually able to accomplish things. I even wanted to get a job, but not a regular job. Besides, I was already a doctor, or at the very least a pharmacist, in my own mind. Before this time, my resume consisted of a summer job at a gas station and my experience as a beach lifeguard. While high one day, I decided to register at the local community college and major in criminal justice.

Being high made it possible for me to pay attention and do well in class. One day, my teacher recommended that I look for a job with law enforcement. Although, technically, I was on the other side of that issue, it still seemed like a good idea to me.

I have always been a big dreamer. I would see a movie and imagine myself living the life of the main character. I remember watching the movie "Donnie Brasco" and thinking it would be a lot of fun working as an undercover FBI agent. So, one day I saw that the DEA was hiring. I tried to get an interview by applying at a local field office, but the only way to apply was to fill out a lengthy application online. After I filled it out, I waited but heard nothing for months.

Finally, I had had enough of waiting for the DEA. I drove to their local field office and decided to tell them how much they needed me (the person who was high on drugs) to help them. These two agents came out and talked to me. I think at first, they thought I was a crazy person, which would not have been too far from the truth. I told them that I wanted a job working for them and that they should hire me now. They both looked at me as if to say, "What the hell are you talking about?" Then, they said, "You need to go through the entire hiring process. You can't just jump in at this level."

I said, "Come on, guys! There must be something I can do." I read about how the CIA contracted with agents and how the FBI used business informants, and so why wouldn't the DEA need some help from someone who knew the drug world? They said the only way that would happen is if I could prove to them that I could be an asset.

At this point, I really didn't know too much about the drug world. I did know how to make up stories and act, so I decided to do my best to convince them that I could be useful to them. After about an hour of telling them that I knew the inner workings of all the drug outfits in the area from marijuana to heroin dealers, I explained how I could help bust them. They decided to give me a shot, which put me in a state of complete disbelief and still does now that I think about it. They said they would do a background check on me first and would get back to me.

Sure enough, a few days later I received a call from them inviting me to come down to the office. When I showed up, they told me that I would be working with them, but on a limited basis. They wanted me to help them purchase narcotics, so they could learn about the different drugs being sold all over the South Jersey area. They said they would see how I did, then we would go from there. This was a fine arrangement for me.

To get the ball rolling, I had to fill out a ton of paperwork, then sign numerous documents promising to keep everything a secret, and that I would never do anything illegal while working for them. As I was signing, I remember thinking about how high I was already on Percocet.

I was also informed that I was not going to be paid by check for the purpose of secrecy. They would pay me in cash, and it was my responsibility to report my earnings to the IRS. I was told I would also get a percentage of all the cash we recovered from drug arrests. They told me that some of the people who worked undercover made up in excess of a million dollars a year and that one person had recently received a $250,000 bonus by helping them bust a big drug ring in our area. They gave me a special beeper that they would use to contact me. I was expected to have it on me at all times. They also used special codes after texts, like 616 for emergency or 777 for one agent and 888 for another. All this "James Bond" type stuff seemed really cool to me. Most importantly, they told me that I was never to tell anyone that I worked for the DEA. Naturally, the first thing I did when I got home was tell my parents I had gotten a job working for the DEA.

The first "drug buy" I did for the DEA was with an agent named Darren. We met up with a guy under the pretense of wanting to buy two ounces of cocaine from him. Our real goal was to buy methamphetamine, but this guy wanted us to buy cocaine from him first before he would sell us the meth. I don't think he had access to meth, but he used the "buy cocaine before he would sell us meth" story just to get us to buy cocaine from him. We pretended to be big spenders, so he would think we could afford to buy a lot.

The DEA used money from drug arrests and seizures to buy more drugs in order to, in theory, get them off the streets. The money had to be strictly accounted for and all the serial numbers were photographed and logged. Just getting ready to go on a drug buy took hours. There were a lot of moving parts. The DEA would get tips from people who ratted their friends out to save their own butts after getting arrested. Then, guys like Darren and I would show up wanting to buy drugs from the person they ratted out. Normally, we would tell them that they were recommended to us by that friend. This was sometimes a very dangerous situation as the friend could always rat us out as well. If they would tell on their own friends, what would stop them from telling on us? After all, it was not like we were dealing with the most honorable people. They were drug dealers who were already lying to friends and setting them up.

Once we bought the drugs, they would either arrest that person or let them go. If they let them go, it was so we could buy more drugs later and create a bigger case. When that person was eventually arrested, there would be so much evidence against him that he would have little choice but to flip on someone else higher up the drug ladder and they would go after them next.

This is how this never-ending game would continue trying to reach the "top guy". Sometimes the guy they arrested would rather go to jail than tell on someone else, which rarely ever happens. Even if they did arrest the top guy, there were a thousand other guys waiting to take his place in a second. Fighting the War on Drugs was like a cat chasing its tail, which is exactly how it felt working for the DEA. We were accomplishing nothing; actually less than nothing. We were just making the situation worse and everyone knew it.

The most important part of the job was to look as though we were not working for the DEA. The first time I met all the agents, I realized how very valuable I was to them. Darren obviously knew very little about the drug world. The first time I went out with him for a drug buy, he wore these shoes that no person in the drug world would ever wear. They looked like very cheap 1980's basketball shoes that you could get at the Salvation Army. Drug dealers pay attention to things like shoes. We were supposed to be buying these drugs to flip them and make money. This wasn't a huge buy. I think we spent $2200, but no drug dealer was going to wear such out-of-style shoes and have the kind of money we were supposed to have. It didn't make sense and looked very police-like.

This was completely lost on Darren and the other agents for that matter. He just figured that because they were in the drug world, things like shoes didn't matter. Maybe the addicts didn't care, but the dealers sure did. I said something to him about it, but he said I didn't know what I was talking about.

Sure enough, right after I said that, we were at a drug buy and I was alone with the dealer when he said, "What is with your boy's shoes?" Because I was wearing a recording device, Darren and the other agents got to hear this question, too. After that, they all started listening to me more. I couldn't believe they were going after big drug cartels and didn't know this stuff. They were also oblivious to a lot of the lingo. The way they talked sounded very rehearsed and scripted, like they were regurgitating lines from a movie. I tried my best to get them to talk like I talked.

The first drug buy happened in the parking lot of a busy supermarket. It took a while to alert the local police that we were doing a drug buy. We did this because we purposely wanted the guy to get away, so we could follow him to wherever he went. We had to make sure the police didn't see us and think we drug dealers, or they'd try to make an arrest. If this happened, things could go south–quickly.

Imagine if undercover plainclothes cops with guns witnessed what they thought was a drug deal going down. Now, Darren and I are in our car and not only do we have a gun, but this dealer has a gun, too. Now, if cops run up in plainclothes with guns, the dealer could get spooked and start shooting at them, us, or both. It's also possible that the cops could get spooked and shoot us, especially if they saw a gun. Not to mention if we just saw men with guns rushing us, the agents watching us could shoot them. It was a very dangerous situation! We tried to lower the risks, but there was no way to eliminate them.

Once we informed the police, Darren and I drove to meet the dealer. We parked in the parking lot as far away as possible from cars and people. The dealer pulled his car right up to the front of our car. Darren got into the back seat so the dealer could sit up front. The dealer then pulled out the drugs and Darren weighed them on an electronic scale. They were right on the money weight wise, so we gave him the $2200. We asked him about buying a lot of meth soon. As he was impressed with how smooth this deal went, he said he would sell us the meth now and set it up for next week.

After the buy, we drove back to the office. On the way back, I remember cruising down the highway going about a hundred miles per hour as we followed a group of cars filled with DEA agents. This was the first time ever I was not worried about getting a speeding ticket. I remember asking Darren if it was okay for me to drive that fast. He said, "Andrew, if a police officer pulled us over and interfered with us, I have the power to arrest him!" I thought that was pretty freaking cool. This job was most definitely meant for me.

I also think the DEA was proud of how I handled myself. The only part that no one knew was that I was high on Percocet and Klonopin. The day we did that deal, I had taken at least twenty-four Percocets and three two-milligram Klonopins.

THE KATE SITUATION

WHEN MY FRIEND John graduated from Notre Dame, he had a graduation party at his house in North Jersey. He invited me and shore Kate to the party. Kate lived in Pennsylvania and decided she would drive her car to my house, then we would ride to the party together.

There was always something about Kate that I liked. Probably the fact that she never fell for me caused me to be even more interested. We would hook up at random times and then not see each other for a while, but she had a cool personality that I liked.

Two years earlier on the last night of summer break before she left for college, I was home alone at around three o'clock in the morning. I heard this knocking on my back window, it was Kate. She said she saw my light on and wanted to hang out and get high and drunk together. I have no idea what I was doing up at that time, but of course it didn't take much convincing on my end. We started pounding shots of hard alcohol and drinking beer. We eventually decided to go in my bedroom and smoke weed under my glow stars.

We went into my bedroom and turned off the lights. The room lit up like we were outside. Then I put on Pink Floyd's "Learning To Fly" and we started passing a bowl of marijuana back and forth. I remember we had a tube we were using to blow shotguns into each other's mouth. At one point, I just put the tube down and put my lips on hers and we started kissing. We laid in my bed and started making out. This is when I started to panic! If I cared for someone, even if I wasn't disgusted by them, sex felt like I was doing something wrong to them.

Luckily, right before it got to that point, she sprang up and ran outside, then started throwing up. We pounded the hard liquor so fast that her stomach could not handle it. I guess she was so embarrassed that she left without saying goodbye. I was relieved.

So now, fast forward three years and here I am with Kate, but now I am high on Percocet, so my anxiety is gone, and I didn't have to be completely drunk to make this happen. I knew if someone had liked me even a little bit when I was like that, they would enjoy being around me even more now. For some reason, I wanted to have sex with her even though it scared me to try to.

We drove up to John's house for the party and even stayed the night up there. The next morning as we drove back to my house in Moorestown, I could tell things were going well between us. The next weekend, I went down to the shore. All our friends including Kate were going out to drink at a bar. I was so content being high that I just stayed home. In the middle of the night, I received a call from Kate saying she just got home from the bar and wanted me to come over to her house. I went right over and went up to her bedroom. She took off all her clothes and we started kissing in her bed. I could not get turned on. I kept trying, but I could not stop feeling as though I was doing something bad. I just kept stalling in the hope that a miracle would happen. She noticed I was stalling and exclaimed, "Just give it to me already!"

But it was impossible. I was not drunk, so there was no way I could do it. It was such an awful situation to be in yet again; the ultimate Catch-22. I didn't wanted to hurt Kate and I knew if I left her without having sex, it would hurt her. Girls take that kind of stuff very personally. I told her I had to leave. I remember the look on her face was like, "What the hell is wrong?". I felt really terrible for that. After that night, I think she started to hate me.

We saw each other a couple of times after that, but our friendship was never the same. She was cordial with me the first time we bumped into each other, but the second time, she had found out I was an addict and stayed as far away from me as possible. I felt really bad for the situation with her especially because I had known her for so long. In reality, I probably did hurt her feelings, but she never liked me enough to care and probably did not think too much about it. Years later, I even tried to apologize, but I didn't know exactly what to say. She just thought I was crazy and didn't care what the hell I was apologizing for.

BREAKING MY HAND ON PURPOSE

AFTER TAKING PERCOCET for almost a year straight, my dealer Mike finally ran out. At this point, he was my only source. Being that I could not get my hands on any, I started going into withdrawal. I was sick for about two days straight until I couldn't take it anymore and decided I was going to figure out a way to get more no matter what.

My friend Brian provided me with a small miracle when he found some in his parents' cabinet. It was a bottle containing only forty pills, but it gave me some relief for two days. After Brian's parents' pills ran out, the withdrawal came back. Getting more pills was the only thing I could think about. At this point, nothing else mattered.

During withdrawal, drugs become as important as air because you feel like you are drowning. I tried taking more Klonopin to offset the escalating anxiety, but I soon ran out of them, too. I was now going through benzodiazepine and opiate withdrawal together. The combined withdrawal from those two drugs is beyond bad, and words can't describe it.

This is when I started considering hurting myself, forging a prescription, or anything. Never before had I seriously thought about breaking the law by forging a prescription. This never would have ever crossed my mind. Once in full-blown withdrawal, I am suddenly ready to do almost anything.

I tried going to the ER, but the doctor told me that unless I had some real injury, I wasn't getting any opiates. He thought I was "drug seeking," which is like telling a person at a gas station that they are "gas seeking."

I left the ER and headed home. During the ride, I got the idea to break my hand, then go back to the ER. As soon as I got home, I went into the garage and found a hammer. I put my hand on the bench and stared at it for a while. Finally, I said, "The hell with it," and brought the head of the hammer down on my hand hard. My hand swelled up, but nothing was broken because I could feel that the bones were still intact. I knew I had to hit it harder. The pain from a broken hand is nothing compared to opiate withdrawal. I just wanted it over with and fast. This time, I swung the hammer with all my might. It landed on my hand with a crushing blow and I let out an awful yelp. After that, I was confident that I had broken it and that made me happy.

I drove to a different ER and the first thing I asked for was painkillers. The ER doctor told me the worst word an addict can hear in a hospital "Ibuprofen." He told me that unless the x-ray came back positive, that was all I was getting from him.

When the x-ray came back showing that I had a broken hand, I was so happy that he almost didn't give me Percocet, but he really didn't have a choice. He wrote me a script for twenty pills, and I left with a broken bone in my hand. I told myself that I was only going to take Percocet when things became dire because I wanted to wean myself off slowly. My idea of "slowly" was to take the whole bottle in twenty-four hours and not twelve. Opiate addicts always start out with great intentions, but things never work out as planned.

After smashing my hand and almost not getting any, I mostly gave up on the self-injury thing, thank God. Later, I heard a guy in AA talk about how a dentist would give him a prescription for Percocet every time he had a tooth pulled. He smiled and he had no teeth!

No one I knew had any left in their parents' medicine cabinets, hospitals were out, and even my own family doctor was on to me. So, for the next month I had no choice but to stay bedridden and kick this sickness. I didn't want to talk to anyone or go anywhere. I was a ghost at the DEA and told them I had mono. It was an awful, agonizing month, but on day thirty-three, I finally started coming around.

With the sickness gone and no opiates, my anxiety and depression came back with a vengeance. I started drinking heavily again and smoking weed with the same people as before, but it wasn't the same. I was going through post-acute withdrawals but was completely unaware of this.

During Post-Acute Withdrawal, or PAWS, you are like a raw nerve. To have an orgasm, all you need to do is touch yourself. And you can forget about sleeping. I saw this doctor on TV talking about how it is impossible for a human to go more than three days without sleeping. Maybe a non-drug addicted person can't do this, but I have personally gone well over 30 days without sleeping for one minute. No naps or anything, which is enough to make you go temporarily insane.

When you are in PAWS, time becomes unbearably slow and the depression is unrelenting. You feel like you have no Serotonin in your brain at all, which is why it is easy for people to commit suicide during PAWS. Everything is super boring. I remember thinking I could win the lottery and not feel the least bit excited. This is because you have practically no dopamine in your brain at this point.

The anxiety in PAWS is also overwhelming. Your GABA levels are reduced to almost nothing, so there's nothing to help you keep calm. It feels like everything is scary and even the slightest noise will make you jump. On the other hand, your norepinephrine levels are through the roof. Because they were numbed by the opiates, they have come back full force, like an extra strong shot of constant caffeine. This very uncomfortable balance of chemicals only adds to the anxiety and agitation.

The only thing that can get these chemicals back into their normal balance is time. Exercise, eating healthy, and staying clean also help the process, but time is really the only way they are going to become normal again. Meanwhile, in the back of your mind, you know that if you just take one Percocet, all of these awful feelings will be gone almost instantly. Not only will they be gone, the exact opposite will occur. All the extremely bad feelings will morph into extremely good feelings within minutes, if not seconds. Knowing this, your natural instinct is to try to escape the agony, which is another reason why it is so hard to beat an addiction to opiates.

I don't think there is any drug on this planet that is harder to break away from than opiates—and stay off them for good. All kinds of famous, smart, powerful, and accomplished people have been brought to their knees by opiates! Now that I was past the physical withdrawal and back to my old ways, I had an amazing coincidence happen that brought me back together with someone from my past.

VALERIE RETURNS

NOT LONG AFTER getting clean of the opiates, I reconnected with Valerie, who was the girl I had dated in Haddon Heights that caused so many problems. I was at a friend's house getting drunk and started looking through one of his yearbooks. I saw that he had one from Haddon Heights High School because he had gone there for one year. I immediately wanted to look through it to see who I knew.

As soon as I saw Haddon Heights, that familiar sick feeling came over me again. In the back of my mind, I had always wondered about Valerie. I had heard that she'd started dating my old friend Jess who had turned against me for Luigi. I heard they basically became King and Queen of the class. I was sure that she was probably married by now and had long forgotten about me, but a part of me still wondered about her.

I looked and saw her picture in the yearbook, and it even had a directory with her phone number. Being drunk, I had no problem picking up the phone and dialing. The phone rang and rang. I never thought she would answer, but suddenly I heard a female voice say 'hello.' I asked to speak with Valerie, the girl replied, "This is her." My heart started racing, and I blurted out, "This is Andrew. The guy you dated when we were little kids." She was completely blown away that I called her. She said that we had to get together and catch up.

She told me how amazing this was because the phone line I called only rang in her basement and no one ever answered it. She was down there getting a drink, and something told her to pick up the phone. She said she never answers that phone, but today she did. It truly seemed like fate had intervened. We agreed that we would meet up for drinks. For the first time in what felt like eons ago, I started to feel some good natural chemicals in my brain, and I was even a little happy.

Two days later, one of Valerie's girlfriends drove her to meet me. I showed up in my Mustang to pick her up. She ran up to me and we gave each other a big hug. Valerie had been a very pretty girl, and she still had the same beautiful lips, gorgeous eyes, and dirty blonde hair. She, too, had done some modeling. Although, I could not help but notice that she looked like she had aged more than most people our age.

I took her out to a local bar. We drank beer and did shots. We didn't even make it out of the parking lot before we were kissing each other. We even came close to having sex that night. When she got home, she called me to say what a great time she'd had and couldn't wait to go out again. Not too long after, Valerie and I decided we were going to be a couple. In my mind, it felt like she might be the person I was meant to be with, or so it seemed.

PARADISE WITH VALERIE GOES DOWN HILL FAST

ONE MONTH AFTER Valerie and I started dating, I received a message on my pager. The only two people that had my pager number were the DEA and my drug dealer, which was ironic to say the least. Every time I heard a message come through, I would get excited hoping it was Mike and this time it was. He put 777 after his page to let me know he was back in business and had Percocet. He used codes just like the DEA did. I had been off opiates now for about three months. I was even feeling semi-normal again, but as soon as I saw that code on my pager, I headed out the door within seconds. I didn't even take the time to tell anyone where I was going.

On my way there, I got this amazing expectation high. It felt like my brain was producing its own opiates. This feeling only happened this strongly after being clean for a while, then suddenly you find out you are about to get high, this incredible rush happens. I was amazed at the strength of the drug's stranglehold on me.

I struggled through a month of absolute physical agony and three months of mental hell, yet here I was not even blinking an eye at the thought of putting myself back in that predicament. I simply told myself that I would not let it get out of control again. I decided to only buy ten, but when I got there, Mike informed me that this might be the last time Percocet would be around for a long time, so I better buy at least fifty to be safe. I left with two hundred and fifty for the bargain price of $900.

As soon as they were in my hand, I popped two. By the time I got home, they had kicked in. The mental high I had going on was nothing compared to what that first high felt like after being clean for three months. The depression and anxiety were gone. My energy level was through the roof and I was riding a wave of euphoria that made me feel like I could conquer the world. The painful memories of the last three months floated far from my mind.

People always have this disillusion that opiate addicts spend the whole time nodding out and drooling on themselves, as if in a coma or zombie-like state. Some do that occasionally, but for addicts like me, opiates were like cocaine minus the anxiety. I wanted to do things on them, like talk to people and go places. They also made me act very loving. I called Valerie and told her how much I cared for her and all this stuff I had never said before. When she came over, we had sex. Opiates helped my sex life because I could last a lot longer, and they numbed the pain of abuse better than alcohol. So, between the great sex life and the opiate induced words and actions of love, Valerie seemed to become addicted to me. She started saying how we were meant to be together and that we ought to get married.

Mike's assertion that he was going to run out of opiates could not have been further from the truth. In fact, he ended up with a seemingly endless supply. In no time at all, I was taking six at a time, five times a day for a total of thirty Percocets a day, which is a crazy amount! To put it into perspective, if I had never taken them before and just decided to pop all thirty in one day, my liver would have shut down and I would have overdosed. Being that I gradually took them overtime, it gave my liver time to build up enzymes to fight off the Tylenol and of course my body had built up a tolerance to opiates by now.

My mind started becoming severely affected by the drugs in ways I had not experienced before. The combination of thirty Percocets and six Klonopin tablets a day was starting to take its toll on my memory and other brain functions. I started to become paranoid and forgetful. I started asking Valerie about her past and doubting if she really did love me. After finding out about her past, I wished I had not asked.

Valerie broke down one night and told me all about her past. First, she told me about how that Luigi clown had basically stalked her. When she started dating Jess, Jess begged her to sleep with his friends. She told me how she had lowered herself by sleeping with Jess and three of his friends at his request. She then told me that she had slept with upwards of fifty guys in college. It bothered me, but I decided then and there to not let anything they said change the way I felt about Valerie.

But now, every time we slept together, I knew I would be thinking about the other hundred guys who have been here. I didn't feel I had any right to judge her, but it was hard not to. She also told me that she had an eating disorder. She suffered from bulimia and had been regurgitating her food for years. She explained that her mother obsessively told her that she needed to lose weight as a little girl, which caused her to develop this eating disorder. Her mother would constantly weigh her and even put locks on the refrigerator. She would tell her that if she gained weight, no one would ever love her.

My image of Valerie as this perfect girl who got away and was now magically back in my life disappeared. I still cared for her and felt bad that she had so much to deal with, but this is when I realized that people who have been abused are drawn to each other. Valerie also had all the signs of being a sexual abuse survivor. She had become interested in boys at a very young age. She also became extremely promiscuous at a very young age, had self-hatred, and developed an eating disorder, which could have been a direct result of her mother's verbal abuse, but it is also a sign of sexual abuse. She also started drinking and taking drugs because she was suffering from depression.

Bulimia is a horrible disease. Not only does it cause you to lose weight, it also makes your teeth and hair fall out, gives you bad breath and unhealthy skin, raises your chances of having a heart attack, and your face becomes super puffy. I also suffered from body issues because of my brother calling me fat, but I never developed into full bulimia. While there were many times that I did attempt to throw up after eating, it just never stuck.

I sympathized with Valerie, but most importantly, I was just too high to make a good judgement. I should have realized that not only was I sick, but so was Valerie. The last thing we needed was a relationship with each other. "Two dead batteries won't start a car" as they say in AA. But our relationship continued, and we started fighting often. Valerie and I lived at my parents' house and never really had any plans to move out. I would just get high and spend time with Valerie, and I was content with this being the extent of my life.

Now that I was back on Percocet, I am back to working with the DEA and have made such a large amount of money that my pill habit was getting worse by the day.

FIRST STREET BUY

WHEN I LEARNED how to buy percocets off the street corner, I had reached a real turning point. Before then, if Mike ran out, I had no other way to get drugs, which meant I was forced to stop. That all changed one day when I met Mike's brother.

I had run out of Percocet and was waiting very impatiently for Mike to get more because I could feel the withdrawal creeping over me. He got his pills from a man who wrote fake prescriptions and got them filled at pharmacies all over the area. Mike would help him sell the pills, then they would split the money. For some reason, either he ran out of scripts or the pharmacies would not fill them, but he had no pills. Every time I called him, he would tell me to check back in an hour.

Normal time doesn't exist for drug dealers. Fifteen minutes could be two hours. One hour could be two days. I had them tell me they were one block away but it took three hours to reach me. I thought I was the only person this happened to, but apparently everyone who has ever bought drugs on planet Earth has dealt with this same thing! I am sure drug addicts reading this are nodding their heads in agreement. I don't think it has anything to do with them not being able to tell time. I think drug dealers enjoy having people waiting on them, needing them. They enjoy having someone call them constantly. While most of them try to act like big shots, it is mainly a defense mechanism. Drug dealers are some of the most insecure people I have ever met. They may get mad when people call them constantly, but without this, they would be nothing. Not to mention they could solve this problem by simply showing up when they say they will, but that reality was completely lost on them.

Not being aware of "drug dealer time" yet, when Mike told me one hour, I drove right over to his house and waited outside for him. I parked down the street in anticipation of the pills to be here in an hour. Finally, after not hearing anything from him, I walked up to his door and knocked. He answered shocked that I was there and again told me they would "be here in an hour," which he had already told me over an hour ago. Six hours and six attempts later, I was losing hope until his older brother pulled up to the house with a friend. The crazy part is that the friend he was with turned out to be a local cop who was looking to buy Percocet, too.

After the friend left, Mike's brother Dan asked him who the hell I was and what I was doing there. Mike said he was waiting for his connection to get there. Dan then asked if I had money and Mike said 'yes' and that I was a "spender." As soon as he heard this, he said, "Why don't I just take him to the city?" Mike immediately replied, "No way. You just got arrested for doing that one week ago!" But the mention of this didn't seem to faze his brother one bit. His brother then asked how many I wanted and how much money I had. I replied that I only had $800 on me but said I could get more. Without saying anything, he jumped in my car and said, "Let's go!" To Mike and Dan, $800 was a lot of money.

On the way there, I didn't have much hope that he was going to be able to get Percocet off some dealer on a street corner. Although, I was willing to try anything at this point. I had never heard of anyone buying pills off the street before.

As we were driving, Dan told me he would do all the talking and for me to "not to say a word." He kept reassuring me that he knew what he was doing and that he was a "pro" as he excitedly rubbed his hands together. I also remember being so sick from the withdrawal that I could not even take a drag of a cigarette without throwing up, but Dan kept nervously lighting them up one after another. This didn't help my confidence in the situation either, especially after learning that he was arrested in the same place just last week. I prayed that we didn't get arrested. Above all, I did not want to go to jail while drug sick. This was probably my ultimate fear at that point, which was second only to continuing to feel the way I was feeling.

We drove down to 8th and Girard Avenue in North Philadelphia. We stood out because it was an all-black neighborhood. As soon as we turned onto the first street, he told me to "be ready to stop." He looked in the rearview mirror to see if a cop saw us turning onto that street and told me to "just keep driving." What I saw next amazed me. As soon as we turned onto that street, people started looking at us and yelling, "Percs! Percs for sale!" I couldn't believe there was a place like this. Percocets were so big here that you could just pull up on a street corner and buy them. I wanted to stop at the first person saying "percs", so that we could get the hell out of there, but Dan was very choosy. He kept telling me to "keep driving." Finally, he saw a guy and told me to pull up to him. He asked him if he had a hundred and the guy said he did. He then jumped into the backseat of my car.

He pulled a big plastic bag out of his pants and I saw it was filled with white pills that I could clearly see were Percocets. As soon as Dan saw them, he said, "No, I don't want them, I want the larger 325s." The dealer said he had them upstairs and if we waited a minute, he would run and get them. I couldn't believe he expected us to wait here where it was painfully obvious what we were doing to anyone with eyes. When I saw he had Percs, I was so happy that I wasn't going to be sick anymore, I didn't give a damn if they were the bigger Roxicets or just normal ones. They were all the same to me. Any number of bad things could happen waiting for the "larger ones."

They call this area "the badlands" for obvious reasons. As we sat waiting for him to return, my heart was beating through my chest as I nervously watched every car that passed because I was sure it was being driven by a police officer who was going to arrest us. Finally, after five agonizing minutes, I saw the dealer come walking down the street toward us. As he was getting back into my car, I went to pull the seat forward and noticed that he had left his whole bag of pills sitting on my back seat! We were just too caught up in the moment to notice. We could have driven away with over a hundred Percocets without even paying a penny, but it was too late now. He got back in and I paid him $500. We left with one hundred Roxicets. Roxicets were the same as Percocets, but they were made by a different manufacturer. Otherwise, there was no difference between them and the pills with the brand name 'Percocet.' I gave Dan ten for bringing me here, then immediately started popping them. I took eight without any water.

This trip was a mixture of good and bad. The good part was that it showed me where I could buy pills anytime I wanted. This was also the bad part depending on how you look at it. The only thing that would stop my addiction now was lack of money. So long as I remembered how to get back here, I would never run out again. Although, Dan told me to never go there without him because it wasn't safe. He said I could be robbed, beaten up, shot, or arrested, and only he knew who to trust. I really believe he didn't want me to go alone because he got something out of it, which was what I suspect he really cared about, not my well-being.

Not long after that I decided to go to North Philly by myself to buy Percocets anyway. I basically drove to the same area we went and asked a guy on the street for Percocets. He got into my car, but I knew nothing about buying pills from off the street. There are a lot of things you need to look out for. Certain people would take your money and run. Some would sell you fake pills. Others would put rocks in a pill bottle. Some would pull a knife or gun and try to rob you.

Most fledgling street drug buyers have had to deal with at least one of these situations. People on the street can spot newbies a mile away and target them. Luckily, he didn't try to rob me or give me fake pills. I got the pills and his number, which was important. I was now able to call him anytime I needed pills. His name was Rome, short for Jerome. He said he would meet me outside of the 8th and Girard areas, so it looked less suspicious for a white guy with Jersey plates to be there.

The only problem with meeting Rome was having to wait for him, which could take anywhere from twenty minutes to an hour. He always had me meet him in the parking lot of a strip club called Delilah's Den. Sometimes he even had me meet him inside the strip club. One time I was at the DEA office in Philadelphia after a big bust and went directly from there to do a drug deal with Rome.

DEA BUST IN PHILLY

WE DID A big undercover drug bust in Philadelphia and the whole situation was both exciting and crazy. I took the last of my Percocet stash before going into the office and was very high by the time I got there. Here I am surrounded by all these DEA agents and local police that were working with the DEA to try to set up this drug buy and I am completely lit up on drugs.

To make matters worse, or better depending on how you look at it, I was told that I would be going alone to buy the drugs from our mark. I would have no one to watch my back if something went wrong. The guy only wanted one person to come with him for the exchange. Normally it was me and another person with me like Darren. This time, I would be all on my own with the jackass setting up the buy. We were buying two kilos of cocaine from these guys he knew. We had originally met this guy when we were looking to buy methamphetamine. For some reason, the government's top drug priority was methamphetamine and they wanted us to buy some anywhere possible in New Jersey.

The problem was that in New Jersey, methamphetamine is very rare. The main way people got it up here was through motorcycle gangs. The main suppliers and users of meth were in the southern parts of the country. A few people in New Jersey had tried and failed to start meth labs in their homes. They ended up blowing up themselves and sometimes half of their neighborhoods.

Crystal meth is an absolutely horrible drug. If you have ever been in a meth lab, you know exactly what I am talking about. The smell is like nothing I have ever smelled before, it's beyond awful. Being around it for just a few minutes makes you feel like your skin is going to peel off and it's hard to breathe. They make meth by mixing ingredients that were never supposed to go into a human body. Basically, chemicals like battery acid are combined with cold medicine to extract meth. When people ingest it, they get an extreme high that lasts anywhere from one to twenty-four hours and it can keep them awake for weeks at a time.

Even one of our top agents suggested that we would be doing everyone a favor if we just let people buy the damn stuff from pharmaceutical companies. At least this way they would not have the meth labs and crazy ingredients. You would also put a stop to drug dealers, theft, and people would not be going to jail for buying it. For half the money we spent on all these things, we could put these people in permanent rehab centers and save hundreds of millions of dollars every month, not to mention lives.

Homemade meth and its ingredients do awful things to the human body. They have taken pictures of people when they first started using meth and then another photo, usually a mug shot, was taken two years later and their appearance is horrifying. When you look at the pictures, it's easy to see just how awful this drug truly is. A beautiful twenty-year-old girl who is addicted to meth will resemble a sixty-year-old toothless, ragged woman in two years. There is a whole website devoted to mugshots of people who have gotten hooked on meth and it's aptly called "Faces of Meth."

Meth is so addictive because of the initial rush it delivers, which is the strongest jolt of dopamine you will get from any drug on the planet. An orgasm is around 200 on the dopamine scale, crack cocaine is around 750, and meth is as high as 1800. So, people will chase that high and, in return, it will ruin their lives and their bodies. The government didn't care so much about the people killing themselves, what got their attention was them blowing up their homes and neighbors' houses. When people make meth in a home, it is not only awful to smell, it also becomes quite dangerous because the fumes are extremely flammable. People don't use proper ventilation because the strong smell could alert police. If these people were not so worried about getting arrested, they would probably only hurt themselves.

That is how we got involved with meth. We were told to do whatever we had to do to find out who was selling meth in New Jersey and arrest them, so that we could find these meth labs and make the DEA look good on the news for closing one down. The crazy part is that by putting it on the news, more people started to look for meth and some considered operating their own labs. Every time the DEA busted a meth lab and boasted about it on the news, twice as many labs would pop up immediately afterward.

The pursuit of meth was what got this current guy into this predicament. He was supposed to be selling us meth, but instead called us and said that some big-time dealers he knew had kilos of cocaine and pounds of marijuana for sale. He wanted to know if we wanted to buy some of this stuff in the meantime. Our bosses decided that we did. We eventually came to a verbal agreement to buy two kilos of cocaine for $50,000. The guy who was supposed to sell us meth, we will call Don. "Don" told us to meet him and he would take us to meet the big dealers to buy cocaine, but there was one condition: he would only bring me. He did not like or trust Darren. We agreed and I drove to meet him with about fifty agents in undercover cars following me.

I picked Don up at his house in New Jersey. Right away he wanted to know if I had the money. I told him that I would go with him and once I saw the drugs and verified that they were real, I would have my business partner, Darren, come meet us with the money. He bitched and complained, but I insisted, "There was no way in hell I was going to bring $50,000 to some strange house in Philly by myself and get robbed." I think it made sense to him and he finally agreed. The car I was driving had video and audio surveillance. It also had something that looked like a radar detector but was a camera and audio recording device all-in-one.

During the drive, Don gave me a big lecture about how the dealers we were going to meet were "niggers" and how bad it was dealing with these "niggers." Don was what he described as "one hundred percent old-school Italian" and he disliked black people very much. I knew that there were at least five black agents and two black police officers listening to this conversation and it made the situation very uncomfortable. He wouldn't stop and it just got worse. He started saying horrible things like "black people are fucking animals" and "these monkeys are only good for dealing drugs." Every time he wanted me to agree with him, he would say, "You agree, right?" and I would just nod my head because I didn't want to start an argument with this nut job. But things got so uncomfortable when he continued saying the worst things possible about black people. This clown made the Ku Klux Klan look friendly toward black people in comparison.

Most people would have been nervous and very worried about the dangers of doing an extremely large drug deal with unknown people, but the thing I was most concerned about was that I had run out of pills and this was consuming my mind. I had the DEA listening and watching my every move, I had Hitler Junior in my car preaching to me, and on top of everything, I was about to do an undercover drug deal with two very powerful and dangerous drug dealers by myself... and all I could think about was getting it done, so I could go buy more pills.

Before I got to the office, I had called dealer Mike because he told me that his "Perc guy" had been there today and dropped some off. Normally, I would have driven to Philly to meet Rome for Percs, but going to Mike's was safer, closer, and easier. As we were crossing the bridge into Philly, Mike started paging me saying that he'd missed my call and that I could come now and get the Percs. I was not supposed to give that pager number out to anyone unless they were part of the DEA. I am sure the agents listening were all thinking, "Who the hell is paging him?" The pager also made Don nervous and he started saying, "What the fuck is that? Damn it!" He kept repeating this over and over again. I tried to reassure him by saying it was a pager and that another dealer was trying to reach me, which was true, but he started yelling, "Shut that shit off! All I need is that shit going off around those niggers and we might get shot! If they hear loud noises, they can't control themselves you idiot!"

He then proceeded to tell me how he never got caught dealing because "he wasn't dumb like me and I needed to listen to his advice." He then explained that black people had brains like monkeys and if they heard a loud noise, they might just start shooting because that is what monkeys do in cages at the zoo when they hear loud noises. I said, "Really? How do the monkeys get the guns in cages?" and he replied, "Oh, you want to be a smartass, huh? You ain't gonna make it in this business!" Then, he said, "Unlike me, you'll be arrested!" He was partially right, I guess. I certainly wasn't going to make it in this business, but not for the reasons he thought. The saddest part was that he believed everything he said.

I wasn't looking around to see if the other agents were following us because I was trying to act as normal as possible. We drove to South Philadelphia to a set of row houses and parked on the street. Don told me to follow him inside. He was really nervous. I was, too, but not nearly as much. He was even looking into the trees to see if people were hiding up there as we walked in. That bewildered me! When I saw him doing this, to amuse myself, I pointed to a tree across the street and exclaimed, "What the hell is that?" He reached for his waist band like he was going to start shooting the tree and I almost burst out laughing. He looked at me angrily and said, "You pull that shit again and I will fucking shoot you! Do you think this shit's a game?"

We walked up to the house and knocked. Two big fat black guys with guns in their waistbands answered the door and let us in. They told us to sit down at the table. Another guy came out of the back and put two kilos of cocaine on the table. This was the first time I had seen a kilogram of cocaine in person. It looked like a small Bible. He then took out a knife and stuck it through the plastic coating and told me to try it. Now I couldn't snort it because I was working for the DEA, but I really wanted to! It was pure and uncut, which you could never find on the street. I just put it on my finger and rubbed it on my gums. I told them it was good and said, "Now, I'll call my friend and tell him to bring me the money."

I called Darren and told him we were good to go. He asked me if it was stamped. That is what cartels use to mark their kilograms. It's like a brand name. I told him it had a scorpion stamp. He told me to bring the cocaine to a neutral area nearby to do the deal. They asked why he didn't just come to the house and I told them it was because he didn't want to get robbed. I asked them if it was okay and the guy said, "Just stick the kilos down your pants and pretend you have a really big dick." So, that is exactly what I did. Between my belt and my stomach sat $50,000 and twenty-five years in prison for a regular person. The dealers said there was no way they were driving in the same car with us and the coke. They told us they would follow us in their car. I walked out of their house and into my car with all that cocaine and we drove off.

I couldn't believe what happened next. I thought the two drug dealers were right behind us, but we lost them somehow. Had this been a real drug deal, we could have just taken off with the drugs and they never would have caught us. Regardless, we drove to the location and parked. Soon after we got there, the dealers finally caught up to us in a big Lincoln and parked on the opposite side of the street. I think they were relieved to see us there and happy that we didn't take off with their drugs.

Then, another crazy thing happened. I looked down the street from where we were parked and saw Rome, my North Philly drug dealer. He came walking down the street with two guys and it was an "oh shit" moment for me. He walked about twenty feet from my car and started yelling, "Boo Boo, Boo Boo!" At first, I thought he was talking to me because this was before it became mainstream for people to call other people their "Boo." So, when I heard "Boo," I thought this was some code word he had for me. He must have said it one hundred times, or at least it seemed that way, so I just stared at my lap praying that he would leave and amazingly he did. He ran across the street to see some girl. I couldn't believe he didn't see my car and noticed it was me. Luckily, the girl across the street he was trying to flirt with distracted him. I don't know how I would have been able to explain to the DEA why a random guy who basically had the words 'drug dealer' emblazoned on his forehead came up and started talking to me like we were best friends, and during an undercover drug deal. Thankfully, I didn't have to.

Immediately after Rome left, I noticed the DEA cars driving by scoping out the area. After about forty-five minutes of them driving around, Don was starting to get really impatient. He kept asking, "Where is your guy with the money?" and saying things like, "This motherfucker better get here or these guys are going to kill us because they are gonna think we lied and are trying to rob them." It was really becoming tense when, finally, Darren called. I answered and said, "Hurry up with the money. They are getting antsy." About ten seconds after I put the phone down, I heard an engine rev followed by screeching tires, then all hell broke loose. Cars started skidding out on all sides of the road and DEA agents with guns were suddenly everywhere yelling, "Put your hands up now, motherfucker, or I will fucking shoot you!"

Darren skidded his car to a stop directly in front of mine as the agents got out with their guns pointed at both of us. They wanted to make it look as though I was a bad guy in case something went wrong. They all started screaming, "Get the fuck out of the car and put your hands up now, motherfuckers, or you're dead!" I immediately got out and was forced to the ground by another agent who ran up to me. He put me in handcuffs, then searched me and found the two kilograms in about two seconds.

They got Don on the ground and had a gun pointed inches away from his head. Don started yelling that he knew nothing about the drugs. While pointing at me, he said, "It's all his drugs, not mine!" Then, he started accusing me of forcing him into the car while sobbing, "Sir, I swear. He forced me! It was all him. All him!" It was such a cowardly thing to do after all that tough talk and gangster bullshit. I didn't feel bad at all that he was going to jail.

They arrested the two drug dealers after a short foot chase. They drove us to the federal building in Philadelphia. When we got there, we all had to ride a huge elevator together, which was uncomfortable to say the least. They purposefully did this so the dealers would think I was being arrested just like them. I tried to look as upset as possible. Still, my main concern was getting out of here and meeting my dealer. Once we got upstairs, they separated us and let me out of the zip-tie handcuffs. Everyone, even the agents from Philadelphia, said what an amazing job I did. I then asked them if I could leave early and they said I earned it but didn't understand why I wanted to leave so quickly. After all, they had raided the house I was in and uncovered a ton of drugs, money, and guns. Everyone thought I would at least want to know what they found, but I had another drug deal to attend to.

By now, the pills I had taken earlier had completely worn off and I was almost sober, which was an awful prospect for me. I left the DEA office and called Mike. He told me he sold out. Luckily for me, I was already in Philadelphia. I called Rome and drove as fast as I could to meet him to get more. After seeing Rome, I had to get home quickly because Valerie and I had plans to go to a play in Philadelphia. Valerie and my mother wanted to see this play, but I could not have cared less. I had a stressful day. Aside from being "arrested" in Philadelphia, I was involved in two drug deals there. I never told Valerie or anyone else about my day. At this point, I was dangerously close to forgetting what character I was supposed to be around who.

BEING MANY DIFFERENT PEOPLE EVERYDAY

DURING THIS PERIOD in my life, I was at least four different people on any given day. I was one person around my parents, and I tried to avoid them as much as possible while acting like a son who was trying to figure his life out, and they believed it. I was a completely different person when working with the DEA. I acted as if I was this law-abiding citizen who cared about the "War on Drugs" and wanted to stop these drugs and the harm they were causing. I would be a completely different person around the drug dealers. I would act like I was this badass law breaker and even act as though I was a dealer myself. I was buying so many Percocets at a time that Rome didn't believe I used them all myself. So, I just pretended that I was a drug dealer, so he would stop asking me questions. When I would come home to Valerie I would play the role of a loving and caring boyfriend who was going to marry her. I pretended that I didn't have anxiety, depression, or a drug problem and that I was well enough to help her with her problems. I also played a fifth person once a week when I went to see my psychiatrist Dr Blum. There I pretended to be someone who didn't use illegal drugs and was far from being an addict. I acted like I wanted to work on my depression and anxiety, and that things were getting better.

Being five different people on the daily is a very exhausting thing to keep up with, especially when you're a drug addict and your memory is not the best. You can't remember what you told to whom and on what day. It is kind of like your life is similar to watching a movie you have seen before, but you have forgotten the lines.

THINGS COME TO A HEAD

My parents decided to go to Florida for the winter, leaving me home to take care of the house while they were away. Valerie was living with me at this point and things were rocky, but when my parents left, things spun further out of control.

Within any given twenty-four-hour period, I was taking enough drugs to cause an overdose and death to about thirty people, maybe more. I was taking a minimum of sixty-four Percocets every day. I would wake up at 7am and take eight Percocets and two Klonopin tablets. At 9am, I would take eight more Percocets followed by eight more at 11am. Before noon, I would have taken at least twenty-four Percocets and four milligrams of Klonopin. By 3pm, that number was at forty plus another two milligrams of Klonopin. At 5pm and again at 7pm, I would take another eight Percocets. Finally, to round out the day, I would take eight Percocets and two Klonopins at 9pm. As my daily pill regimen concluded for the day, I would eventually fall asleep around 11pm in an opiate induced euphoric stupor, then repeat the same cycle starting promptly at 7am the next day. Give or take a few pills, this was how it went day in and day out for months straight.

There were a few major problems with this lifestyle, one of which was money. Being that my family was wealthy, money was not a problem at first, but I was spending at least $300 a day on Percocets alone. That is over $2,100 a week and $8400 per month, and that is just the cost of the Percocets. I was also paying $5 for the bridge toll, $15 a day in gas going back and forth to Philadelphia, $16 on two packs of cigarettes (I smoked a lot while on opiates), not to mention I bought breakfast, lunch, and dinner, which was at least another $30 a day. I had been spending at least $11,000 on drugs every month for the past year and now the money was running out. I started taking money that was around the house.

My mother had money stashed all over our house. It would be inside drawers, purses, and coat pockets, anywhere really. For about a month, I had no problem finding $300 a day every day, but that even started to become scarce. I had never thought of pawning jewelry or anything like that. To me, that was truly stealing and for some reason I just never considered it.

The second problem with taking that many drugs is that it affects your mind and you start doing things you normally would never do and behaving strangely. At night, I started getting paranoid thinking that people were coming to get me. Valerie, still unaware that I was on drugs, believed me when I said people were outside and that they wanted to hurt us. I had four guns in the home at this point. A .40 caliber Glock handgun, a 12-gauge shotgun, an AR-15 semi-automatic assault rifle, and an SKS/AK-47. Drugs, guns, and paranoia are not a good combination.

The paranoia would start around 9pm every night. I would hear some noise outside and it would set me off. I would tell Valerie, "Get down and follow me!" Then, I would shut off all the lights in the house and run upstairs to my room to get my guns. I would give her my AK-47 loaded with a thirty round clip and yell at her to "back me up goddamnit!" Valerie would become frightened out of her mind by this point. She would take the gun, which she had no idea how to use, while crying her eyes out and shaking.

Poor Valerie had never shot a gun before and here I am handing her a loaded AK-47 while barking at her to back me up like a Navy Seal on a mission. I would creep in front of her with my Glock handgun in my belt and the M16 assault rifle in my hands ready to fire. I was also carrying about four extra clips in anticipation of this massive firefight that was sure to ensue.

I would sneak down the stairs as quietly as I could. Valerie would be holding the gun awkwardly away from herself while following me with a deer-in-the-headlights look on her face. We would get to the first floor, then creep through my kitchen to the back door that led to the deck. We would crouch down beside the door in a firing position. I would then turn to Valerie and whisper, "I'm going to light this fucking backyard up like a Christmas tree as soon as I see these motherfuckers." I would then say to her, "Three round bursts, quick magazine changes, and headshots." She had no idea what the hell I was saying, but she was so scared that she would try her best to nod while frozen in fear.

Then, I would start counting down with my fingers and I could hear her tears start hitting the floor behind me. Finally, at the last second, I would flip the backyard light on to blind "the intruders," then kick the back door open as I charged outside with my M16 leveled only to find a completely empty backyard. The fact that it was empty would amaze me each and every time.

I would yell to Valerie, "Those bastards got away again, but don't you worry, we'll get them next time." It really is a miracle that no one ever got shot, including myself and Valerie. This same mission played out night after night, almost like clockwork for weeks.

I also stopped going to the DEA on a regular basis, or even leaving the house for that matter. Amazingly, all of this was fine with Valerie and it didn't seem to bother her. I think she just became completely enamored with me and went along with all this craziness out of love. I have no other explanation for it.

The next week it snowed, and I didn't even bother doing any shoveling. I was too high to give a damn. Not long after that, my parents came back from Florida and all hell broke loose.

As soon as they walked in, I could see my mother's disgust, and I told Valerie that she should go home for a couple of days while I smoothed things over. As soon as she left, my mom started yelling, "You have not shoveled around the house and you haven't called us in Florida for weeks now." I had not called them on Sundays, they took it very personally because it was a sign of disrespect to them. She said, "You have one week, then you are out of this house." I said, "Fine. How about I leave now?" She told me this was fine, but I was not to take the car because, "Remember we bought it for you?"

At this point, I was completely broke and had no way to get to Philadelphia to buy the drugs I desperately needed. To make matters worse, the transmission on my car went out that day, too. Not having a way to get around was a scary feeling considering how bad my habit had become and the withdrawal that would surely follow. When you are an addict and you get caught, you always seem to be at your lowest point.

That night I ran out of Percocet. When I awoke the next morning, I could feel the withdrawal creeping up on me. By nightfall, I was so sick I could hardly walk. I heard my mom scream at me to come upstairs. I yelled that I couldn't eat. My dad said, "You need to come upstairs now and face us." As soon as I came out of the basement, my dad knew immediately that something was horribly wrong. I was hunched over like an old man and looked as if I was dying. I don't know what came over me, but I just came out and said, "I think I have a drug problem." At this point, everything looked very bleak and I didn't know what else to do.

My mom went absolutely crazy and started yelling, "How could you do this to me?" Over and over like a broken record. She yelled, "You are an embarrassment! Your whole life, you have been nothing but an embarrassment to me!" She then told me yet again that she was cutting me out of the will and everything would go to Adam. When my father went upstairs and she was done yelling, she stated matter-of-factly, "Why don't you just kill yourself. I will not have a person in this family who's taking drugs." My mother's brain did not let her see the glaring hypocrisy of that statement.

She got on the phone and called my brother and angrily said, "Your disgusting brother is now taking drugs," then let him know that everything was his. He replied, "I said you should have kicked him out when he turned 18." To which she replied, "You're right, Adam. As always, you are right and I will be taking your advice from now on, and you better believe that he is gone for good! How dare he spit in my face after all the money we spent on him."

She exclaimed, "He probably got them from those scumbag friends of his!" She didn't even realize that I was taking the same pills she fed to me as a child, and the same pills I got when she took me to the doctor.

MY FIRST DETOX

THE NEXT MORNING, my mother told me I had two choices. I could leave the house and find somewhere else to live or go live on the streets because no one taking drugs would be allowed in or near her family even though she indulged in Valium, Xanax, Ativan, Klonopin, Temazepam, and drank Canadian Club whiskey till she passed out every night. Not many people consider alcohol to be a drug, but it most certainly is.

Little things like facts or the truth never mattered to my mother. My father had the sense to call Dr. Blum. The doctor basically told my mom I was not well and needed help. Had my dad not called him, I would have been kicked out in full opiate withdrawal during the winter with nowhere to go. He told them they had to take me to a detox center immediately!

I am sure Dr. Blum couldn't understand why in hell they had not jumped on this idea earlier. When a child has drug problems, parents will go to the ends of the Earth to help them, even if they don't have insurance or other means. So, he said to my mother in disbelief, "You have both money and insurance and you are not considering this?" None of that made sense to him im sure, especially since my mom had portrayed herself to be such a loving parent when they first met.

Other children have robbed their families blind, stolen all their jewelry, and much worse, but the parents still do anything they can to help. Here my parents just found out I was using drugs for the first time and they were willing to kick me out onto the street while I was so ill that I could barely walk. I know he was blown away by their lack of compassion, especially by my mother because this contradicted everything she had told him. I am sure he saw that she could put on a good show in his office when he met her, but now he saw some of the reality I faced.

My mother was able to keep her true side hidden because she was able to convince anyone that she was a truly sweet, loving mother. She was just like those preachers who have a bunch of followers who love and worship them, but behind closed doors they abuse children.

So thankfully, I ended up at a local hospital's detox. My mother was furious and kept going on about how much this was costing her. My mother told the intake woman what I had put her through. The woman told me later that she felt sorry for me and said, "You are the one in detox and all your mother wanted to talk about was herself." This had become a common theme.

I could tell that the first doctor I saw in the ER didn't believe me when I told him the amount of drugs I had been taking. At that point, the opiate epidemic hadn't hit New Jersey, so doctors were not aware of how bad the problem could get. If this had happened today, he would have seen many other people like me already and probably some on the same day.

They admitted me to the detox center and immediately put me

back on Klonopin. They told me that I had been taking it for so long and at such a high dose that I could easily die if I stopped it cold turkey which I already knew. This detox did not use methadone or Suboxone for opiate withdrawal yet. They just gave you a cocktail of muscle relaxers, pain killers, blood pressure medicine, anti-anxiety drugs, diarrhea medicine, and things like that to treat the symptoms. Treating the symptoms is a good approach to anything else except opiate withdrawal because it provides very little relief.

The only way to withdrawal from opiates in a non-excruciating way is to use other opiates, then wean off them very slowly. The problem is that doctors viewed it as counterproductive to use the same drug you are addicted to, to break the addiction to this drug. This is true with some drugs, but not opiates. Sometimes the only way to safely get a person off opiates is with another opiate. There have been instances where people have done so much damage to their brains that they are unable to enjoy life at all unless they take an opiate substitute. Opiates are really in a different league all together.

My habit was different and unheard of by most people at detoxes back then because most opiate addicts had other habits, too. Most did heroin, yet the withdrawal from it can be much shorter than Oxycodone and other pharmaceutical drugs. Back then, people were mainly taking five Percocets a day on average. There just wasn't a lot of access to pharmaceutical opiates during this time. The drug companies did not start pushing Oxycontin on the country just yet. So, treating their symptoms in a medical detox was not completely unbearable.

Another reason they didn't use opiates was because most of the people who came to that detox had problems with alcohol. They give you something called Librium, which is a benzo like Klonopin that helps ease the withdrawal from alcohol. Alcohol has a short, intense detox, but it is nothing compared to opiates. It is especially dangerous because of the potential to have seizures, which is just like Klonopin withdrawal.

If someone wasn't there because of alcohol, they were most likely coming off cocaine. Cocaine was a drug that I never understood why anyone needed a medically supervised withdrawal because there were practically no physical symptoms and most people just needed sleep.

This would all eventually change as the opiate epidemic took over. Eventually more and more people started coming in with serious opiate habits that involved Oxycontin and other pharmaceuticals. The drug dealers even had to start making heroin stronger by adding pharmaceuticals like fentanyl. The strange thing is that while heroin has the worst name, these pharmaceutical drugs could be much stronger and more addictive, and their withdrawal was more intense and prolonged than heroin.

Striving to make a huge profit, the pharmaceutical companies gave millions of potential addicts some of the most addicting substances on the planet. This led to not only millions of people becoming addicts, but also millions of deaths and destroyed families. People got divorced, lost their children, became convicted felons, and many other people suffered needlessly in crowded jails while others overdosed and died. The idea that they were pushing pain killers to stop pain is so ironic because these drugs literally caused about a million times more pain than they ever stopped.

But for now, I was an anomaly at the detox. The first few days I just sat in my bed shaking and throwing up. By the seventh day in detox, a full ten days without opiates, I felt a little bit better and my head started to clear. I was still very weak and skinnier than I have ever been. All I wanted was to leave the detox and get high.

The girl that ran the place was the sister of a girl named Ashley who was in my high school class. When my parents showed up for a family meeting, she recommended that I immediately go to rehab after the detox. My dad asked her which she recommended and she said Hazelden in Minnesota. It was very expensive and many famous people went there. She asked my parents if they had the financial means to send me to such a place. My dad didn't hesitate and said, "Yes, we do." A rehab was the last place I wanted to go, and I tried to talk my way out of it, but their minds were set. The next day when my parents picked me up from the detox, they informed me that I was getting on a plane first thing in the morning to Hazelden.

Valerie was going crazy the whole time I was in detox. She didn't know exactly what was going on and kept trying to call the detox. She kept coming by my parents' house about forty times. When I got home, I told her to come see me, so I could let her know that they were sending me to rehab in Minnesota because I needed to get off these pills I was taking. She freaked out and said she couldn't survive without me for a month. I told her that she would get through this and I would be home before she knew it. It took me six hours to say goodbye before she finally left.

In the morning, I boarded a plane. I had to take twenty-two Klonopin tablets just to get on the plane. The fear of flying was another phobia I had developed in addition to my anxiety. Now that I didn't have opiates in me, I knew my anxiety would be rearing its ugly head and the last place I wanted to have a panic attack was at 35,000 feet.

HAZELDEN

I LANDED IN Minnesota during a bad snowstorm. The first thing I noticed besides the snow was that the people talked funny and seemed to move very slowly. They said, "Eh," and, "Oh, yah," a lot. It was also extremely cold, which was nothing like the kind of cold we have in New Jersey.

Hazelden was about an hour's ride from the airport. It looked like a ski lodge and a college mixed together. As soon as I arrived, the intake people asked me a million boring questions. They also took away my bottle of Klonopin, which was completely unacceptable to me. I had been on Klonopin for over seven years. No one ever told me I had to stop taking it; it was my lifeline. I was here to get off drugs I thought, not to stop taking Klonopin. I immediately called my dad and said I needed to leave. To which he responded, "I'll come get you and bring you home—when pigs can fly."

I was given a room in the detox and my roommate was an alcoholic Calvin Klein model named Jamie. He was a nice guy who was about forty years old. As soon as I went a day without Klonopin, I experienced an all-day panic attack and was in no mood to talk to anyone.

Luckily, Jamie had a wife and he was really in love with her. She was a model, too, and he showed me pictures of her. He wrote her love letters all day long and did not bother me too much.

I kept begging the doctors, nurses, and a counselor to let me have my Klonopin. After a week in the detox without Klonopin, I started to feel like I was in a dream world again because I was hallucinating. They were giving me the weakest possible medication I could take to wean off the Klonopin without dying. I remember there was this man who worked there who kept telling me that it would get better. He would say, "It can't go on like this forever!" This all sounded great but provided me with no relief and very little comfort.

Feeling like this again really upset me and I thought to myself, "I got sober to live in this permanent hell again?" It really was like, what is the point? I did not want to live with the belief that I was going to drop dead at any moment!

After fourteen days of hell in the detox, they put me in a unit of the rehab called Silkworth. It was named after Dr. Silkworth who helped start Alcoholics Anonymous. It was an all-male unit of about thirty guys. I remember reading the book A Million Little Pieces and knowing that the author was lying after the first page. He claimed to have been in the same unit called Silkworth, but the things that he said happened were not possible. For instance, he mentioned women but they were in a completely separate unit.

I was the youngest male in my unit by about ten years. The average age was around forty. Most were nice guys, but I was completely lost as to what the hell they were talking about. It was like they were speaking a different language with all this AA talk. They were mentioning the twelve steps and repeating sayings like "It works if you work it" and "no cross talk" and "wait for the miracle to happen." This was all very strange stuff. Everyone except me seemed to know and understand this talk, which made me feel even more like an outsider.

My roommate was a guy named Ron. Ron wore ripped sweatpants and went around all day looking like he had just rolled out of bed. He kind of resembled Bob Dylan, but in a homeless kind of way. When his wife arrived to visit him, I was amazed to see that she was drop-dead gorgeous and could very well have been a model. One of the guys said, "How did he pull that off?" Another guy explained that Ron was part of one of the richest and most famous families in the Midwest. Ron's dad started a national pizza chain and owned two sports teams, plus a bunch of casinos. They were billionaires, which certainly explained how he ended up with such a beautiful wife, but you would never know that Ron even had one dollar to his name.

They assigned me a counselor who was a big biker-looking lady with manly tattoos. She was about fifty years old and on the harsh side. I wanted them to give me the pretty counselor I saw around, but fate put me with this woman. She did say something to me that I will never forget.

She called me into her office to meet me and have a chat. I decided to tell her that she and everyone else had this all wrong and me being here was a big mistake. I said, "After being around the guys and evaluating the situation, I realize that I'm not like any of these other people. They've all been to multiple rehabs and are much older than I am." She turned to me and said, "You're right. You are not like them!" For a moment I thought she was on the same page as me and she would soon be calling my family to come get me. But, the next words out of her mouth were, "You are the sickest one here! They were all able to make it forty years before coming here, and you didn't even make it to twenty-three, which definitely makes you the sickest one here!" I immediately felt like a deflated balloon. I have never forgotten her words and it turned out that she was right. I was the sickest one there.

While I was at Hazelden, my mother called and accused me of ruining Valerie's life. She told me that Valerie had stopped eating because

I had left. My mom was the one who sent me here and now she was yelling at me for it. In my mother's eyes, I couldn't win no matter what I did. She said that I had caused her to worry about this poor girl now, too. She told me that Valerie was so skinny that she was worried about her health. I felt bad for her, but what could I do? She would not let me come home, so I wondered what her point was.

After talking to my counselor, she saw things in a different light. She said very bluntly, "Why is she even bringing this girl up and not worried about you? If this girl doesn't want to eat, that is on her, but you are fighting one of the hardest things there is to fight. You have a deadly disease that will kill you and the last thing you should be worried about is some stupid girl at home. Shame on your mother for calling you with this." My counselor was blunt, but she could not be more right.

Every phone call from my mother was about how much I had put her through, how embarrassing it was for her to have to tell her friends that her son was now a drug addict, how worried my father was, how expensive the cost of the rehab was, and how my poor brother was feeling about having a drug addict for a brother. The whole time she wanted me to focus on her "suffering," which she said I had caused. I really should have been focusing on myself and getting myself healthy, which is what a loving parent would have insisted upon. To my mother, the most important part was me feeling bad.

When that counselor said these things to me, it was the first time someone had ever suggested that I think about myself. It was such an awkward feeling for me. I never thought about myself. Everything I did, except getting high, was to please someone else. The counselor told me, "Your mother needs to put the past behind her. She needs to focus on you getting better, and the future. That is what people who love each other do." I think this was when my counselor realized that there was not much "love" in my family because it was so unnatural to me.

Most, if not all, of the other men's families were behind them and showed their support. They wanted them to get better and that was all that mattered. So, it was hard for me to find someone to relate to and, frankly, I was embarrassed that no one in my family really cared, especially my own mother. All these guys talked about was how their families couldn't wait to have them back and were behind them all the way.

Eventually, Valerie also got on my mother's last nerve. She kept coming by every day. Sometimes she would just knock on the door to say she left something at their house, then stay there for hours crying and saying how hard this was on her. She would say how hungry she was, but that she could not eat. Eventually my mother stopped feeling so bad for her and told her she needed to stop coming over. That was when Valerie called Hazelden and got an operator to get me. This was a huge no-no in rehab because there was supposed to be anonymity, especially in a place like Hazelden that had a ton of celebrities. They were never supposed to admit that a patient was there.

Valerie told the operator that she was going to kill herself if they didn't let her talk to me. Once I got on the phone, she told me that she couldn't take it anymore and that if I didn't leave right then, she was driving out to Hazelden to get me. No one, not even the cops, would stop her. My counselor was listening to what Valerie had told the operator and then jokingly said, "Wow, you must be really good in bed!" After that, she became very serious and said that she was prohibiting me from speaking to Valerie again during my stay, and if she showed up, they would have her arrested. At first, I was really upset by this, but deep down I knew I needed a break from Valerie. After a few days of not talking to her, I felt so much better. I had a whole host of other problems to focus on. The last thing I needed was to worry about Valerie, too. That was the last conversation I ever had with Valerie.

At the request of Hazelden, my parents came out to visit me like Ron's wife had done. The crazy part was that the rehab allowed them to take me out to dinner. When we got to the restaurant, my mother asked if I wanted to order a beer. You're damn right I did! So, here I am at this expensive rehab for drug and alcohol addiction and during a visit with my parents who sent me here, I was now indulging in alcohol. So, I drank with my parents before I ever left Hazelden. Later when I told a counselor at another rehab about this, she could not believe my mother would encourage me to drink when the first thing Hazelden told parents was not to allow us to drink or take any over-the-counter medications while away from the rehab on a visit. Had I been caught I would have been kicked out.

FIRST "RELAPSE"

AFTER COMING HOME from Hazelden, my first thought when the plane landed was about getting high. As soon as I smelled the air in Philadelphia, it reminded me of getting high. Driving back to my home from Philadelphia reminded me of the route I took to buy drugs. Everything I saw reminded me of seeing it while high. Just driving in a car reminded me of driving to buy drugs. Every minute since I had landed, the urge to get high became stronger and more intense. By the time we pulled into my driveway, I was sweating, and my stomach was full of butterflies and knots. I could not think about anything except getting high. There was a part of me that truly did not want to do the wrong thing. The problem was not my desire to stay clean, it was the way I felt inside. I had not done anything in my time at Hazelden to work on the real problem, which was what was wrong deep down inside of me. I had just removed the drugs, which were only a symptom of the real problem.

I was home for about one hour and could not take the craving anymore. I told my parents that I needed to go visit a friend. My dad gave me his car keys and a hundred-dollar bill. I drove right to Philly and called Rome, who was ecstatic to hear my voice. After all, I was one of his best customers, and he thought I had died or gotten arrested. While I sat there waiting for Rome to bring me drugs, I literally felt high. He showed up not long after I got there. I bought the pills and immediately took five before he even shut the car door. On the way home, they started to kick in. It was such a great feeling! I started talking to the bottle of pills like I was just reunited with a long-lost lover and saying things like, "Please don't ever leave me again!" The people in the car next to me must have thought I was crazy. Thinking back, they would've been correct in their assumption.

I had gone months without taking anything. I suffered horrible withdrawal from opiates and terrible withdrawal from Klonopin, which were compounded by raging anxiety, severe depression, extensive suffering, not to mention boredom, fear, pain, and misery, and all I had accomplished was washed away in minutes by a wave of euphoria. The person I liked was back, I felt free and happy again. By the time I got home, it was as if the last three months had never happened. I said 'hello' to my parents and told them "Erica," who I never went to see, said 'hello,' then I went down to the basement to my old familiar spot as though I had never left.

The fact that my parents had just spent $50,000 on me going to this rehab and everything I had learned there about how I was an addict and needed to stay clean, was lost on me. The most important thing in my mind was feeling normal, which was only going to happen if I was taking a narcotic. I viewed my stay in rehab as if it was a mere pit stop, so I could learn to use correctly this time. I also did not believe I was a drug addict. In my mind, a drug addict was someone who landed on the side of the street, was homeless, dirty, and committed all sorts of horrible crimes to get their drugs. I really believed that if I just had an unlimited supply of pills, I would be fine. I promised myself that I would not let my usage get out of control again, which I truly believed I could do.

KICKED OUT AGAIN

I WAS ONLY home for about two weeks when my mom found a bag of pills that she knew were Percocets and she kicked me out on the spot. The big problem for me was that I had nowhere to go and no way to get there. While I was at Hazelden, my parents sold my car to a friend's brother as punishment. So, my mom told my dad to drive me to the bus stop and wish me luck.

My father took me to the local bus station, and I could see he was sad. I asked him for money as I barely had enough to buy a ticket. He handed me a couple of $100 bills and I gave him a hug and said 'goodbye.' My dad was smart enough to know that this wasn't the right solution and things were only going to get worse, but he had to listen to my mother.

I would always cringe when I hear people advising parents to immediately kick their kids out as soon as they discovered they were using drugs. Drug addiction does not have a one size fits all solution and when you kick an addict out, you can create a whole new set of problems for them and their situation usually becomes worse. There needs to be more thought and consideration. After all, it is always easy to tell someone else what they should do. Unfortunately, my dad really didn't know what else to do, so he took me to a bus station and left me there.

I bought a ticket to California and took a Greyhound bus all the way there. While I had always wanted to go there since I was a little kid, taking a Greyhound long distance was an awful experience. They stop every couple of hours, so you have to get off and wait in stations for up to eight hours at a time and sometimes there aren't any seats to sit in. By the time I made it to Los Angeles, I was completely sober. I was also completely broke and out of drugs. The reality of my desperate situation hit me, and I decided to call my father with my tail between my legs and beg for help. I could not believe he said he was going to get me a plane ticket home without much argument. I happily accepted.

Later, I found out why they were so willing to bring me home. There was a woman I had saved from drowning years earlier and she was looking for me. My parents' friends were over when she stopped by and everyone started asking where I was. It would have been very embarrassing for them to say that they had kicked me out without so much as a place to go.

SAVING THE DROWNING LADY

When I was about fourteen, I was sitting out on the back deck of my parents' house in LBI getting a tan in just my jeans. Suddenly, I heard a car screeching its tires and I looked up to see it swerving all over the road before finally coming to a stop. A woman jumped out crying and screaming and ran at full speed away from the car. She saw me on the deck and hopped right over our little fence and into my arms. She started hugging me and asking me to protect her. The person driving the car saw her reach me and quickly sped away.

She started saying, "Thank you, sweetie! He was trying to hurt me, so I had to get away from him." She was obviously drunk, and it was only about three o'clock in the afternoon. She said he was her boyfriend and they had got into this big fight because she had lost his car keys. He had just bought a new BMW, so he flipped out. He hit her and said all kinds of horrible things, then told her to go kill herself. She said she'd had enough of him, everyone else, and her own life in general. I brought her inside and tried to calm her down. Then, she started taking off all her diamond rings, earrings, and necklaces and told me to keep them and said, "Tell my family I love them," then ran out my door toward the beach.

I couldn't believe this was happening. I followed her to the beach but as soon as I got up there, the beach was covered in a blanket of fog. I searched for her everywhere on the beach and then scanned the water. After a few minutes, I finally saw something floating nearby. I jumped in and swam out as fast as I could in jeans. Once I reached the object, I could see that it was her. I grabbed her and swam her in like I was trained to in lifeguarding. I kept trying to keep her head above the water, so she could breathe, but each time I let go, her face would go back under the water. I finally decided to put her on her back and swim with her on top of me while side stroking in.

I reached the shore with this unconscious woman and immediately started breathing into her mouth. After about twenty seconds, she coughed up some water and started breathing again. She looked scared to death, but I was also just as scared. She grabbed me and started crying. Eventually I got her up and I held her hand as we walked back toward my house.

There were now multiple people watching and trying to figure out what the hell was going on, which made me uncomfortable. An old couple watching started giving me the thumbs up and saying, "Great job!" Another man asked if he should call an ambulance while three girls nearby just stared at us. I didn't want this to turn into a big thing, especially because I had plans to try mushrooms for the first time that night and did not want anything interfering. When we finally made it back to my house, she didn't want to leave. My girl-friend kept calling, so I had to answer. She heard this woman in the background and asked who she was. I told her it was a long story because I did not want to embarrass the woman. My girlfriend got furious with my answer and said she was coming over immediately.

I told this woman that I had to take her home right away. I gave her some dry clothes and even my favorite Moorestown football sweatshirt. She asked if she could stay the night, but I told her if my parents came home and found a thirty-year-old woman in the house, I would be in serious trouble. She agreed and I walked her to her friend's house. Before she went inside, she asked me to wait a minute to make sure she was okay. I could tell there was a big group of friends staying in this house because there were about eight cars parked out front. I was surprised that none of her friends were looking for her.

Then this angry man who was at least thirty-five years old came out of the house. He was drunk and started yelling at me. He screamed, "She said you pulled her out of the water. Big deal! Do you see this BMW? That's a $50,000 car. I bet you don't have one of these, right? You probably don't even make that much in a year!" The fact that I was only fourteen was completely lost on this clown. He held up his car keys and said something like, "On a scale, my car is worth more than her life any day." I told him to go fuck himself, then he got in my face. His cologne was ridiculously strong, and I almost punched him. I think he was a little surprised when I just stood there and didn't back away. He then said, "If you touch me, I will sue you and own you!" I just laughed.

One of her girlfriends came out and started thanking me for helping her. I asked her to please get my sweatshirt back. She said it was probably best if I left now and she would get the sweatshirt to me later. I left and never got my football sweatshirt back. That was the last I would see of this woman until much later.

Years had passed when she decided to come back and thank me for "saving her life." When she showed up at my house, she encountered my parents and their friends. They all got to hear the story. That was the reason things changed when I got home. Within a day, my parents took me out car shopping. They said I could use it to get around and find a job. I told them that I had made up my mind and I was done with drugs. I truly did feel this way and meant what I said. I had only used for two weeks and the worst of the withdrawal was now over. I started feeling better and stronger and more determined than ever to stay clean.

The next night my parents decided to take me to the casino for dinner and gambling. I ended up winning $3300 dollars playing blackjack. On the way home, I decided to get five Percocets to celebrate, just this once. I called Rome, but he refused to meet me for just five pills. The minimum he said he would come out for was fifty. So, I bought all fifty and said to myself that I would save the others for a rainy day. That rainy day came the next morning. After that, I continued using again nonstop. Not long after, I was caught again by my parents. They asked me to leave and told me to go live with my uncle. They also said they did not want to hear from me for at least a year.

GOING TO LIVE WITH MY UNCLE

UNCLE JIM WAS my mother's brother. He was a strange man who lived alone in Virginia. He looked like he could win the 'Pedophile of the Year' award. He was also a super religious man, of course. My experience up to that point with overly religious people convinced me that most of them were not great people. They get by with being that way by believing God will forgive them. They use religion as an excuse to escape their misdeeds. They claim they are just flawed, but no matter what they do, God will forgive them. They also believe that everyone is evil and stealing a piece of gum is the same as murder. This is just the façade of a bad person and most people see through this.

Uncle Jim had super pale skin that made him look like a ghost. He always wore a white shirt with a pocket protector. He had these strange Velcro shoes that were a mix of dress shoes and sneakers, which he must also have bought at Pedophiles R Us. He lived off my grandfather's money, too. Ironically, his interests were the church, computers, and Halloween. He even had his own online business called "HauntMaster" where he sold lights that are used in Halloween decorations. He was a very socially awkward man who apparently had an evil side just like my brother did with a super jealousy sickness. I also believe he was sexually abused by my grandfather.. He used to be married but is now divorced. His ex-wife had an adopted child who lived with my uncle and eventually committed suicide for reasons unknown. I think my uncle did have a good side to him deep down but it was difficult to understand him.

Because I had nowhere else to live, I went to live with my uncle. He told my mother that he was going to do a Bible study with me every day and this would get me off drugs. As soon as I got there, I was weirded out by all his religious stuff. It was super easy for him to read the Bible all day because he had nothing else to do. He didn't have to work, didn't have kids, didn't have friends, or anything else counting on him. When he would say, "All these sinners are out there who don't read their Bible every day," When I was high, I could somewhat tolerate the religious stuff. Had I been sober, this would have been unbearable for me. That is not to say that I do not believe in God. I absolutely believe in God, it is just at that point religion was at the very least hard to understand.

When my parents kicked me out, they thought me going to live with my uncle and Jesus might be the answer to my problems. My mother even wrote me a $5000 check to put in my bank account because she said she felt so strongly that my uncle could help me after speaking with him. The crazy part was she knew I was doing drugs. Giving $5000 to a drug addict who has just relapsed is like putting gasoline on a fire.

On the drive to his house, I spent $3000 on eight hundred Percocets thinking that they would carry me through my stay there. They lasted about three weeks. I then had to drive back to Philadelphia to buy more. Philadelphia was about a six hour drive each way. In under a month, I was out of money. Then, I found a whole book of my parents' checks in my luggage bag. I decided to write myself one check.

This was the first time I had ever done anything of this magnitude. I went and deposited the check into my bank account. Within a day, the money cleared, and I was on my way to buy more pills. I told myself that I would repay them and would never do this again. As soon as that money ran out and I started getting sick, I decided to do it one more time. Eventually, I was forging checks and driving up and back to Philadelphia at least twice a week to buy drugs.

Meanwhile, my uncle was telling my parents that I had found Jesus and he had cured me. I felt awful about taking the money and fooling everyone into thinking I was well again. I knew it was just a matter of time before my parents found out it was all a lie, then I would be screwed. I had a better chance of Jesus rising again to stop me before I stopped on my own. Although, I did start praying to God to help me. The minute the drugs took effect, I would be completely determined to stop, but when they wore off and the sickness hit, all my good intentions went right out the window. I knew I needed something stronger than myself if I was going to stop using drugs for good.

I was driving overnight to get the pills, so my uncle wouldn't know I was gone. One morning, I was driving back from a night trip to Philadelphia and my phone kept ringing. I eventually answered it and it turned out to be my parents saying they knew I was stealing checks and that they were pressing charges. I told them they were crazy, and that there must be a big conspiracy against me. They told me that my uncle would have all my stuff waiting out on the back porch for me. Luckily for me, I had just bought a lot of pills, so I did not have to worry about that for the moment. Strangely, the thought of going to California popped into my mind again.

Collecting my things at my uncle's house was a very uncomfortable situation. For all his faults, I still felt bad about lying to him. I think he thought Jesus had really saved me and, for the first time, my uncle looked great to the family because he had helped me. Now, all of that had been crushed by my parents' phone call and the realization that my addiction was worse than he could have imagined. It was hard to look him in the eye. I was glad when I got back in my car and turned the corner.

HEADING TO CALIFORNIA

So, I was back on the road to California. Thankfully, I was driving this time instead of traveling by bus. I bought about six hundred Percocets and thought they would last me a long time. I promised myself that I was only going to take them when I absolutely needed them. I was going to make them last for as long as possible. I didn't even make it to California before I ran out. I was somewhere near Las Vegas when I took the last of them. I decided Sin City was as good a place as any to find some Percocets.

I got a room at a dirty little motel on the Vegas Strip. I was up all-night sick from the withdrawal. As soon as the sun came up, I was out driving around searching for anyone who looked like a drug addict or dealer. I saw this guy standing on the street who was obviously up to no good. I asked him if he knew where I could get Percocets. He didn't, but he said he was waiting on a heroin deal and that might help me. I gave him money and he bought three bags of heroin from a man in an old Trans Am.

Before I saw it, I figured I could just snort it, but I soon found out this was not going to work. It was a little ball of black tar, so taking it up my nose would have been impossible. I asked how we were supposed to use it and got my answer when we went inside his apartment. There were needles everywhere. His girlfriend was in the apartment and they immediately started fixing up the heroin in spoons. It was black tar heroin, which could only be injected with a needle. I was too scared of needles at this point to shoot it. Especially after what I saw next.

The guy showed me his arms and it looked like some flesh-eating virus had gotten to him. He had huge open gashes all over his body. His girlfriend had them, too. It turned out they were abscesses from shooting up black tar heroin. They completely expected me to shoot it, but I said, "Hell, no! There was no way I was going to inject that crap into my body." He replied, "Well, then you're going to have to stay sick." So, I left with my heroin still in the bag instead of in my veins. I eventually did try eating a little bit, but it did nothing. The next day I gave up on Vegas and drove to LA.

When I got there, the first thing I did was drive to Tijuana. I had heard that you could buy Percocets easily down there from any pharmacy. Tijuana was a crazy city. I found a pharmacy that sold me a bunch of fake ones called Percogesic, but at the time I thought were real. Thankfully, right before leaving, a woman talked me into buying a couple ten-milligram pills of Oxycontin. She said they were better than Percocet. I did not know anything about Oxycontin, or I would have bought more of them. I wasn't even going to buy any of them because I thought I had real Percocets already, but I felt bad for her because she said she needed the money to feed her family. I bought two Oxycontins and went back to LA.

I immediately took the fake Percocets, but quickly realized I felt no different. I was already back in the United States by this point and did not want to go back because I had problems crossing the border on my return trip to the US. The border police searched my car, which scared me because I had the Oxycontins when they searched, but they didn't find them. So, there was no way I was going back. Luckily, the Oxycontins I bought from the lady were real and I decided to give them a try. Within fifteen minutes, the sickness was gone, and I felt great. The drive back to LA was peaceful, short, and beautiful now that I was high. I found a hotel room and knew I had a couple hours of peace before the sickness returned with a vengeance.

For the next three weeks I laid in that hotel room bed and kicked my habit. The withdrawal was hell but knowing I had nowhere to get pills made it possible. Now that I was sober and in post-acute withdrawal, I became so depressed that I decided to commit suicide.

I drove my car to the Pacific Ocean via the Pacific Coast Highway and pulled out my Glock .40 caliber handgun. I sat there wanting to do it, but the fear of going into that oven for eternity was too much for me to bear. While holding the gun to my head, I could not bring myself to pull the trigger, then broke down. I decided to call a friend from high school named Brian who now lives in Los Angeles. When he answered, I told him I was in town and he invited me over. I drove to his house and told him I needed help.

He let me stay at his place and I started calling rehabs out of the phone book. At this point, I still had health insurance and found a place in Florida that offered to take me. They even sent me a plane ticket. I left my car, my gun, and most of the money I had with Brian. The next morning, he drove me to the airport. I was still feeling sick when I got on the plane, but when we landed in West Palm Beach, I was not sick anymore. It was pretty amazing considering it had only been twenty-seven days since I had been in opiate withdrawal. This was the only time I stopped using and was ever able to remember exactly when the withdrawal stopped, and I felt better.

PATHWAYS/FLORIDA

PATHWAYS WAS A decent rehab. It was right on the beach in Delray Beach, Florida. It was co-ed and was generally a fun place to go for rehab. When I arrived, I made my first smart decision toward drugs and was serious about getting clean.

At this point, rehabs like Pathways started using Oxycontin in their detoxes. Oxycontins were time released, so they offered a good way to wean off other opiates. The detox offered me a week of Oxycontin to detox with, which I turned down.

The rehab center was paid more by insurance companies for the days you spent in detox rather than the days spent in the rehab section. I wasn't sick anymore, so the only reason to be in detox would be to get a high from Oxycontin, which many people in the detox were doing. They would keep them in their cheeks after the nurses handed them the pills to swallow. They would later crush and sniff them to get high. I was really upset about where these drugs had taken my life so far and was fed up, so I declined them. I was also not sick, so without that monkey on my back, it was a lot easier to say 'no.'

ALEXIS

PATHWAYS WAS THE first time I started to pay attention to AA and NA and understood what they were talking about. I never really believed I was an addict, but it seemed like everyone else did. I decided to sit through the meetings and listen as best I could.

We used to have meetings at night on the back porch. One girl who came to speak really stood out to me. Her name was Alexis and she was beautiful; what most men would consider perfect. She was blonde, about twenty-one years old, big boobs, perfect body, tan, and the absolute last person you would ever think was a drug addict.

When she got up to speak, the guys were all saying things like, "Oh, wow! This little rich girl probably got sent to rehab after smoking too much weed one day. What the hell is she going to tell us?" After she started speaking, we were all left with our jaws on the floor by what we heard.

She was an amazing speaker and was brutally honest. She told us that when she was just six years old, her father started having sex with her. He got her older brother to join in and they would both have sex with her. Her father would film the abuse, then sell the tapes to "sickos." By age of nine, her father started selling her to other men for sex. At age twelve, she started shooting heroin to cope with this nightmare. Eventually, she ran away and went to live on the streets of Baltimore where she became a prostitute.

In Baltimore, she sold her twelve-year-old body for heroin. She was raped multiple times, beaten up, stabbed, kidnapped, and shot—all before the age of seventeen. When she was nineteen, a woman rescued her from the streets and sent her to Pathways to get help.

She had stayed in Florida ever since and had now been clean for three years. She devoted her life to staying clean and helping other addicts. She was the most impactful speaker I had ever heard. I could not believe how brave she was for sharing this with a group of strangers. I thought I would never have the guts to tell people what had happened to me.

Sadly, less than a year later, I attended her funeral. Hers was the first of many fellow addicts' funerals I would, and still do, attend. Alexis relapsed and her heart stopped. I did not see her father at her funeral, but if I had I would have punched him in the face. Although, it was not like she ever really had a father in the first place.

As horrible as her death was, I still think Alexis is in a better place. She suffered horrors worse than I had, which is extremely rare when I can say this about someone. For that reason, I felt a connection to her even though we never spoke to each other.

I know the abuse she dealt with and the devastation it causes a child. It cripples them with an unbelievable handicap forever and the pain never goes away. The pain is overwhelming for an adult, but for a child to deal with something so horrible and calamitous is simply too much. Sometimes death seems like a much better option than a lifetime of suffering.

Shortly after hearing Alexis speak, I completed Pathways and went to a place called the Florida House. It was a halfway house in Deerfield Beach. The rules there were very simple: you had to live in an apartment with three other guys, pay rent, and stay sober. You also worked, went to meetings, and tried to support each other.

I started working at a sporting goods store and eventually started waiting tables too. After a couple of months of promising myself I would stay off drugs and trying to remember the pain it had caused me, I started to forget. The longer I stayed clean, the more I started to daydream about drugs and soon forgot about the bad aspects of them.

One day, I even went out walking around hoping to find someone who would show me where I could buy Percocet or Oxycontin. "Oxys," which is slang for Oxycontin, were the only thing people talked about in rehab. They said they were the new thing, raved about how great they were, and insisted that everyone was doing them. They told me all I had to do was find a doctor and pay him cash. They said I could easily get an unlimited supply because doctors everywhere were prescribing it.

I met a guy named Jackie at the Florida House and we agreed to move out and get an apartment together. Although, not having any necessary life skills made this a little difficult. I wasn't aware of credit, savings, or other things that normal people needed to get by in life. I had to try and do my best to learn.

SEPTEMBER 11, 2001

I WILL NEVER forget 9/11 and what happened on that day. This was also the day that I got my first apartment and moved out of the Florida House with Jackie. It was in a nice complex in Deerfield Beach, Florida, that had a gym, a pool, and a whirlpool spa.

I remember waking up that morning and hearing someone say that a plane had hit the World Trade Center. Ever since I was a child, I loved those buildings for some reason. When I heard a plane hit them, I knew right away it had to be terrorists. It was unbelievable watching the towers fall. As sad and awful as it was, there is something about such events that cause me to get very interested in a deep, thoughtful way that most people never stop to consider.

I wanted to know what those people were thinking about when they jumped. I wanted to know if anyone on the planes felt pain. I remember thinking very deeply about the situation and being impacted by it more than most people. There was some connection I felt to the ones who died on that day, which I can't explain.

Now that I was on my own, I had complete freedom and it wasn't long before I met some neighbors. One neighbor's name was Joe and he lived with three Brazilian girls. Apparently, he took money to have an arranged marriage with one of them. Joe and the girls immediately started inviting me over to their place. I started to notice that Joe would go outside every time I was over to meet someone for about three minutes, then come back. I knew immediately what he was doing, I just didn't know what kind of drugs he was selling.

It turned out to be Lortabs. Lortabs are like Percocet only not as strong, but still addictive as hell. Eventually, I just came out and asked him to sell me some. He did and I started taking them. He would only get a few at a time because his connection got one prescription a month. That kept my habit from going out of control until I met another "drug dealer" named Mike.

Mike was the guy Joe knew who could get Oxycontin. Mike was a little squirrely guy with a high-pitched, squeaky voice. He was about forty years old and still lived with his parents in a retirement village. He drove this crappy little car that was painted five different colors. He had been a TV cameraman, but when he got hooked on drugs, his career and any chance he had at a normal life was ruined.

Mike was able to get Oxycontin from these two old Jewish brothers named Stewart and Mike. They were retired car salesmen who lived together in an apartment. They had become what Mike thought were "big time" drug dealers. They sold cocaine, Xanax, muscle relaxers, and opiate pain killers.

South Florida would eventually become the pill capital of the world because of fancy drug dealers or as they are sometimes also called, well-respected pain doctors and the "good" people at Purdue Pharma were not pushing their drugs hard enough yet. So for now, Stewart and his brother were two of the biggest suppliers of Oxycontin in South Florida.

This is how my drug deals with Mike went: He would drive to meet me, so I could give him my money. He would then drive to Stewart and Mike's apartment and buy the drugs, which he would bring back to me. They would give him pills free of charge as a reward for bringing them the business, and I am sure he charged me more than what he had bought the pills for. Mike was basically a runner, or "middleman," who got high and made money all day by running around getting people drugs.

There is this huge misconception that everyone who sells drugs is a "drug dealer." The fact is, they are no more of a drug dealer than the guy who sells his friend a dime bag of weed out of the stash he bought. Real "drug dealers" do not stand on corners and hand out drugs, they do not deliver drugs, or even talk to customers. These were just people who drug dealers use to make money, like the addicts.

Even though I was buying them from a "middleman," I was still getting the Oxys very cheaply. I could get eighty milligrams of Oxycontin for $20. There are sixteen Percocets worth of oxycodone in one eighty-milligram Oxycontin. Eventually in New Jersey, they would go for a dollar a milligram, or $80 per pill.

I learned about crushing and snorting Oxycontin when I was in Pathways and wanted to try it. When Mike arrived with the pills, I took them up to my apartment and crushed them with a quarter. Then, I sniffed Oxys for the very first time. This felt like I was "really" using drugs now because I was taking them this way, but I liked sniffing them much more than ingesting them. They hit me so much faster.

The problem with sniffing Oxys is that you can really do a lot of them without realizing how much you were actually doing. Snorting two pills is the same as taking thirty-two Percocets. By sniffing Oxys, your addiction can get out of control very quickly.

Because I had such a high tolerance before, the amount of Oxys I needed to take increased very rapidly. It wasn't long before I was sniffing three at a time, six times a day. Taking eighteen Oxycontin 80s is equal to taking two hundred and eighty-eight Percocets! Now imagine how intense the withdrawal is from that.

To support this habit, I started to steal at work. I worked at a hotel on the beach delivering room service, waiting tables, and bartending. It was a very lucrative job. I could easily walk away with three hundred dollars a night in cash and I worked six nights a week. But by the next day, I would not even have enough money to buy cigarettes because I was spending everything I made on drugs. Every day I would go through the same routine. I would buy drugs about an hour after I got to work, then I would work all day and night just to make enough money to buy more drugs the next day.

Mike was doing two runs a day to Ft. Lauderdale for me. Once in the morning when I made enough money to send him. Then again later, when I made enough money to send him for more. The problem was, the worse my habit got, the harder it was for me to work without them. Not being able to work meant I didn't make any money, which meant no drugs. Something had to give. It was always a race against the sickness. Then one day, a fellow co-worker got one of the manager's codes.

With his code, if someone paid in cash, I could void their tab and pocket all the cash. I started doing this to the tune of about two to three hundred dollars per day. I tried to take enough money that I would have some breathing room.

I was making somewhere between five and six hundred dollars a day in cash and it was still not enough for me. I never had extra money because everything I had was going toward drugs. The more I made, the more I used. It was like my mind was on autopilot and was being controlled by an addiction monster.

I started working seven days a week to pay for my habit. Taking the

Oxys gave me incredible energy. I was working nonstop double shifts seven days a week. It was a marathon that I could never win. My life consisted of working and getting high, nothing more. Then, it all came crashing down—again.

I was literally bringing home more money than someone making $200,000 a year and I couldn't find fifty cents in change if I needed it. My roommate Jackie knew I was getting high and started avoiding me. My parents had come around about the whole stolen check thing and they thought I was doing great in South Florida.

One day, I arrived at work and was told to go to my manager's office. They were all waiting for me. They said, "We know you have been stealing and are so disappointed."
The one manager I was friends with looked so angry and upset, I felt awful. They told me to get my things and never come back. When I got home, I saw a note Jackie left saying he had gone home for a couple of weeks and when he got back, he was moving out.

My roommate leaving was upsetting, but losing my job was a real problem. I had an astronomical habit by this point and my job was my only way of feeding it. I went into complete panic mode and called my parents. I told them I needed help.

I am not sure if my mother was just in a strange mood that day or what, but she seemed concerned. I received a call back from both of my parents saying there was a detox in Boca, which was one town away and that I was going there in a couple of hours. They had a driver coming to pick me up soon and I had to be ready. I did not let them know that I had lost my job and my roommate. I just asked them if there was any way they could Western Union me some money, so I could get some things I needed to go into the detox. The things I needed were drugs and they said, "Absolutely not."

The driver arrived at my apartment and drove me to a place called the Watershed in Boca Raton. By nightfall, the sickness enveloped me, and it felt worse than ever before. I was using about ten times as much as I had been at the peak of my worst use by this point, so this sickness took things to a different level.

They tried to get me to fill out paperwork, but I was too sick to write, eat, sleep, or do anything else. That night I did not see the doctor as he had already left for the day. A nurse said she could at least give me valium and a cocktail of things to help take the edge off. In the morning, I would see the doctor and get methadone, which I had heard of but had never taken before.

Even with everything she gave me, I still didn't sleep a wink. I sweated so badly the whole bed was soaked, and I just moved back and forth in the bed all night long while throwing up non-stop. By the time they came to take me to see the doctor, I could barely walk.

I could not understand how everyone else there seemed completely fine. They were happy and walked around laughing. When I finally got in to see the doctor, he asked me a few questions, but I interrupted him and said, "Doc, I am too sick to talk. Could we please do this after I get some medicine in me and feel better?" He told me he was giving me only twenty milligrams of methadone now and twenty milligrams tonight. This seemed so little that it scared me, but I was too ill to argue. I had never taken methadone before, but I was sure that twenty milligrams would not do much of anything for me.

I took the dose and waited for about a half hour but felt nothing. A person came to my room and said I had to meet with my counselor. I told them I was too sick, but they insisted I go. When I entered the counselor's office, I curled up into a ball on a chair. I had on two pairs of sweatpants, two long sleeve t-shirts, and was also wearing two sweatshirts. I was sweating like crazy but freezing cold. He started to talk to me and said that I had to answer these questions and the sooner I did, the faster this would all be over. All I could do was answer him with a 'yes' or a 'no.'

After about twenty minutes in his office, I started to feel this familiar warm feeling flowing through my stomach, then it radiated throughout my whole body. First the chills and shaking went away, then my skin became dry. The pain disappeared and I sat up straight. I was warm now, so I took off both sweatshirts. The volume on everything decreased. This scary, overwhelming facility suddenly became a safe and pleasant place to be. This good feeling was very similar to the high I got on Oxycontin, just not as intense and drug-like, but it was still good in its own way. I didn't feel like I was high on drugs, just really content and at peace within my own skin. To a normal person, this is no big deal, but to me, finally feeling tranquil again was amazing.

Only moments before, I had felt so awful, so I started worrying that all this was too good to be true. I kept thinking this wonderful feeling was going to disappear at any moment. I also started talking the counselor's ear off. He stated that he had just seen the transformation of a person who looked like he was dying of the plague who became a happy, healthy, good-looking person in five minutes.

When I went downstairs, my appetite had returned. None of the girls could believe I was the same guy that they had brought in. The pretty girl in the detox said loudly, "You are actually really sexy," and they all started laughing. Now I understood why everyone was walking around happy, they were on this methadone. Methadone was not like being on Oxys or some other powerful opiate. They were not high, knocked out, or nodding out, like I had seen at some detoxes. They just seemed like normal, happy people.

I was sure that within a couple of hours this feeling would go away as it did with all the other opiates and I would be asking, or more like begging, the nurse for more. But it didn't, in fact it stayed the same all day. When they came to give me the second dose, I didn't even think I really needed it.

I woke up the next morning bright-eyed and bushy-tailed. I had energy and I wasn't feeling sick, anxious, or depressed, and I was not thinking about drugs. I felt so motivated and ready to face the world. It was the best I had felt for an extended amount of time since, well, forever.

I decided that this was the miracle cure I'd been needing. If I could feel like this every day, I would never touch another drug again in my life. There would be no reason to as I didn't take drugs to get high. I took them to change the way I was feeling.

I told my roommate about how great I was feeling, and he said, "It's a shame you didn't get to a methadone clinic before. You probably could have saved yourself a lot of pain and misery. As much as you use, you sound like the perfect person for methadone." The more I thought about it, the more I realized how right he was.

For the next seven days in the detox on methadone I paid attention in groups, wanted to be involved, and decided that I could really stop taking drugs forever and I meant it. On methadone, I did not want to do any other drugs at all.

I left the detox on the eighth day. The problem was I never really detoxed. They just gave me methadone and weaned me down for seven days. That is like giving a broken bone seven hours to heal and then trying to walk on it. Had the detox given me a prescription for methadone, I probably would have not used drugs again until it ran out. Sadly, the government and capitalism got involved in the dispensing of methadone and because of that there was no easy way to get it.

They made it so that the only addicts who could get methadone were the ones who went to a clinic and paid eleven dollars a day. They treat methadone differently than any other drug because no other drug that carries the restrictions that methadone has; absolutely none. I believe there is probably no other drug on the planet that could save more lives than methadone! Can people use it to get high? Sure. Are there problems with using other substances with it? Yes. But overwhelmingly, methadone is a much better alternative compared to anything else.

The sad fact is that there are even complete idiots who want to put an end to methadone clinics and using methadone at all. These are the same people who are behind the reasoning that makes methadone so inaccessible in the first place. You can find something wrong with any drug, but vilifying methadone is the absolute worst and most braindead thing I have ever seen in my life in terms of treating drug addiction. Whoever decided that people who are suffering cannot just go to a doctor and get what they need is going to have a special place in Hell.

If doctors were able to write me and a million other addicts a prescription for methadone, they probably would have saved a minimum of 250,000 lives by this point. That is five times the number of Americans who died in the Vietnam War.

Instead, they stopped giving me the methadone on the sixth day and wished me luck. By the time I got back to my apartment, I was starting to go back into withdrawal. So essentially, all the detox did was hold off the withdrawal by a week and lessen my habit slightly. There is no way you can rush withdrawal for someone who used as much as I did in one week, or even one month.

My chance of success after leaving a detox in withdrawal is about zero even though my eight-day stay had just cost about $8000. When someone has a bad opiate habit, they need at least two weeks of weaning down in a medically supervised setting. Then two weeks after that to deal with the symptoms of post-acute withdrawal in a safe environment. The only way a weeklong detox works is if the person goes straight from the detox to a thirty or ninety-day inpatient rehab clinic.

Weeklong detoxes are fine for an alcoholic or a cocaine user, but I can't believe a medical professional wouldn't realize that more time is needed for opiate addicts. I saw so much money wasted by families, insurance companies, and the government on these programs, which absolutely don't work. For instance, the government pays $5000 for you to go to a weeklong detox and that's all they will pay for, so after the week is over, you are told to leave.

Now if you use opiates, you will go back to using and the $5000 was a complete waste. For the next two years, that same person comes back to the same detox about twelve times for a one week "tune-up" and relapses every time he is asked to leave. The government has now spent $60,000 for nothing and they still have a person who is using drugs. I have seen this happen many times.

If they were smart and hired someone like me to advise them, they would learn the truth rather than blindly following a politically correct assumption. They would end up saving millions of dollars and just as many lives. I would tell them to give the person enough time to get clean the first time around, which would involve about three weeks of detox and five weeks of inpatient rehab minimum. Plus many other things like therapy for abuse, animal therapy, etc that would increase their chances of staying clean.

One of the easiest ways the government could stop all this madness is to let doctors prescribe methadone to those who are in opiate withdrawal and at risk of relapsing. It is quite difficult for some addicts to get the money to stay at a clinic because it can cost upwards of $200, and then they have to make it to a clinic every day to get their dose. Considering these circumstances, many people just give up. Sometimes they must wait six months to get into a clinic in the first place. This is also the reason why I am in this current predicament during this period in my life.

Before long, I was back at my apartment and sick as a dog. I realized that there was no way I could keep living in this apartment without money or a job. I would start using with any money I got because I was so sick. I had to find a solution and fast.

I called a friend of mine who had been in Pathways with me. He told me that Pathways was opening a new halfway/rehab in Delray and the first people there were going to be a sort of experiment, so their stay would be free. This sounded like the perfect fix for my situation, and I went right away.

PATHWAYS PART 2/SCOTT

I ENDED UP back where I started, at Pathways at a new place they bought. I always remembered something my dad had said to me about going back to rehab. "The more times you keep going to these places, the less nice they are going to be." He was right because this time it was in a small one-story apartment complex far from the beach. A big difference from Hazelden and even the first Pathways.

The good part was that I did not have to pay to be there because they just opened and wanted us to be their "lab rats". It also meant there were fewer rules and groups to attend. In fact, for the first month and a half I just laid in my bed and didn't go anywhere because I was so sick from coming off Oxycontin. It had only taken me only about three days to recover the first time I kicked opiates. Now, it had almost been two months and I was just starting to feel a little bit better.

Eventually, when I could get out of bed, I started going to meetings with a friend named Scott who I had met at Pathways. Scott stayed clean and sober since then and had reinvented himself. He came by when he heard I was at Pathways again and started taking me to meetings. Not long after, he invited me to come live at his house, which I thought was a good idea.

I started living at Scott's house and things were going well. We went to AA/NA meetings during the week. I worked at a local car dealership, which was an awful job. I was pulling car parts out of a hot warehouse in South Florida all day for bad pay, but for the most part, life was pretty good.

I was staying sober and going to meetings. Although I wasn't really getting much out of them except to see the girls there. Above all else, Scott was the closest thing to a big brother I have ever had, and I enjoyed that.

Scott was a forty-year-old Jewish convicted felon. He served five years in prison for dealing LSD. He had a great sense of humor, which I liked. He loved the band Phish and took his sobriety very seriously. He also woke up every morning to lift weights before going to a technical college where he was learning computer programming.

He even called my parents and developed a relationship by talking with my mother, which was awkward for me. After doing well for a while, they invited us over to the house to see them. So, we flew up to New Jersey and stayed with my parents. I remember trying to pretend all the horrible things in my life had never happened. I just wanted my relationship with my parents to be a normal one, but it was like hanging out with an ex-girlfriend who cheated on you. There was always going to be this uncomfortable tension.

Scott and I decided to go to New York City to see the 9/11 memorial. When we got back, my parents took us to the casinos in Atlantic City. I kept telling Scott about these five-dollar slot machines that we would win on practically every time we played. I didn't think Scott believed me, but sure enough, after ten minutes of playing, the first machine hit $1000. Then, I hit another $1000. My mom gave

Scott $400 to play and he just wanted to keep it. Anyway, we left with almost $3000 more than we had when we arrived.

Something about being in New Jersey, being around my parents, and winning all that money, got my addict brain going crazy. On the flight back to Florida, all I could think about was calling Mike and getting some Oxys. I kept telling myself that I could use just this once and stop.

The minute I got home, I used my phone and called Mike. He drove to Delray Beach and I gave him money, then waited. I was supposed to go to this regular meeting later in the day because I wanted to see this girl named Jessica who was going to be there. So, after I got the drugs, I went to the AA meeting.

It was a very strange feeling sitting in a meeting surrounded by people who were trying to stay clean while waiting for my drugs to kick in. Once they did, the meeting flew by and I didn't want it to be over.

I told myself that being high was the best way to do this sobriety thing. Normally, I would be sitting in the meeting looking at the clock but because I was high, I didn't look at it once. When you're high, you could have fun watching paint dry.

I remember at the end when we all held hands and said the Serenity Prayer, this was the first time I had ever paid attention to the words. I was high as hell and the prayer actually made sense now. I even felt more connected to AA while being high than I ever did while sober.

SECOND MAJOR RELAPSE

THIS WAS THE second time I had experienced a relatively long period of being clean from drugs, then started taking them again. Even though I promised myself I was only going to use once, I knew that no drug dealer was going to come out and meet me if I only was buying one. The risk was not worth the reward.

Also, once you start using it, even once, it is incredibly hard to stop when you are an addict. There is this strange thing that happens to addicts' brains when they use just once. Granted, you are not physically addicted, but there is this mental aspect that makes you feel like you need to continue using. I call it the "first use fog." It is not there in normal people and was not there in me when I first began using, but it was damn sure there now.

I bought fifteen Oxy 80s for three hundred dollars and swore to myself that I would only take two and save the rest. After taking the first two, I really tried to go the next day without taking any.

The problem was that the "First Use Fog" was making me feel awful because I wasn't continuing to use. I wasn't sick, but when the drugs wore off, I felt sad and unmotivated. Every cell in my body seemed to be telling me to take more.

It wasn't like I could just take one Oxy to get high, then go back to how I was feeling the day before. So, my holdout didn't last long. Before I knew it, I was calling Mike again for more and I was right back to where I started.

MY BROTHER'S WEDDING

MY BROTHER DECIDED to get married to a girl from college named Vanessa. My dad told me that he had decided that I would be his best man, which blew me away. So, I had to get a speech together.

I had two problems. First, I was back on drugs. Second, I didn't know nor like my brother, so how the hell was I going to give a speech as his best man? I wondered why in God's name he would even want me to be his best man in the first place.

Apparently, all his fraternity brothers who had younger brothers asked them to be their best man, so that was the reason my brother asked me. He wanted to look good in front of other people. The idea of being my brother's best man felt so awkward. It was like Hillary Clinton asking Donald Trump to be her best man. The only bearable way to make it through the wedding was to be high, really freaking high.

I planned on bringing enough drugs to make it through the whole wedding and the trip home. I knew how much I needed and even brought some extras just to be safe. His wedding was going to be in

Greenwich, Connecticut, so if I ran out there, I would be screwed because I was far from any dealers I knew.

Before the wedding, we stayed in a hotel in Connecticut. The trip was now on its fifth day and I was running out of Oxys. No matter what I did, it was impossible for me to ration drugs like I had planned.

With that being said, I was still able to save one for the last moment right before the wedding started. No matter what, I would at least not be sick during the wedding. Well... this was easier said than done!

The night before, I was up the whole night with the sickness, tossing and turning in bed. It took every fiber of my being to hold out and not take that last one. About an hour before the wedding, I finally decided to sniff the last Oxy.

I went into the bathroom and turned the water on because my parents had come to my room and could hear what I was doing. I got out my driver's license and put it on top of the pill, then pushed down to crush it. Instead of crushing the pill, it slipped and shot right into the sink and down the drain with the running water. It was gone in a second. My heart dropped and I screamed, "Nooooooo!"

My parents started banging on the door and asking what the hell was going on. For the next forty-five minutes, I tried to take the sink apart, but eventually had to give up. It was the worst feeling ever.

Now, I had to face this whole wedding and make a best man speech while in full opiate withdrawal. As far as real-life awful situations go, this was about as bad as it gets. Even when I think back on it now, I shudder and feel my stomach start to turn.

EVERYTHING FALLS APART AGAIN

AFTER THE WEDDING, I went back to Florida and things went from bad to worse. Scott realized something was wrong because I was acting completely different. I stopped being myself and I am sure he suspected I was getting high.

One day while in withdrawal, I decided to pawn Scott's laptop computer. I was expecting my paycheck later that day and was going to get it out of pawn before he came home. But when I got to work, my boss said they were not giving out the checks until the next day. Things like that always happen when you are getting high. So, I went home and had to face the music.

Scott was pissed, but he took me to a detox. It was a county-run facility in West Palm Beach and was by far the worst detox I had been up to that point. They gave you no helpful medication, the food was horrible, there were no TVs, groups, or anything else to do. Basically, all they did was give you a bed and make sure you didn't die.

They put us in this huge room with fifty beds and you never left.

Most of the beds were filled with people in agony as the opiate epidemic was starting to hit Florida now. I spent as much time as possible in a chair under a hot shower. I was awake twenty-four hours a day with nothing to do but think. The thoughts that run through your mind during withdrawal are awful. Everything seems worse than it really is, but there is nothing to do except deal with it.

After a week in detox, I ended up at the Salvation Army Rehab Center in West Palm. It had three different sections: a homeless shelter, a rehab, and a prison halfway house. The first month, I was still in withdrawal and could not sleep. I just stayed up all night listening to my Walkman and staring at the ceiling. I also rarely spoke to anyone. When the withdrawal finally subsided, I actually started to enjoy myself there.

There was a good group of people in the rehab. We all had our past sufferings in common to talk about and there never seemed to be a dull moment. I even started playing softball, which was a lot of fun. I also got a job at a local gym called Club Fit.

SHAWNA

WHILE I WAS in the Salvation Army, or Sally as we called it, Scott had taken a job working for Pathways. He had become romantically involved with one of the female clients, which was completely against the rules. This female was named Shawna and she had won the Powerball lottery and turned into a horrible drug addict. She and her husband David had won when the jackpot of $283 million in August of 2001. Three other people had also won, so after taxes they walked away with about $28 million.

Originally, they bought a huge house in Kentucky, but they did a very stupid thing by going on the news after they won. Everyone in Kentucky seemed to come looking for them begging for money. They had people show up claiming to be long lost relatives. Others came saying their children were dying and they needed money to save their lives. Every day, they had boxes of mail full of letters coming to their house that were from people begging for money.

To make matters worse, they also lived in the worst area for Oxycontin. Doctors flooded Kentucky with it because of financial incentives delivered by Purdue Pharma. They created an incredible number of addicts for such a small rural area.

For David and Shawna, this made getting Oxys easier than buying alcohol. With all the money they had and all their friends doing them, they went crazy, especially Shawna. David would buy his friends unlimited pills, then would pay for their funerals after they overdosed. Things got so bad in Kentucky that they had to move to Florida to get away.

Shawna is the one and only person I have ever met that had a worse habit than I did. She was taking fifty OC 80s a day, which is equivalent to eight hundred Percocets a day! In addition, she was smoking $1000 worth of crack daily, swallowing Xanax bars like they were Lucky Charms, and shooting heroin like it was… well, heroin!

She had even been to some truly amazing rehabs like Promises in Malibu, California and the one with that commercial that claims to make you a normal person again by curing your addiction for the cheap price of $100,000. These places prey on people when they are desperate and at their most vulnerable and in reality offer very little help for addiction.

After relapsing repeatedly, David eventually had a judge sentence Shawna to go to Pathways. She had to stay there or go to jail. This is how her relationship with Scott came to be. Their marriage was on the rocks, so when Shawna met Scott, the timing was perfect. She was looking for a man and Scott was looking for a payday.

Shawna was really into cars. She and David had a Lamborghini Diablo, a Ferrari 360, a Dodge Viper, a Shelby Series 1, a Rolls Royce, a Bentley, a Porsche 911, two Cadillac Escalades, and more. Her neighbors even complained that it looked like a car dealership.

They were completely broke when they won the lottery. David was an ex-con who had spent time in prison for armed robbery of a gas station. Shawna was about half his age and came from a trailer park.

They knew nothing about money, let alone how to save and invest. Some people tried to help them, but most just tried to rip them off. They saw them as backwoods country folk who could easily be separated from their money.

Scott came to visit me and was so excited to tell me that not only was he dating this millionaire lottery winner, but she allowed him to drive her Ferrari whenever he wanted. He said that the next week when he came to visit me, he was going to pick me up in the Ferrari and I could drive it. He was so happy it was as if he had won the lottery.

Just as he had promised, the next Saturday he picked me up at this homeless shelter/rehab in a new Ferrari Modena Spyder convertible. When we drove away, people were looking at me as if to ask, "What the hell is going on here?"

The really cool thing about Shawna was that she never looked at the Ferrari like most Ferrari owners do, like they are afraid you are going to damage the paint by breathing on it. Amazingly, she let me and Scott drive it as much as we wanted. I loved driving that car, it was incredibly fast and so much fun. I told myself that one day I would be cruising around in one of my own.

Soon, paradise between Scott and Shawna went sour. She used an unbelievable amount of drugs every day. Her purse would be full of $50,000 in one-hundred dollar bills until she met with her dealer and then her purse would be empty. Less than a week later, she would do it again. She was paying $100 for an OC 80 and buying five hundred at a time. One night, she even stabbed Scott with a crack pipe when he tried to stop her from smoking it.

Not long after they broke up, she called me and asked if my dad would buy her Ferrari for $50,000. It was an amazing deal, but she had one stipulation, she wanted the cash that day. I called my dad and right away he knew it was for drugs. Even though he easily could have made $100,000 off it, he refused. This made her furious at me. I never heard anything from her again after that, but I eventually found out that she and her husband had lost everything.

There was a story in the paper called "From Rags to Riches to Rags" and it was about Shawna and David. They had lost everything. They were evicted from their home, sold all their cars, and were arrested while living in a storage unit using buckets in place of a toilet. This was less than seven years after winning one of the largest lotteries in history.

David died not long after that from his drug and alcohol use. His liver basically failed him, and he died completely broke. Shawna was sentenced to prison for stabbing another person in the neck with a crack pipe.

I read in the paper and online about people calling them "junkie scumbags," "hillbilly losers," and things like that. People who never even knew them were calling them horrible names. I wondered how those people would feel if they knew that Shawna had grown up in a trailer park and had been sexually abused as a child. Yes, they were drug addicts, but they were also kind hearted people. They gave a waitress who was down on her luck a $5000 tip. They donated $250,000 to firefighters after 9/11. They gave so much money to so many people that I would have to write an entire book just to tell you about it. But still, people only wanted to focus on the negative aspects about them and I found that sad.

BACK IN THE SADDLE AGAIN

I RELAPSED AFTER nine months of sobriety in the Salvation Army Program. I was at work one day when a homeless guy came in asking for money and I gave him a dollar. He told me he had a bottle of pills from the VA clinic and couldn't read the label. He asked if I could read it for him and let him know what he was supposed to take. The pills turned out to be Percocets. Just seeing Percocets up close got my brain thinking about getting high, almost like I had just popped one.

I had stayed clean this whole time, but I had done nothing to work on the root of the problem. Drugs were not my problem. My problem was the reason I took the drugs in the first place. I needed to fix that hole, or I would never be able to resist drugs. This is another reason why the War on Drugs is ridiculous. We are treating this as a criminal problem instead of the real mental problem that it is.

Every day during the next week, all I could think about was getting high. I went back and forth debating about whether I could or should use just one more time. This was an improvement. In the past, I would have been high already. It just took a combination of an anxiety attack, a couple of bad things happening during a bad day, and I gave in and called Mike.

I was so excited about getting high that I drove with Mike to get the pills to Ft. Lauderdale, so I would not have to wait any longer to take them. On the way there, the Aerosmith song "Back in the Saddle Again" came on the radio and I thought to myself how fitting that was. Before long, I was "back in the saddle again" taking multiple Oxycontins every day.

I left the Salvation Army shortly after relapsing as I knew I would be caught sooner or later. I figured it was better to have a place to go when I got kicked out, so I moved in with a guy from work. He let me use his car to get to work and I lived rent free because I was doing so well at work, which was making him a lot more money than rent was ever going to bring in.

After only two weeks of using Oxys, I stopped and started having bad withdrawals again. I quickly realized I didn't have it in me to do another detox. This staying sober thing was just not working out. No matter how bad I wanted to stay sober, something was always leading me back to drugs. Something was missing from my life that made it impossible for me to stay sober for an extended amount of time.

Right after a relapse, the pain of using, the consequences, and the awful withdrawal were all still fresh in my mind, which made it easy to find the motivation to resist urges and stay sober. But as time passed, it was like I had a built-in "forgetter" and all those things did not seem so bad anymore. Then, I would start remembering all the good times more than the bad ones. After six months, it became a completely one-sided situation.

All I thought about when I thought of drugs were the good times and how incredible they made me feel. Having to fight these urges while not seeing any negatives was incredibly difficult and practically impossible.

I needed to find a compromise. That is when I remembered how great and normal methadone made me feel. Now that I had a car and a job, I decided to try to enroll in a methadone clinic.

METHADONE

THE FIRST MORNING at the Methadone Clinic was a five-hour process. It felt like it was going to last forever, especially since I was in withdrawal. Eventually, I was enrolled, and they gave me a dose of forty milligrams of liquid methadone. That was the most they would give you the first day. After that, you could go up ten milligrams a day until you felt stable.

I left the clinic and headed to work still sick, but since I was riding an anticipation high, I had just enough energy to get to work. An "anticipation high" is a natural high you get when you know you are going to have drugs in your system soon. It can be so strong that it will alleviate many of the withdrawal symptoms. Sadly, there is no way to trick your body into having this feeling, but I have a suspicion that when they find the cure for opiate withdrawal, it will come through this knowledge.

I was still not sure if the methadone in the detox was a fluke and if it was really going to help me out or not. I waited anxiously and started losing hope because it seemed like a long time had passed and I still felt the same. But after one hour, my whole life changed.

As soon as the methadone kicked in, I felt that same familiar feeling I had felt that day in the detox. The sickness went away followed by a feeling of being content, but not high. The happiness I felt was like nothing I had ever experienced without the help of drugs. I had energy, looked forward to my day, was motivated, and the thought of having to use more drugs obsessively was gone. This feeling lasted until the next morning and I knew my life was about to change for the better.

Ideally, no one wants to be on a drug, but when you are as sick as I was and nothing helps you to stay clean, it is beyond words to describe how great it feels to be somewhat free. I imagine that this is how a slave in Egypt must have felt after being freed from the chains. It was the first time in my life I had ever felt hope for my future. I even cracked a real smile for the first time in as long as I could remember.

At this point, methadone was the only thing that enabled me to live a semi-normal life and have some peace. While on methadone I did not steal, I had nothing to lie about, and I went to work, saved money, and acted just like a normal person. The only exception was that I had to go to this clinic and get my dose five times a week, which was fine with me considering the alternative.

Methadone gets a bad name from people in AA and NA who have gotten clean and now feel the need to tell people that they are not clean because they are taking methadone. Meanwhile, the critics smoke cigarettes, drink eight big cups of coffee for breakfast, drink twelve Red Bulls for lunch, are on five different antidepressants and antipsychotics, eat fast food daily and, most importantly, have never had a bad opiate habit.

Yet, some people feel that they are now experts and their opinion is what matters. AA and NA people are not doctors and are never supposed to get involved in medical affairs. Although, this does not stop many of these "holier than thou" people who want to show everyone how great they are by telling people to be clean like them. The best people I met in AA were the ones that shared what worked for them and not tell others what to do. There example said more than a million words ever could.

I had a friend who listened to these hypocritical people constantly berate him about being on methadone. He decided to hurry and get off it just to please them. Shortly after stopping methadone, he relapsed on drugs. After relapsing, these same people all turned their backs on him. A week later he was found dead in his bathroom by his mother.

I would never tell an alcoholic that they should not take Antabuse nor would I ever tell anyone else that they should not take something that could save their lives, just because I don't take it. I have not walked in their shoes and have no right to judge or advise them on matters I am not qualified to speak on. I wish more people would come to realize this. These jailhouse lawyer attitudes have harmed more people than they have helped. Also, the ones who do the most judging always turned out to be the worst people themselves. When you judge someone for something it says more about you than it does about them!

Methadone has a thirty-three percent success rate of keeping people clean after two years. While that is not a great success rate, it is still a lot better than the three percent of drug addicts who stay clean after two years from a rehab or the six percent from AA/NA. Any other program on the face of the planet with a three percent success rate would be considered a huge failure.

MEGAN

Now that my life wasn't being consumed by drugs, I met a girl in Florida named Megan during a hurricane, which I should have taken as an omen of things to come. This happened while I was sharing an apartment with a friend from work named Matt. This massive hurricane came and everyone in the apartment complex started partying together. These people who lived across from us invited us up to their apartment to party.

When we got there, there was this one girl who wouldn't look at me. Her name was Megan and she did not say one word to me the entire night. She was the prettiest of the girls there and had a boyfriend whose name was also Andrew.

Throughout the night, we had a fun time during the hurricane. The next morning, I heard a knock on my apartment door. It was Megan who asked if she could come in. I wasn't sure why she was at our apartment, but quickly started to realize that this girl was obviously into me. We ended up hooking up a few nights later.

My friend Matt tried to warn me when he said, "She has a boyfriend and is hooking up with you? That is not a good sign for the future," but I didn't listen. Eventually she broke up with Andrew and got together with me.

Megan was from Ohio and went to college at Florida Atlantic University in Boca Raton. We eventually got an apartment together, which I paid for because she was in school. She also told me she had no money because her father drank away their family business, so her mom was working at a fast food place for money just to survive.

While in Florida, things went pretty well between us. I was working while she went to school. I loved the warm weather and the new freedom methadone provided me. I enjoyed being a regular guy who went to work and paid his bills. We eventually decided to move back to New Jersey because of Megan and my parents.

Megan did not like being in Florida because it was so far from where she grew up. She also did not like some of my friends. My friend Noah from LBI became a male model lived in an awesome house with a couple of other models and they threw parties non-stop, which Megan hated. She did not hate the parties, but she had a problem with the girls who would attend.

Megan kept saying how she really wanted to leave Florida. She explained how her dad would drink all day and night and that she was worried about her mom. My parents also wanted us to come back to New Jersey, which seemed odd. I had been on the right track now for over two years and I think my parents figured that Megan must have been the reason for that. The reality was that the methadone had more to do with it than anything else, but this didn't matter to them. They said there was a house near them in LBI for rent and they would rent for us if we moved up there.

I didn't want to leave Florida, but Megan was miserable, and my parents even bribed me by saying that my grandfather had left me a lot of money and if I came up, they would give it to me to buy a house.

Later I found out the real reason my parents wanted me there so badly. My brother had lived near them for a long time and only dealt with their bullshit because he wanted money. After a while, he and his wife could not take it anymore. My parents expected them to be at their beck and call twenty-four hours a day. If they weren't, my mother would berate them and always held the money over their heads.

My mother would give them all the money they needed and then some, but as soon as they did something she did not like, she would take the money away. Being that my brother didn't have any real concept of money and saving, it made them dependent on my parents. Eventually, even my brother had had enough.

I wasn't getting into trouble, so all my mom had to talk about was how awful my dad was. She called my brother everyday complaining about him. Adam was also going over to shovel snow, cut grass, move things, be her psychiatrist, and lots more on a daily basis. If he couldn't make time when she asked, she went absolutely nuts and would tell him he was a no-good son just like his brother.

Adam and his wife finally said enough was enough and moved all the way to the West Coast and even left a great job. My mother saw this as the ultimate betrayal. She said to him, "How dare you leave me with your father all alone here!" He responded by yelling at her and my mother did what she always does. She told him she was done with him and not to call or talk to her and, of course, he was now out of the will. I was used to being told I was cut out of the will, but this was a first for Adam.

Anytime things got bad, my mother would always stop talking to me or say our relationship was over for good. When she felt badly done, you were out of the will and she never wanted to talk to you again. Now that neither of our names were in the will, my mother claimed she went to a lawyer and had it arranged so that my cousin Christopher would get all her money. This cracked me up and I bet the lawyer was probably saying to himself, "How long is this one going to last?"

My cousin Chris had never said two words to my parents except for a brief 'hello' at Christmas and Thanksgiving. He never sent them birthday cards, presents, or anything else. I don't even think my parents knew where he was living when they decided to make him the benefactor of their will.

My brother had helped them for years and my mom knew all he wanted was the money from that will. She knew this would hurt him more than anything else. For me, I couldn't care less and busted out laughing when I heard the estate was now going to a cousin. It was such a sad, pathetic thing for my mother to do, but it is exactly what my brother deserved. Karma had finally started to come around.

This was the reason my mother was now being so nice to me. It was not because she was happy that I was staying clean or even that she wanted to be near me. She wanted to hurt my brother and she knew if I was home helping them, it would hurt him more than anything. Even if it meant giving a drug addict a quarter of a million dollars, she would go to any length after someone wronged her, especially someone in her family.

Sadly, the idea of me having a lot of money combined with Megan's hatred of Florida was enough motivation to make me move. So, we packed up and moved to Long Beach Island in a home right down the street from my parents' house. At first, things were going well. Then, my mother demanded that I get off the methadone.

The nearest methadone clinic I knew of was in Atlantic City, so it was about a two-hour drive there and back each day. Had I done a little bit of research, I would have discovered that there was a clinic close by, but I didn't find out about it until years later.

My mom convinced Megan that I should get off methadone, too. I had read about this stuff called Suboxone, which supposedly worked like methadone except you could get a prescription for it from a doctor. That sounded like the perfect solution. I called a doctor near Moorestown named Dr. Baruch and set up an appointment.

Dr Baruch was a very good man and he went above and beyond the call of duty as a doctor for me. There were times that I could not pay for his services many years later and he always helped me. He even gave me money one time! I will forever be grateful to this kind man and a great doctor.

The day I walked into Dr. Baruch's office, I had taken one hundred and sixty milligrams of methadone and had been on it for about three years. He asked me if I had taken any opiates recently, I lied and said, "No." I told him I was in withdrawal, thinking he wouldn't give me Suboxone if I told him I took another opiate. I thought he was like all the other doctors who would not give you an opiate if they suspected you had taken other opiates the same day because they didn't think you had enough of a tolerance to handle both. I found out later that wasn't why he was asking me if I had taken other opiates. He was not worried about me overdosing. He was worried about the exact opposite.

He gave me the Suboxone to put under my tongue and told me to let it dissolve. About fifteen minutes later, I told him I felt fine, so he gave me a prescription for Suboxone and another for Klonopin. He said Klonopin would help with the transition to Suboxone as there could be some serious anxiety involved. I should have never accepted the Klonopin. It had been years since I had taken one and had a horrible addiction to them. I took the prescription but convinced myself that I would not take the pills unless it was absolutely necessary.

My parents drove me to a local pharmacy to get the prescription and the girl behind the counter was a friend from high school. She started talking to me, then all hell broke loose.

Everything suddenly got really loud and bright, then waves of panic and fear like I had never experienced before washed over me. Meanwhile, everything just kept getting louder and louder. I ran to the bathroom and threw up all over, then I had such bad diarrhea that I almost couldn't make it to the toilet. Everything just ran out of my system like water. I started hyperventilating and immediately was covered in sweat from head to toe. I felt unbelievably cold and started shaking uncontrollably. I was sure my heart was about to explode.

Twenty minutes passed before I finally stopped going to the bathroom and throwing up, so I could leave the restroom. By the time I got the prescription and got back into the car, I felt like a 100-year-old man who was dying from some horrible disease.

What happened was that Suboxone put me into precipitated withdrawal. The reason the doctor asked me if I had taken anything before is because Suboxone will throw a person who is addicted to opiates into immediate and agonizing full opiate withdrawal in a matter of minutes. You must be clean from opiates or in withdrawal before taking Suboxone.

You go from feeling completely fine to feeling like you went through three full days of intense withdrawal in minutes and now you are stuck this way. Some people's hearts have actually stopped because it is so intense and such a shock to the system. To this day, I have never felt so sick in my entire life. Especially because it was precipitated withdrawal from such a high, prolonged dose of methadone, it was the ultimate sickness.

The big draw back from methadone is also its benefit, and the reason the withdrawal is so bad is because it has an insanely long half-life. It builds up in your system, so the next day when you take it, you still have half of the previous day's dose still in your system. While this is a useful tool for addiction, this is also why it is one of the most horrible opiates to withdraw from, which can take six months to a year or longer in some cases.

SUBS & THE RETURN OF MY OLD FRIEN-EMY, KLONOPIN

It took a week of lying in my bed in absolute agony until the Suboxone finally overtook the opiate receptors that the methadone had been occupying, then the sickness went away. Because Suboxone is an opiate-like drug, I did not have to wait months to feel better, thank God.

I also started taking my old friend Klonopin. That first day when I went into precipitated withdrawal, I took over twenty of them. I had no tolerance to Klonopin at this point and took over forty milligrams in one day. It didn't calm me down one bit or let me close my eyes for one second. If a normal human with no tolerance was given 40 milligrams of Klonopin, they would probably have slipped into a coma. You could probably knock out ten people easily with that much Klonopin. My system was that amped up from the withdrawal, so it barely fazed me.

I started taking Klonopin on a regular basis with Suboxone, I believed it was helping me transition. Very quickly I became addicted to it again, which is something I didn't want. Benzodiazepines like Klonopin messed with my mind and changed my behavior more drastically than opiates, but it was too late to stop now because I was already having withdrawal symptoms. There was no way I was going through another benzo withdrawal right now. After all these years, I was right back where I started, on Klonopin and an opiate. The only difference was that I was on a stronger opiate.

Suboxone is a combination of an opiate called buprenorphine and an opiate blocker called naloxone. They add a blocker, so you won't crush and inject it. However, taking it under the tongue works just like any other opiate and the naloxone has no effect.

Buprenorphine is a very strong opiate that is almost forty times as strong a morphine and eleven times as strong as Oxycontin. It also has a longer half-life than methadone. There was this rumor that you don't get sick when you come off it, but that is a complete lie.

The more I took Suboxone, the more I wanted to keep taking it. I started by taking one eight-milligram Suboxone three times a day. Then, four times a day, then one and a half four times, and then two four times, and finally three tablets four times a day. That is twelve eight-milligram tablets or ninety-six milligrams of Suboxone, which is an incredibly high amount. A milligram would be enough to get a non-addict completely trashed for days. In fact, hospitals give patients a quarter of a milligram for severe surgical pain, and I was taking four hundred times that amount every day.

To make sure I always had enough, I started paying three different doctors for prescriptions and I would also buy them off the street. Getting off methadone was turning out to be the worst thing I could have done.

INHERITANCE/STOCK MARKET/ ENGAGED

I RECEIVED MY inheritance from my grandfather, which was around $200,000. My parents gave it to me because they wanted Megan and I to buy a house near them, and we almost did.

The house was right off the island. I put money down on it, but the loan officer pulled some shady stuff at the last moment to get us into a higher rate. Most people would have gone for it, but I saw it as the perfect opportunity to back out. I had recently started working at a Mercedes-Benz dealership, but knew nothing about home owner-ship. I also dreaded living close to my parents on a permanent basis.

By this point I was also getting tired of Megan. She was definitely not the person I wanted to spend the rest of my life with, which was about the only thing I was sure of at that time. Megan only wanted me to take care of her and was extremely selfish. She also never made me feel as though she was someone I could trust. There was something about her that was very fake. I felt trapped with her and my only solution was to take more drugs.

One day, I came home from work and my mother met me at my place. She said we needed to go for a ride and talk. Whenever I was alone with my mom, I would get this awkward, sick feeling. This time it was different though, but I still knew something was up. It was not long before she started telling me that it was time for me to ask Megan to marry me. She explained that all her friends' children were getting married and great things were happening for them. She said it is about time she had something good to say about me.

I told her that I would consider it, but now wasn't the right time. I was not in the right mindset to ask anyone to marry me. Then, she explained that the only reason I received the inheritance was because she told her father to put it away for me. If she hadn't done that, it would have gone to her and then she asked, "Now, why can't you do this for me?"

She compromised, "Well, why don't we just go take a look at rings?" She took me to a store called the Diamond Mine. I saw a ring that looked nice, but it was the last thing I would ever give to my future wife because it was yellow gold. I didn't like engagement rings made with yellow gold. I only liked the way platinum looked. Before I could say anything, my mother whipped out her credit card and said she would pay for it. I was shocked but could not turn that offer down.

When I got home, I literally tossed the ring to Megan and said, "Marry me," and she replied, "Yes." It was such an awful feeling. I wished I could just take the money and drive to California. I had recently bought a new Mercedes-Benz and dreamed about leaving Megan and my parents and going back to California to start a new life.

WATCHING MY FATHER SLOWLY KILL HIMSELF

NOT ONLY DID I have to deal with my mom and Megan, I also had to deal with my father who was falling apart. It was hard to watch. He had type 2 diabetes, which my mom blamed on Agent Orange exposure in Vietnam. While type 2 diabetes was a symptom of Agent Orange, telling my dad this was the only reason he was suffering from the disease gave him the green light to keep eating anything he wanted. When you have diabetes and eat like you are in a contest, your blood sugar becomes dangerously high and destroys most of the organs in your body.

His eyesight got so bad that the state took away his driver's license, so now he had to depend on my mother, which was sure to make her angry. His feet started eating away at themselves. He also put on a ton of weight because of the diabetes medication and his eating habits. It was a vicious cycle. It also hurt his heart, which was weak in the first place.

My mom would be so hypocritical when it came to my father. She would tell us how awful it was that my father wouldn't eat right. Then, an hour later, she would take him out to dinner when she knew he would eat everything he shouldn't be eating. It was like crying about someone hitting you, then ramming your face into their fist. I started to feel like she wanted him to eat himself to death, so that she would not have to deal with him.

Watching him eat was like watching a drug addict take drugs. He started doing this thing where he would eat so much and so fast that food would get all over his shirt. He would sweat like he was at a gym. He would even start taking insulin shots in his stomach in front of everyone. The whole time my mother would act like this was fine and never say anything to him directly.

Once dinner was over, she would go home and tell us how awful it was that my father was doing this. The next day, she would complain about it all day long, then like clockwork, they would go out to dinner again and do the exact same thing. I was taking enough drugs to sedate half of the island we lived on and I was really starting to feel like I was the sanest person in my whole family. I did realize that food was the only thing that brought my dad any joy at this point in his life, but it was also killing him.

My mom became even more resentful that she had to drive my dad everywhere and walk him around like a child, a very angry and large child, but I rarely sympathized with her. You are supposed to be there and tell your partner when they are doing something wrong; not go behind their backs and talk badly about them to get sympathy. Most importantly, you were supposed to be there for them in sickness and in health. That's what family does.

They eventually sold the Moorestown home and moved to LBI full time, which no one their age was doing. The only people who retired to Long Beach Island were much older people. My parents were young compared to them, so this gave my mother another reason to be resentful toward my father.

My parents completely expected my brother and I to live near them for life. They looked at their children as servants who were born to take care of them forever. Anything else was unacceptable to them. Had they been loving, supportive, healthy, non-abusive parents, this probably would not have been so much of an issue. The reality was that they were incredibly unhealthy to live around. Their love was expressed a dollar at a time and never in a more appropriate way.

HELLO, OHIO

AFTER A FEW months of living near my parents, Megan had finally had enough. She couldn't take it anymore and wanted to move near her family. I also had it up to my eyeballs with my family. This was about the only subject that Megan and I agreed on.

One morning it snowed, and Megan and I walked over to my parents' house to shovel, but the driveway had already been taken care of by the time we arrived. When I knocked on the door, my mother had that evil look in her eyes. She yelled, "How dare you make me shovel snow," then, "Get the hell away from me! I don't want to talk to either of you." Megan didn't understand what was going on. She asked, "Why didn't she just call and ask you to come over?" and, "Why did she get so upset at having to shovel snow?" She said her parents would have done it and not said anything. She could not comprehend this. She also could not believe my mom just told us that she never wanted to talk to us again.

Megan then went off on a tangent and listed about a hundred things that my parents had done so far that were completely insane. She said, "I thought my parents were bad, but your parents are insane and impossible to deal with. I would go crazy living near them. Money is nice, but this is unbearable." She wanted to leave as soon as possible. I also wanted to leave, but not with her.

I was in a situation where I was engaged to someone I didn't want to marry. No matter what I did, I was going to make someone very angry and this whole time no one cared about what I wanted. Not once did she ask what I wanted to do. It seemed as though my only option was to move to Ohio with her, but I was definitely not looking forward to being around her family either. My solution was the same as always, just take as many drugs as possible and hope for the best.

My parents were furious when I told them I was leaving. My mom said she should have never given me that money and she would find a way to get it back from me if I moved. I left for Ohio anyway and, of course, I was out of the will this time for good again and was told not to talk to them for at least eighteen months. I am not sure where she came up with the number eighteen, but she did.

When we first got to Ohio, we lived with Megan's parents. Megan's family was definitely not like any families I grew up around. Her dad kept a keg of beer in the house. He drank every day and every night. Her mom was working at a fast food place with high school kids. The way they talked and acted was kind of culture shock.

Megan's dad was not someone she was proud of. He was jealous of the fact that I drove a Mercedes, had a job, and had more money than him, which was not that big of an accomplishment because he was broke. Around town, people didn't respect him very much. He eventually got a job picking up trash for the town, but he had caused problems about some union thing and local people now called him a loser, a liar, and a storyteller.

The second week I was there, I got into a conversation with a man from her hometown. As soon as he found out I was dating Tim's daughter, he said, "Good luck," and started laughing. He said, "For your sake, let's just hope she isn't like her father." That was really comforting!

Our first weekend there, we played in this football pool that Megan's dad always played but had never won. The first time I played in the pool, I won big. Her dad became extremely upset about this even though, technically, his own daughter won half of it. You could tell he wanted to prove that he knew more about football. In all reality, these pools are just games of luck because they involve gambling, this was lost on him, too. I couldn't understand why he could not at least be happy we'd won. After all, we were all on the same team.

I could tell Megan was embarrassed by him, but she said, "He is my dad and I have to deal with what I got." That was the good thing about Megan, even though she said what an embarrassment her father was, she still showed him love. Some stuck-up people like an evil neighbor of ours would have been too embarrassed to even admit that they knew someone like her father, let alone reveal that he was family.

To make my living situation bearable, I started taking insane amounts of Klonopin. I was taking twenty-two milligram Klonopin tablets every night. I was buying them for two dollars apiece and had un-limited funds for the most part. While my self-induced Klonopin coma started to make everyone nervous, Megan's mother was the first to become worried because of my alarm clock. I would set it for 8am on the loudest setting possible. It would go off and stay on for at least an hour before they would come in and physically wake me up. This was strange and I could tell it upset her because nobody with a heartbeat could have slept through that incessant noise.

When I overheard her parents talking about what was happening, I laughed. Her father was not bright enough to figure out what was really going on. It was like listening to a bunch of country bumpkins trying to figure out how an iPhone works. "Maybe he has a brain tumor," and, "Maybe he's deaf," or, "Maybe he's an alien!" Basically, just off-the-wall things like that. I felt like I was in the Twilight Zone. Thank God we moved out shortly thereafter.

By this point, the damage was done with her parents. I was praying they would convince her to leave me. My prayers were answered in a way. One day, I heard her talking to her father on the phone when she thought I was asleep. She said that I was passed out on drugs. She told him that she was going to leave me. Her dad encouraged her to at least get me to buy her a car first and, "To get as much money as possible." This completely didn't shock or upset me. I was so relieved to learn she was leaving that I decided to have some fun with her. I acted like nothing happened and immediately went and told her that I had made a million dollars in the stock market and she believed me.

I had been investing in stocks for a while now and had bought in to Monster Energy Drink at the very beginning, so the notion that I had made a million dollars was not beyond the scope of reality. As if on cue, Megan told me how much she loved me, and I told her I couldn't wait to buy her that fancy sports car she wanted. I even told her I was going to buy her parents things, too. I was already helping to pay some of their bills.

Megan's parents could not afford to pay their bills, so of course, we, meaning me, volunteered to pay for them. They never said thank you, not once! Had I been in my right mind, none of this craziness would have ever happened. The first time they didn't say 'thank you' would have been the last time they received a penny from me!

I knew her dad didn't have a chance at being declared Father of the Year, but I couldn't believe he was encouraging his daughter to stay with me just to get money. He knew by now that I was on drugs, so any kind of disaster could have happened such as falling asleep with a lit cigarette and burning the house down with his daughter in it. Although, I started to worry because if she told him I now had a million dollars, he might never let her leave without getting that money.

When things actually finally came to a head between us, I actually fell asleep while she was talking to me. I found out later that she came back to my place and stole a bunch of money from me and cleaned out the bank account I had, which was really an awful thing to do! She knew I had a drug problem and never once tried to get me any help. She just took as much as she could. It was such a scummy thing to do, and I could imagine her father doing that but not her.

As soon as I found out the money was gone, I also saw that my name was used to fill out two credit cards that I had no idea about and were not to my address. I remembered how she hated it when people signed her up for things and always used my name when she applied for credit. I was so angry that I went online and filled out about ten applications in her name for stupid things like 'Dildo of the Month Club' and the exact same credit cards she had applied for to get back at her!

What happened after this made me realize that getting away from Megan and her family was a bright spot in my life, and the greatest gift she could have given me. I also realized that I should have listened to everyone who was trying to warn me about her and her family.

LETTER TO MOM/ARRESTED

AFTER MEGAN LEFT, I received a letter from my mom saying how horrible it was that I was back on drugs. Megan called her and said she did everything she could to try to help but was unable to stop me. This was an unbelievably low thing even for Megan to do. She conveniently left out the parts about how she had stolen everything, cleaned out my bank account, applied for credit cards in my name, conspired with her father about getting me to buy her a fancy car, and she never once tried to help me in anyway.

My mother said, "How could you put this poor, sweet girl through all of this?" I just laughed as my mom she had no idea what the hell she was talking about. One of the saddest parts about being on drugs is that rotten people feel they have the right to do whatever they want to you just because you are an addict. Megan robbed me pure and simple and she should have been sitting in jail, not calling my mother.

Of course, my mom felt awful for her and couldn't care less about me or anything Megan had done. I am not exaggerating when I say that I truly believe that had Megan murdered me to steal all my money, my mother would have said I deserved. Megan knew this very well. My mother also told me that Megan was asking for money now because she and her family had none. I told my mom that she was just trying to con her and wondered how she could not see Megan for what she was. For how dumb her family was, Megan could be very cunning and manipulative.

My mom also stated that she wanted payment for the credit card she had given me and if I didn't take care of it, she was going to call the police. My mother gave me the credit card to use before I got my inheritance and encouraged me to buy things for Megan, and even for her and my father's birthdays. Little did my mom know that Megan had spent thousands on that credit card and left me to pay it. Now, because she had no legal right to the inheritance, this was her only means of getting back at me.

After Megan had the nerve to claim she was wronged and asked for more money, and my mother claiming she was going to call the police on me, something inside me snapped. This was too much to handle, they were such hypocrites. I decided to respond with the truth about everything and I didn't care about the consequences anymore. She went too far when she said she would bring the police into the situation. It was just too ironic for her to be threatening me with the police when she was the one who should have been in trouble!

I wrote her a letter stating that she had some nerve threatening me with the police, then I just came out and said it: "You sexually abused me as a child and are the cause of me being in this whole predicament in the first place." I told her that they had things called lie detector tests and I would love to see her take one. I finished the letter and sent it.

About two months went by, and I was in horrible shape. I had not heard from my parents. I was fired from JP Morgan because I couldn't keep my eyes open or show up on time. I just sat in my condominium and got high day in and day out. I had bought three dirt bikes and an expensive street motorcycle people often called a "crotch rocket" because of its intense speed. For some reason, I brought them inside and took them all apart in my living room.

This was just one of the crazy things I did while high, like spending over $50,000 in one month alone on drugs. My days started fading away into a sort of dreamlike state. I remember going to sleep, then waking up as it was just getting dark again. The only time I left my place was to get more drugs. One day, the phone rang, and it kept on ringing. I wasn't answering my phone anymore for anyone. I just let it ring as I got ready to take my two dogs out for a walk.

When I opened the back door, I saw a police officer standing there with an assault rifle pointed at my head telling me to put my hands up. I turned around and saw that the police were in the process of raiding my house in full SWAT gear. I could not believe what was going on and was sure they had come to the wrong house.

Apparently, Megan had been so upset with me for filling out those online applications that she went to the police, but only after speaking to my own mother who encouraged her to do this. My mother had received my letter and gone into panic mode. What she did next was unbelievable. She got so worried that she decided the best way to protect herself was to have me arrested and declared insane. She went to anyone who would listen and told them I had gone nuts and that she was fearful of me.

She never mentioned the letter I wrote and how I said she was abusing me. She just told everyone that I went completely insane and needed to be put in an institution or jail to "save myself." I am not sure how she convinced people I was dangerous, but I think she told them about the guns and immediately they thought it was something it wasn't.

She did this because she wanted to protect herself. She even retained a lawyer. I never even went to the police about the abuse she subjected me to, but she was paying a lawyer for advice. That lawyer must have thought she looked pretty damn guilty, and I'm sure it was obvious that she was worried sick.

What made no sense was that she was never afraid of me before, but as soon as she got the letter, I became a threat. The only real danger I posed was to her freedom. Had anyone found out the truth, she knew damn well that she would be in deep.

Most people who didn't know the whole story just automatically believed her. They thought I had indeed gone crazy because, well, why would a mother lie about such a thing? Since no one knew the truth, they had no reason not to believe her.

Then, she convinced Megan's family that they needed to call the police for their own protection and tell them about the guns I owned. She said because I was using drugs that I was a danger to them, which was all a bunch of crap. The only person I was a danger to was myself. My mother was worried about being found out and nothing more. I would love for her to face God and tell him that she was indeed afraid of me hurting her.

I had never threatened anyone with physical harm, including my mother. I was not a convicted felon and completely within my rights to own a firearm. All the drugs I was taking were completely legal as far as anyone knew, but Megan was able to get the police to arrest me because she said I had filled out credit applications in her name. I never received or used anything from the forms I filled out. After I talked to a lawyer, he could not believe the police arrested me because of this. They had absolutely no proof of a crime except for Megan and my mother's accusations.

Meanwhile, Megan never mentioned to the police that she had done the exact same thing to me, had stolen money from my house, cleaned out my bank account, or that one of the guns in my possession was a gift from her, which she purchased with my money. It is completely illegal to buy a firearm for someone else, and you can go to jail for doing this! Yet, she called them anyway and, just like my mom, conveniently left out these details. Especially the one about me not having the guns anymore. Megan knew I sold all of those guns months before this! But she lied to the police and told them I still had them.

While this retaliation gave Megan the opportunity to get revenge on me, she also felt wronged because she still thought I had millions of dollars. I found out that Megan's father had this big plan to sue me after I was arrested as a lame attempt to get a chunk of my imaginary millions. He was irate because I stopped paying his bills after Megan and I broke up and now Megan was never going to get a free car. He thought this was his big shot and he must have been seething when he discovered that I had nowhere near a million dollars!

He even went so far as to ask my mom if she wanted to sue me, too, once it got to the point that even my parents felt terrible, or at least my dad did. What happened was this: Megan's father wasn't too bright, so after talking to my mom, he thought she must have been totally against me and that she would help him sue me. At this point, my dad realized how awful Megan and her family was and could see that they were doing this out of spite and greed, and not because they were concerned for my well-being. This was when my dad told my mom that Megan and her family were complete "pieces of shit". Even my parents friends, were like wait a minute here… Sue him? They saw their true colors now. They weren't afraid of me or feeling they were criminally wronged, they were low-lives looking for a payday from a sick person by using the police.

The police had decided to bring SWAT to my house based on the baseless words of my mother, Megan, and her father. I pointed this out to the police after they brought me to the station, but all they said was, "Well, you still filled out credit card applications in her name."

Not only did I not get any of those cards, but I had entered fake addresses and everything else. The only thing that was real was her social security number. No one, especially me, would have ever gotten those cards and used them. I said, "If she was allowed to do the same thing to me and then go into my bank account and empty it, I was damn sure allowed to fill out a credit card application in her name."

I told them how "someone" had filled out a credit card application in my name. They could not believe what I told them and tried to show them on my computer but they refused to look. The only person who could have done this was Megan. So, on top of making up the story about all the guns I had, she was guilty of the exact same crime she was accusing me of doing. I could tell that the cops were embarrassed after hearing this.

I then explained to the police officer how ironic it was that Megan would report all these "illegal guns" when she had purchased one of them. He was in disbelief and said, "Wait... she really bought you one of those guns and then called the police on you about the same gun?"

First off, it is illegal to buy a gun for someone, so they should have been arresting her. The officer said, "Considering who her father is, I'm not surprised by any of this," and then they let me go without charging me with anything.

Although, before they let me go, another officer stated that he couldn't believe that my own mother wouldn't call and ask me to give the guns to the police or at least warn me that the police were coming, so "I wouldn't get shot." He asked me, "So, she didn't tell you we were coming or to lay the guns down?" I said, "Nope!"

Apparently, my mom told the cops that she was going to call and tell me to put the guns down because the police were outside, so they wouldn't shoot me. I looked on my caller ID and saw that she'd never called. He said, "Geez, it's almost like your own mother wanted you to get shot!" That didn't surprise me. What surprised me was that my dad hadn't called me either! Megan's father is a lowlife and Megan is an awful person, but for my father to not step-in was shocking, but also freeing in a way.

When I left the police station and got home, the news got even worse. Megan had broken into my place after the police took me away. She stole everything of value and even let her new boyfriend try to steal my motorcycle. He was driving away with it when a neighbor stopped him. Megan tried to intervene by saying, "You know he filled out credit card applications in my name, right?" My neighbor replied, "So, that gives you the right to break into his house and steal his motorcycle?" She had no answer and stormed off angry as hell.

When I found out about this, I called the police and told them, but they did nothing! They refused to send an officer to my house. To this day, I cannot believe that the Westerville Police Department of Ohio turned a blind eye to this. After all, she and her boyfriend broke into my home, burglarized it, and attempted grand theft auto, yet the police weren't interested in arresting either one of them. My neighbor was so flabbergasted about the police not arresting her that I think he was even angrier than I was. He said, "You told the police that I saw them rob your home and how I stopped them from stealing your motorcycle, right? I can't believe they still won't do anything!"

This was yet another example of how wicked people take advantage of those who are in a bad situation, especially when it comes to someone who is on drugs. Megan and her family are the perfect example of people who are sober and still capable of committing criminal offenses. They got away with it for no other reason except for the fact that their victim was addicted to drugs.

Megan should have been arrested for burglary, filing a false police report, lying to the police, buying a firearm for someone else, and grand theft auto. But because I was on drugs, the police let her get away with all of this. I had always thought the police were supposed to be there for people who couldn't protect themselves and were at a disadvantage. Not in my wildest dreams did I think the police would ever be fine with not bringing a criminal to justice, even when there was an eyewitness who managed to stop a part of the crime while it was in progress. But that is exactly what happened.

After the police refused to arrest Megan, I went back into my house and filled out more applications in her name. If the police were not going to arrest her for what she did, there was no way they could arrest me. To my complete shock, this is exactly what happened. Even after everything she did, they chose to come and arrest me and let her keep her freedom.

A few nights later, they came back to my house and took me to jail. A female Westerville police officer who was aware of everything that had happened so far, told me how she thought this was complete bullshit. She almost let me go and tried to get the male officer to leave without arresting me. She told him she knew this situation and that I was not the person they should be arresting, or at the very least, they should be arresting both of us. He said because they had a warrant, he had no choice, but he also said that if his partner felt I should not be arrested, then this really must be some "bullshit!".

They did not search or handcuff me, so I managed to arrive at the police station with a bottle of Klonopin and a bottle of Suboxone in my pocket. I took half the bottle of Klonopin while at the Westerville Police Department. By the time they got me to the county jail, I finally told them I had drugs on me. The cop who drove me was shocked and said, "If they'd found these on you inside the jail, you would have been charged with two felonies."

I stayed in the county jail for the night, then was released when a local lawyer named Steven Ames bailed me out. Steven Ames is still someone I need to make amends with. Had he not bailed me out, I would have died from withdrawal in jail without a doubt.

Jails do not give you anything to ease withdrawal. I would have had to do a cold turkey withdrawal in a jail cell from sixty milligrams of Klonopin and ninety-six milligrams of Suboxone taken daily for over a year. I would have started having seizures followed by a heart attack. I spoke to a doctor who told me that the level of Klonopin I was taking was the highest dosage he had ever seen a human consume. He told me I would have gone through suffering that probably would have thrown my body into shock and then I would have convulsed and died. The sad part is that I would have been given a death sentence for the crime of filling out applications online. Something about our criminal justice system is very wrong, especially when it comes to drug addiction. My real crime was putting a substance into my own body.

When the case went to the grand jury, they couldn't figure out what the hell I was even arrested for and threw it out. To this day, this is one of the biggest injustices I have ever faced, but I am sure God will make it right, if he hasn't already.

I must also mention that Steven Ames saved my life and he doesn't even know it. I feel bad because he put up $1000 to bail me out and, by this point, I didn't have the money to pay him back. Had the grand jury not thrown my case out, he would have been stuck paying for it. Either way, one day he is going to receive a check from me and a thank you note.

COMING HOME AFTER THE LETTER

MONTHS PASSED AND I eventually ran out of money. I also crashed my Mercedes. So, I drove back to New Jersey in a rental van because I needed drugs. I was making this trip at least once a week and I had rented this big van, so I could travel with my dirt bike in case I wanted to ride it.

Once I got back to New Jersey, I was high and in need of money, so I decided to stop by my parents and see them. Being broke, I didn't know what the hell else to do. I drove by and saw my brother's car in the driveway. I decided that it wasn't a good idea to stop while he was there, so I drove to my friend John's house and, strangely enough, I saw that someone was home at Kate's house, which was three houses before John's. So, I decided to stop in and say 'hi.' I knocked and a voice told me to come in. I knew it was Kate.

As soon as she saw it was me, the look on her face said, "Oh, no! It's him." I thought, "Oh, great. She still hasn't gotten over that one night." She let me in, but was very cold towards me. Considering the circumstances, I managed to get up the nerve to apologize to her for not sleeping with her that night so many years ago. I told her there wasn't anything wrong with her and that the problem was with me, but she didn't seem to care either way. I could tell she wanted me to leave, so I said I was going to go, and she said, "Good." or something along those lines, and I agreed.

I left Kate's thinking she simply hated me ever since that night because I wouldn't sleep with her. So, I drove to my friend Greg's house and saw he was home. When I went to his door, I got the same look from him that I had gotten from Kate. Shocked and confused, I asked what the hell was going on.

He said that Kate had called him and asked if "I was stalking her or had plans to kill her or are you in the mafia." I said, "Greg, what the hell are you talking about?!" He insisted that I show him what was in the van before he said anything else. I let him look inside the van to prove that it only held my dirt bike. After he saw this, he looked confused and said, "What's going on?" Then, I found out why everyone was acting so strangely toward me.

What happened was that after my mom got my letter, she went around telling everyone I was crazy. She said I had guns and planned on killing people. She warned that if anyone saw me, they were not to believe anything I said and to get to safety. This was her way of making sure no one ever heard or believed anything I said. She even told them I was driving around with machine guns in my car. So they would never find out what I said about her. Even after the police her they were sold.

So, this false information spread through everyone and rumors were now out of control. Greg said he heard I was in the mafia now, some white power gang, and had killed someone at a Wawa, was stalking Kate, and had killed a preacher last year, and all this other ridiculous stuff. I couldn't help laughing my ass off when I heard this. The fact that he seemed to believe it made me laugh even harder, which was the first time I had laughed in quite a while.

Apparently, Kate had gotten this love letter from me, which wasn't from me it was a friend getting back at me for joke we pulled on him and decided to write letters to girls I knew and even called others saying he was me and loved them. By the time it spread through the rumor mill, I had become a stalker, too. I think even Kate believed it. That made me laugh, too, because it was so ridiculous it was funny.

Kate had this wimpy brother named Scott that looked like a little weasel and was probably the biggest coward I have ever met in my life. One night I was at his house because local kids told him they were going to use his house for a party and he let them. While there they all went through his mom's underwear and were even wearing on their face. He did nothing about it. He would also start fights with people from cars and then run away. He was basically this skinny little rich kid that had this inflated sense of ego for absolutely no reason. I knew he must have been scared to death and heard he was telling people some of these lies, which didn't surprise me.

I said, "Greg, I was just apologizing to her for turning her down when she asked me to have sex with her!" Then, he said, "Oh, yeah. She said that was true. I wondered why people told Kate you were stalking her, yet she never mentioned that."

He looked disappointed afterward and let his guard down. He said, "People always spread gossip about negative things and it never turns out to be true. I always believe things and am so gullible!" I could tell he was upset, and I asked, "What, did you want this to be true?" He replied, "No, it's just disappointing how people lie!"

I really didn't blame him or anyone else for thinking something was wrong with me. After all, it was coming from my own mother and I did have a well-known problem with drugs. Some of my friends had problems, but their parents didn't broadcast this to everyone and damn sure didn't tell everyone they were insane and worthy of being feared. Greg let me stay the night with him. The next morning, I drove to my parents' house.

I saw that my brother was gone and decided to stop by. At the very least, this visit was going to be beyond awkward. I started walking around back and saw my mother. As soon as she saw me, she came outside. She was acting a bit odd, but not angry. It was more like she was spaced out on drugs. My dad came out and, thankfully, right then the neighbors did, too. No one could believe how skinny I was. At this point, I stood five feet eleven inches tall and weighed one hundred and eight pounds, which was a lighter weight than when I was eleven years old. Regardless, I had no idea I was so skinny. I told my parents that I needed to go back into rehab and was going to Florida.

I knew things would never be the same after that letter, but we just acted like it didn't happen, which was how we normally dealt with things in my family. Still, it was incredibly awkward.

BACK IN REHAB

ABOUT A MONTH later, I ended up at the Carrier Clinic in Belle Mead, New Jersey. My mother's brother Doug even agreed to pay for it. I decided to call him out of the blue one day. He had not talked to my mom or our side of the family in years, so I figured what could it hurt?

He had cut off my mom and our family when her father left his land in Gettysburg to our family. My grandfather did that because my mom was the only one with children and he wanted us to have the land to enjoy. He also felt his own sons would just sell the land for the money. My mother blamed me for years because Doug wouldn't talk to her, but I had never asked for the land and was only ten years old when he left it to us.

When I called him, I was surprised that he agreed to help. It truly seemed like an angel was watching out for me. I had nowhere to go and my habit was so bad that I could not have made it while detoxing out on the street. I probably would have died one way or another.

While in Carrier, the doctor told me I had the longest and most severe case of withdrawal he had ever seen. He brought me down from the amount I was taking, but even after two months, I was still nowhere near being completely detoxed.

After Carrier, I went to a halfway house, but I had not stopped taking Suboxone. After forty-five days in detox, they quit giving me Suboxone, which was about forty days longer than anyone else was on it. I was a cash paying client, so they didn't care. After they cut me off, I was so ill that I could not get out of bed. A girl in the rehab started giving me Suboxones she had sneaked in. I guess she was forced to be there and decided to bring some just in case. Most addicts will help other addicts out if they can. After experiencing the sickness, no one wants to see another person suffering like that.

She was even nice enough to give me twenty Suboxone when I left detox and gave me her number in case I needed more. Luckily for me, the halfway house didn't test for Suboxone yet, and they let me in even though I was taking Suboxone. I didn't last very long and I soon decided to leave and go live with the girl from rehab.

Moving in with a girl from rehab is never a good idea. They have a saying "Two dead batteries will not start a car," which they won't, and rehab relationships rarely work out either. After living with her for a few weeks, I decided to try heroin. Everyone in the rehab had been using it and said how cheap and powerful it was. When the Suboxone ran out, I tried heroin for the first time.

HEROIN

THE FIRST TIME I sniffed heroin I was not impressed by it. I had used incredible amounts of opiates by this point in my life and barely felt the heroin because it was not the good stuff. By this, I mean it wasn't powerful or potent.

There is this huge misconception in the media and with the police that when someone dies of a heroin overdose it is because they got a "bad batch" or "bad bag" of heroin. This could not be further from the truth. The reason they overdosed was because it was very good and extremely potent.

The police and the media became the best advertisers ever for drug dealers. They would make an announcement on the news that eight people had overdosed on a certain type of heroin and told people to stay away. The next day, the people selling that heroin would be flooded with customers because they knew it was good.

Heroin comes in little glassine baggies and is a light brown color. It is cut by a dealer with things like B vitamins, baby laxatives, iced tea, chocolate milk, and all sorts of other ingredients. It has a very bitter taste and the more bitter it is, the better it usually is.

The reason most addicts end up on heroin is because you get more bang for your buck, plus it is easier to get than prescription opiates. The problem is that you never know what or how much you are going to get. The people who deal heroin are less than savory types who you would never trust with your money, let alone your life, but that is the world addicts live in.

I couldn't just stop taking the Suboxone and still be okay. After running out of them, I switched to heroin to avoid withdrawal. People always think that when someone does heroin, they start because they wanted to get high. Most people I know who use heroin did so the first time to avoid withdrawal from another opiate like Oxycontin, not to get high. This is another common misconception.

The only problem I had was that I didn't have much money at this point to keep using heroin and neither did the girl I was living with, and she was more addicted to me than the drugs, which made the situation depressing for both of us.

SHOOTING

AFTER USING HEROIN nasally and basically giving up on myself, I finally decided to give in and use a needle. I remember losing all hope because no matter what I tried, I just kept going back to opiates and was now sniffing heroin. My future did not look bright, which led to my next thought, "Why not shoot? Everyone says it's so great."

Every time I bought heroin, I would go see this guy Chris at his apartment. It was an awful place and everyone who lived there was addicted to heroin. The apartment was a big room in the basement of a building. It was divided into four sections by hanging sheets. Chris was the youngest person who lived there while the rest were in their 50s and 60s. The older men survived on government assistance and odd jobs. Chris worked for a lawn service.

Their apartment smelled terrible because cats lived there, and they would urinate everywhere. They peed all over their clothes and no one washed them. Also, everyone smoked with no ventilation or open windows. The smell was so bad that if I was there for even ten minutes, when I got back into my car it would smell for days.

Here I am pulling up in my Mercedes to this bad area of New Brunswick, New Jersey, and then going into the basement of this hellhole building to buy heroin. I knew sooner or later I was going to be stopped by the police, robbed, or shot.

Chris and all the guys who lived with him shot heroin and they always tried to get me to do it. They said how great it was and how I was wasting my drugs by sniffing them. One day I went to buy drugs and told Chris I wanted to shoot them. So, after I bought the drugs, I held my arm out and told Chris to shoot me up while I looked the other way.

My heart was thumping furiously and felt like it was going a thousand beats per minute, then I felt this incredible rush. When you inject heroin, it hits you all at once and builds to a climax, sort of like having an amazing orgasm during a roller coaster ride, but much better.

The feeling is so great that it's difficult to describe in words. I will say that no matter what horrible thing is going on in your life, after you inject heroin, it will not matter to you anymore.

After you start injecting, you never want to go back to sniffing. The whole ritual of preparing the heroin in the needle even becomes addictive. However, shooting it brings a whole new set of problems.

It is neither socially acceptable nor legal to inject yourself with heroin in public. You need to have hypodermic needles, which are not always easy to get depending on where you live. You also need access to water, a cooker to mix it in, and cotton to use as a filter when you suck it up into the needle.

Then, you need to find a vein to inject into, which can be very difficult depending on whether or not you are hydrated, if the atmosphere is cold or warm, how much body fat you have, if you are male or female, and if you have good veins for shooting in the first place.

You are also supposed to use a new needle each time you inject. If you don't, the tip becomes dull and causes horrible damage to your veins. Most addicts reuse their needles many times over and end up with collapsed veins.

Lastly, you need to find a private place to shoot up. When you are not alone in your own home, finding privacy is not always as easy as it sounds. If you went into a public bathroom, you could get arrested, die of an overdose, or waste your drugs, the last one is probably what addicts dreaded most.

I remember one time I bought heroin from Atlantic City. I was so sick that I couldn't wait and pulled off the parkway into a rest stop to shoot up. I parked as far away from other cars as possible, but once I had everything mixed up in a cap, sure enough, this van pulled up right alongside me.

It was a group of hippie-looking kids who were smoking marijuana. They looked at me and thought I was some uptight businessman because I was in a suit and tie, drove a Mercedes-Benz, and looked clean-cut.

I could hear them saying things and laughing while they were blowing smoke at the window as if to say, "Want a hit? Nah, he's probably doing his taxes," and so on. The whole time I am trying to get a vein. Finally, I saw that magical red blood start to fill the needle, which let me know I was ready for lift-off and pushed the plunger down.

Immediately, I felt the rush and instantly felt amazing! The volume of the clowns next to me was quickly muffled and, with the needle still in my arm, I purposely lifted my arm up so they could all see. When I saw they were all looking, I pulled the needle out of my arm, then put my mouth on my arm to suck up the blood. Their faces dropped and they looked completely blown away! I just drove away laughing to myself.

It wasn't long after I started shooting that I ended up back in another rehab called John Brooks in Atlantic City. At this point, I never had enough time to build much of a life, so if I had a relapse my only option was to go to detox and then rehab. After all, it's not like I had an apartment to lose, a mortgage to fret over, or a job to quit because I could not stay clean long enough to accumulate anything substantial.

MAUREEN

WHILE AT JOHN Brooks, my parents called and said their friend Maureen wanted to come visit me. Maureen was the wife of a friend of my father's, and she'd been a horrible alcoholic. She had also attempted suicide in the most brutal way by shooting herself with a .357 Magnum in the chest. Luckily, she lived and was now sober. She was going to AA and thought she could help by visiting and telling me all about the program.

Maureen and her husband Doug had a house on the beach near my parents' house. Doug was very wealthy and was about thirty years older than Maureen. They married when she was very young. Doug and Maureen were close friends with a couple who lived across the street named Tom and Sue. My dad, Tom, Doug and another friend used to go out for breakfast every week.

The first time I heard about Maureen was before she had shot herself. My mom mentioned that a woman had come over early in the morning to visit her "drunk as a skunk." I didn't think much of it at the time. Later, when she told me that that same woman had attempted suicide by shooting herself, her name stuck out to me, but also because she was very pretty! Maureen had blonde hair and huge boobs. She looked like a Barbie doll.

When she came to visit me at the rehab, all the guys kept saying how hot my girlfriend was. When I said she wasn't my girlfriend, they said well you can tell she likes you, so you better hook up with her.

She started coming to visit me regularly. She would bring me candy, cigarettes, and other things I needed, but everyone kept saying how much they noticed how into me she was, which piqued my curiosity. I was sober, so I would never sleep with my father's friend's wife, but I think I enjoyed flirting with her and it was nice having a regular visitor. I also think she liked that a younger guy was giving her attention.

She told me about her attempted suicide. She said she could not stop drinking and hated her life. It got to the point where she just couldn't take it anymore. So, she grabbed her husband's gun and shot herself in the chest. She missed her heart by centimeters and was still alive, she kept drinking for hours! Then, when she didn't die, she started to get scared and called her husband. He called the police and they took her to a local hospital. Amazingly, the doctor (who sadly was killed in Iraq not to long after) saved her life.

After that, she started attending AA and had been clean for three years now. Her new mission in life was to help people like her. I thought that was great, but Maureen was focusing solely on other people and not on herself. She needed as much help as anyone else did, if not more.

In AA, you are supposed to get a sponsor, work the steps, and focus on yourself. Maureen didn't want to look inward, she said it was too painful. She believed what kept her sober was helping other people and supporting John McCain for president and his anti-abortion stance. I still have not figured out what that had to do with staying clean, but I guess it worked for her.

She had never been able to have kids and had become a strict anti-abortion advocate. I found this a little hypocritical coming from a person who had attempted suicide three times already to be such a pro-life person, but hey, who was I to judge anyone?

After about six months of being in rehab, I was supposed to go on to the next phase, which is like a halfway house where you lived and worked. The only exception was that there were rules, and counselors there twenty-four hours a day to enforce these rules.

The day before I went there, I played a game of football with the guys from the rehab. They all acted tough, but when they took us to a field to play a real game, it was different. Acting tough and being tough are two completely different things. Since I had played football before, I outplayed them. I caught two touchdown passes and intercepted another, then ran it in for a touchdown within the first ten minutes. During one play, I was going for the ball when I fell on my hand. It really hurt and my pinky would not move. I thought it was broken. The next day my hand was all black and blue, so they took me to the ER.

The doctor at the ER said she had bad news. My hand wasn't broken! I couldn't see how that was bad news until she explained that I had torn a flexor tendon and needed to have surgery as soon as possible. She then offered me a prescription for Percocet, which I felt damn good about declining. I had gone through months of horrible withdrawal at the rehab and was finally clean of everything. This gave me the strength to decline them.

When I told the halfway house about my hand, they said that I was a liability and could not stay there. I called my parents who were in Florida. For the first five months I was in rehab, they refused to talk to me until Maureen had asked to visit me. After Maureen, they started talking to me normally and even seemed concerned now that I had nowhere to go. My dad told me he would call me back with a solution in thirty minutes. When he called back, he told me that Tom and Sue were going to pick me up and bring me back to their house. Maureen was going to take me to meetings every day and do everything she could to help me stay sober. I was so excited to hear this great news. I didn't want to be in a halfway house and would be much more comfortable in my own home, and having a pretty woman taking me around places wouldn't be bad either.

Tom and Sue were very nice people. They were good people who had always cared about me. The first day I was home, Maureen came right over and took me to an AA meeting. I was the youngest person at the meeting. Maureen was like a celebrity to the men in the meeting. It seemed like they had never had a rich, beautiful woman talk to them.

She went around introducing me to everyone in the room. Besides another woman named Kara who was a lawyer and also very pretty, Maureen was the hottest thing in any AA meeting on the Island. She flirted with all the guys and they went for it. After realizing that I was going to be coming with Maureen from now on, two men named Dan and Jack started offering their help to me.

They said it was what they always did with newcomers. The funny thing was that I had been to meetings there about five times previously without Maureen and neither one of them had said two words to me, so I knew they were not honest about the whole "newcomer" thing. Dan offered to be my sponsor and Jack gave me his phone number and said to start calling him.

Dan was obviously infatuated with Maureen. Dan was a married man who had been a horrible drunk and was now overly "AA-if-ied." He had gone as far as getting a vanity license plate that said "LBIAA". I guess he forgot about the anonymous part. He had been a horrible father as a drunk. He had even left his little girl and her friend with some drug dealers in the inner city of Baltimore and drove home because he was too drunk to remember they were with him. Maureen was his dream girl and I am sure he thought she really liked him. Her flirting was just the way she was, but to Dan it meant more.

Jack wasn't much better than Dan. He was this little old guy that would start talking to you and literally not stop for hours. You couldn't get one word in while he was talking. It was like he didn't think anything you said was important, but you are going to listen to everything he said whether you were interested or not. I started to realize why these people were alcoholics. It was a completely self-centered disease.

Maureen thought both Dan and Jack were sad, but she would always be nice to them. She would take their calls and would always talk to them at meetings. When Dan started to sponsor me, the first thing he should have said as a sponsor was that men should stay with the men and women belonged with the women. Every AA sponsor in the whole world does this, except Dan.

He noticed Maureen and I were always together and said nothing about it. The same thing went for Jack. Also, Dan really didn't understand drug addiction and Jack knew even less about it. So, there was no way I could relate or feel comfortable talking with them. I just went along with the motions to please Maureen.

Our days became routine. Maureen would drive over to my house at 6:45am and pick me up for a 7am meeting. We would then spend most of the day together attending meetings and talking. We enjoyed each other's company. That is how our days went until I had to have my surgery.

I had told the doctor prior to my surgery that I was an addict and did not want any addictive painkillers during or after the surgery. This was a big mistake for me.

The doctor said I should take a narcotic during the surgery and then after for about three days. He said I should also give the bottle to someone to hold. This would have been the smartest thing possible to do.

So, they gave me nothing as I had requested and when I woke up from the surgery, I was in so much pain that I was going out of my mind. They had to cut my whole hand open and force metal rods through my bones. On the way home, we stopped at a pharmacy where I picked up a prescription for this "non-addictive" drug called Ultram. I took a handful of them right away.

Before I got home, that old feeling came back and all I could think about was getting high, which was too much being that I was already in pain. It turns out that Ultram is quite addictive. The company just marketed it as non-addictive to sell more. It is a horrible medication. If anyone reading this an addict and is thinking about taking it as a painkiller, do not! You will regret it! The pain it dulls is nothing compared to the pain it causes.

Ultram is basically like taking an opiate, which would get my drug-thinking mind cranked up again without the benefit of being strong enough like a real opiate to deaden the pain. So, I got all the negatives and none of the positives. As soon as we got home, I told Maureen I needed a couple of hours alone to sleep. The first thing I did was drive down to Atlantic City to buy heroin. I was in a cast and bleeding all over as it had only been three hours since the surgery.

I met up with a female "drug dealer" and she said we needed to drive to a spot, so she could pick up her stash. She jumped into my car and we drove to the spot. I gave her the money and she got out to meet the guy on the corner, then came back to my car. As soon as she closed my door, I saw police lights behind my car, and I was sure I'd been caught. Luckily, the guy she met told her that she had to wait five minutes for the drugs.

The police saw her getting out of my car, then back in, so they came up and asked us what the hell we were doing. They said they knew the person she was meeting was a drug dealer and they had been watching him. They said if we gave them the drugs, they wouldn't tear the car apart. Being that we didn't have any drugs, we had nothing to give them, so they went through the whole car and found nothing. They could not believe I was driving being that I had just gotten out of surgery hours earlier. "That addiction shit is a motherfucker," the cop said. After not finding any drugs, they let me go.

Hours later, I finally got the drugs. I only bought four bags and swore that it was just to get me through the pain. On the ride home, I sniffed the heroin and it kicked in hard. It had been eight months since I had gotten high, so my tolerance was next to nothing, which made the high feel extra amazing. The pain from the surgery was completely gone and I could barely keep my eyes open. I couldn't believe how hard only two bags were affecting me.

Shortly after I got home, Maureen came over. I remember I was laid out on my couch and she said she was going to take care of me like a nurse. I put on a movie and the next thing I knew she was lying next to me on the couch like she was my girlfriend. It was awkward at first, but I was high, and my shyness was gone. We started looking into each other's eyes, then began kissing. As we were kissing, it became passionate to the point that we were about to have sex, but I stopped it. I told her, "I can't do this. You're Doug's wife."

She started saying, "You are such a good man," and said she was proud of me for saying 'no' to her. She went on to tell me that she and Doug slept in different beds and that he hadn't touched her in years. She said that she couldn't get pregnant and that she wanted me to see her naked anyway.

She took off her clothes and I looked but didn't look. She told me that she didn't shave and wanted to know what I thought about how it looked. Next, she pulled out her boobs that were huge. She told me to feel her scar, which I did while touching her boobs as she sat on me. Finally, I just said the hell with it and flipped her over and we had sex. What a crazy day this had been! Opiates can make it difficult to get an erection, but they can also make you have incredible sex. I could tell she had never had sex like this before and was a stranger to having an orgasm during sex.

Had I not been on some drug, I would have lasted about thirty seconds, which would've been far from a great time for her. After getting "the dope sex," she was hooked! I felt awful the next morning, but I sniffed the last two bags of heroin and had sex with her again. After I sobered up, I promised myself I would never sleep with her again and would stop using heroin. I decided to just use Ultram for the pain whether it helped or not.

The problem with Ultram was that it was getting me high even though they said it wasn't going to. The high was not as intense as other opiates, but it was most definitely a "high." Anyone with a drug problem who takes this "non-addictive" drug will be using again in no time. The doctor had prescribed me two bottles, but when I went back for the two-week follow-up, I ran out. They were supposed to last me three months.

My parents were back from Florida by this time and came to the doctor's appointment with me. The doctor was a nice guy who I liked. When I asked for another prescription, he said, "What happened to all the ones I gave you?" I said, "I threw them out because I didn't think I would need them, but now the pain is back."

My dad asked him if this was something I could be abusing. He said, "Absolutely not. They were no more addictive than aspirin," and he had no problem writing me as many scripts as I needed because it was so safe for people with addiction problems. He was very wrong. I was even starting to feel withdrawal sickness without it. Years later, I heard people sued the company that makes Ultram for false advertising. There is absolutely no way possible that the company did not know this was a very addicting substance that caused physical and mental withdrawals.

Thanks to the "non-addicting" Ultram, I was now using opiates again and for the first time, I didn't know it or mean to. Either way, I was back in the nightmare again and things were getting out of control very quickly.

Maureen was a strict Catholic woman who went to church often. Strangely, after having sex with me, she became a nympho. She would come over as soon as she woke up and have sex with me at a quarter till seven in the morning. Then, after the meeting, we would have sex again.

All these people in the meetings would ask Maureen to watch their homes while they were gone during the week. This was their second home for a lot of people. Maureen would take me to their homes and have sex with me in their bedrooms. I felt bad about this and couldn't believe it didn't bother Maureen. I was high and she was completely sober doing this. It amazed me that she could look these people in the face during the meetings.

She was also sleeping with a "newcomer," which was a big no-no in AA for anyone with a lot of clean time. If I had been a long-time AA member who had been clean for three years and a newly sober girl had come into the meeting and I started sleeping with her, the men in the meeting were supposed to put a stop to it or at the very least say something. But no one did or said anything to Maureen. Not Dan or Jack or anyone else.

Maureen also became very jealous. I remember one time when girls my age came to a meeting. After the meeting, three of them started talking to me. I looked behind them and Maureen was just sitting there staring at me with the angriest look on her face. She walked up and told me it was time to go. I said, "It'll be just a minute." She stormed off, then pulled her car up to us and started beeping the horn. All three of the girls were like, "Wow, your mom really wants you to stop talking to us!" I almost started laughing right there when I heard that. On the way home, Maureen berated me and told me how she didn't like me talking to those "little bitches."

When I got home, my dad said he wanted to have a talk with me. He told me that he knew Maureen was a beautiful woman and what she was doing for me was very nice, but she was his friend's wife and if I was having any thoughts about having an inappropriate relationship with her, I shouldn't. I acted shocked and said, "No way, Dad! It won't happen." This was one of the first times my dad had given me fatherly advice. The problem was that it was a little too late now. I felt bad, so I went to my room and looked for my Ultram solution, then realized I was almost out. I started thinking of the sickness and everything that was happening, and before I knew it, I was on my way to Atlantic City to buy heroin. Once I started on heroin this time, I didn't stop.

Eventually, it all came crashing down when my mom found a trash bag full of empty heroin bags. She couldn't believe how many bags there were and, frankly, neither could I. I didn't pay attention and just threw them in, but now the bag was overflowing.

I admitted to her that I was using, and she called Maureen to come over. Maureen was upset because my mom said I had to leave, which was always her go-to. She also said I was cut out of the will again. I was starting to wonder how many wills she had left to cut me out of. She then said, "After all the help Maureen gave you, how dare you use and put her and me through this!" She thought Maureen was going to say to throw me out onto the street, so it boggled her mind when Maureen said, "We need to get him help, then get him back into the meetings."

My mom looked bewildered by this. She always lived by the mantra: "As soon as you find out they are using, you cut them off and throw them to the wolves." If Maureen had not been sleeping with me, I am sure she would have been fine with that. But now, she did not want to give up her boy toy. They agreed to send me to a detox nearby, then figure it out from there. While I was at the detox, my mom told Maureen that I was not going to be allowed back to live at her house.

Maureen panicked and asked Jack if I could stay with him. Jack, of course, volunteered within a heartbeat. Jack was dying for some company because even his own kids would not visit him. Plus, this was the way he would get to see Maureen every day. After he agreed to take me in, my parents tried to talk him out of it. They spent two days writing him about every bad thing I had ever done since I was two years old. They made Jack come over, then read the list to him.

Of course, Jack didn't give two craps about it. He had been a horrible drunk and had all kinds of ghosts in his closet. I am sure he even thought it was ridiculous for my parents to be telling him all this stuff including things like me not going to baseball practice when I was six years old.

While at the detox, I spilled my guts to a counselor there about Maureen. She said I needed to end the relationship with her now. Once the drugs were out of my system and I sobered up, I knew I had to as well. So, when Maureen called the detox, I told her that the relationship between us was over. She was furious and basically told me that nothing was going to come between us. She said she was going to divorce her husband and take me to Italy where we would start a new life together. After that, I stopped taking her calls. I still had one big problem, my parents were coming to pick me up and drop me off at Jack's place tomorrow.

They showed up to get me at the detox and as soon as I got into the car, my dad turned to me and said, "You're just the gift that keeps on giving!" After I told Maureen it was over, she had apparently gotten drunk and went over to my parents' house. She told them that we were in love and that she was going to divorce Doug, take half his money, marry me, and move to Italy. My dad thought this was insane, but for some reason it didn't bother my mother that much. Doug was rich and I think my mom just saw dollar signs.

My mom said, "I told Maureen that you two should wait at least one year before getting married." I couldn't believe she was okay with this; it completely blew my mind. You could tell my dad was not impressed, he just said, "You have no idea how many problems this is going to cause!" He was right, and the nightmare that followed was awful.

THE MAUREEN AFTERMATH

After protesting and begging not to go to Jack's house, my parents took me anyway. They told me how amazing it was that he still wanted me in his house after knowing everything about me. They told me about what they had told him, and I remember thinking, "I'm sure you left out the most important parts about yourselves."

When I got to Jack's, I was not feeling well because I was still experiencing withdrawal. Jack started to talk my ear off about all this AA stuff. I wanted to jump out the window and end it all after only ten minutes with him. I was oddly relieved when he told me that Maureen was coming over to see me. I figured it would give me time away from Jack. At this point, neither me nor my parents knew Maureen had started drinking again. She was drunk when she went over to my parents' house, but they didn't notice.

When she came to pick me up, she told me to come out to the car without coming inside, so I knew something was up. When I got into her car, she looked awful. When she drank, it instantly aged her about twenty years. She looked like a haggard, beat down old woman. She was slurring her words and could barely drive.

I got behind the wheel and she admitted she was drunk. She asked, "Did you want to drive to Atlantic City to get drugs?" and offered to give me money to buy them. To this day, I don't know why I didn't, but I didn't. I did want to stay clean, but I was also in withdrawal. I guess it scared me seeing her like that when I had a sober head.

She kept trying to kiss me while telling me that she loved me. We parked in the Acme parking lot and she kept chugging Vodka. She said if I stopped loving her, she would kill herself. I was sick, so I overreacted. I knew I couldn't just leave her as she would drive herself around all day and probably kill someone, so I drove her back to Jack's. I went inside and told Jack that we have a problem with Maureen because she's drunk. He said, "Oh, my God! Bring her inside." So, I brought Maureen inside and laid her on a bed.

The next thing I knew my mom showed up with my clothes. We had to tell her what happened and showed her that Maureen was passed out on the bed. She started crying and hugging her. She said, "Awe, honey. Everything will be okay. We'll fix this." I couldn't believe that my mom was showing someone sympathy. If that had been me who was drunk, she would have said, "You awful, horrible person! Get out and never come back!"

Jack called Maureen's friend Joy who immediately started saying it would probably be better if she stayed at my house instead of being alone as her husband was never there. Jack didn't care about her well-being; he was in love with her and wanted her there. Maureen heard that and said, "Yes, I am going to live here for the rest of my life". Jack was so happy to hear this, his face lit up like a light bulb! Meanwhile, I'm sitting there in withdrawal and all of this was so overwhelmingly pathetic to me.

My mom's sympathy was disgusting, Jack's enthusiasm was just as disgusting, and her friend Joy soon showed up and was upset. She was the only caring person besides me who was thinking this whole thing was insane.

Joy asked Maureen what was going on and Maureen told her that she was in love with me and we were having a relationship. Joy then told all of us to come outside. She asked, "What the hell is going on?" and my mother blurted out, "Andy and Maureen are in love with each other." Both Jack and Joy's jaws dropped to the floor. They were speechless.

My mother continued, "But I told them they needed to wait a year before they get married because that's what is says in A.A." I guess she figured this would make her look like a good, caring, and sensible mother. I was waiting for her to find some angle that made her the victim, but Joy lost it when she heard this. She exclaimed, "Married?! What the hell are you talking about? Your son just got out of a detox and you are talking about him marrying a married woman who is one of your friend's wives, and that's okay with you?...What?!"

Then, Jack jumped in and said, "You knew this was happening the whole time and all you did was tell me about your son not coming home on time in fifth grade and things like that? I asked you to tell me something that was important and could help him, yet you left this out? How could you lie to me, Ellen? You said how awful it was that your son was a liar when the whole time you were lying!"

I knew Jack was right, but I felt I had to stick up for my mom, so I said, "Relax, Jack, the only reason you are so upset is because you are in love with Maureen and everyone knows it. How dare you lecture her when you know newcomers should not be together, but you said nothing. You are the biggest hypocrite here." My mother was speechless.

Then, Jack told me I wasn't welcome in his house anymore, which was the best thing he could have said! I left with my mom who was furious at me for "causing" poor Maureen to relapse and by "forcing" her into that situation.

My parents had no choice but to let me stay at home until I could find another place to go. Once this got around to the people in AA, Dan called me and angrily asked, "How could you sleep with a married woman?" He started crying and saying that he and Maureen had a special bond that couldn't be broken by anyone. He said he was going to make sure Jack wouldn't let me stay with him anymore. I told him he needed more help than me and to go back to his wife.

Before I got off the phone, I said sarcastically, "You know what, Dan? You're right. I should've been the bigger person with three minutes of sober under my belt and told this married woman who had been clean for three years to stay away from me." He completely didn't catch on to my sarcasm and said, "Well, at least you know that!" I took a deep breath and hung up the phone.

I left Long Beach Island and went to live with my friend Noah in North Carolina. Maureen found a way to contact me there, but eventually Noah said, "That woman has to leave you alone." One night she called, and my friend answered the phone and told her that she needed to get a life, stop cheating on her husband, and leave his friend alone. He told her that he was having her number blocked by the phone company and if she started calling from another number, he would have a restraining order filed against her.

I guess she believed him because she never called me again but instead started sending threatening emails. One stated that if I didn't call her or write back immediately that I was going to regret it. Another said, "You have no idea who you are fucking with." I couldn't believe that this woman who drove around with a "Family Values" bumper sticker on one side of her bumper and "A Pro-life" one on the other side was now threatening to kill me. It was kind of hilarious and we all started laughing about it and turned it into a running joke. We made a fake bumper sticker that said, "Don't fuck with me. I am pro-life and I will kill you!" I never talked to Maureen again after that.

Apparently, she held good to her promise and told everyone in AA that she was a victim of me seducing her, which completely back-fired. Eventually, someone told her husband what happened because of the bullshit story she made up. People thought her husband knew and wouldn't have a problem with it, especially since she was the "victim," which is laughable at best. I actually think her husband is gay. He really just used her as arm candy, but he was also a very smart man. He saw his wife was following me around and everyone told him how she was with me all the time. He didn't believe for two seconds that I seduced her; he knew her better than that and was rightfully upset with her.

Even their best friends Tom and Sue knew the truth. So, when her husband found out, he kicked her out. She went from living in a four-million-dollar mansion to being on the streets. Eventually he let her back in. She started going to the rooms of AA again, but did the same thing she did before. The same Dans and Jacks followed her around and told her how great she was, but only because they wanted to get into her pants. So, instead of telling her to take responsibility for her actions and worry about herself, they were just happy to tell her she was doing great so long as she kept flirting with them.

She knew deep down that she was wrong for what she did with me. Eventually, she even realized the fakeness of the people in LBI who claimed to be her friends. A friend of hers told me that she said, "Andrew was right the whole time about everyone." After another three years of being clean, she relapsed again.

One day not too long afterwards, I was walking into an NA meeting and my phone rang. It was Kara from the AA meetings in LBI, who was the pretty lawyer that I mentioned before. She told me that she had some sad news. Maureen was found hanging in the stairway of her house dead. She had committed suicide. I was saddened, but not surprised.

Jack was the person who found her after her sister called and asked him to check up on her because she had not heard from Maureen all week. What amazed me is how all these people in AA who were supposed to be her friends didn't stop by and check on her for two weeks. They knew she had relapsed and not one person stopped by to see her.

People like Jack and Dan certainly didn't help Maureen, but I don't blame them. They were just two sad men who were infatuated with this woman. The only reason Maureen is dead is because of Maureen. No one else is to blame for her death. Sure, there are some hypocritical dirtballs in AA, but that shouldn't put people off. It has helped a lot more people than it has hurt!

NORTH CAROLINA

AFTER THE MAUREEN catastrophe, I moved in with Noah around Charlotte, North Carolina. Noah knew he wasn't the best influence to be around when I was trying to get sober. His advice to me about how to stay off drugs was to drink beer and smoke weed. He did both, all day, every day.

For the first two weeks, I got over the withdrawal by laying on the couch and sweating it out. After that, I started drinking beer and smoking weed to get over it. About two months later, I started feeling physically okay, but I would shake and sweat a lot because my anxiety was through the roof. I felt that familiar feeling of no good chemicals being naturally produced in my brain.

For the next six months, I drank and smoked pot with Noah. The problem was I still wasn't feeling normal. After all those years of using, my system was so messed up. Unless I was drinking or using some chemical, I had no feelings of joy. My anxiety was so heightened all day and would cause me to sweat so badly that I would have to change shirts.

I also lost my confidence to talk to women. I would get anxious and my words would not make sense. I would drink to calm my nerves, but then I'd be too drunk to talk. It was like I was either anxiously sober or completely drunk. There was no middle ground.

Noah didn't understand drug addiction and wondered what the hell was wrong with me. He said it was like I lost all my confidence in life and was a completely different person. In a way, he was right.

RELAPSE IN NC

ONE NIGHT, WE went out with these two girls. Noah was dating one of them and she was bringing a friend to meet me. I was especially anxious for some reason. We went to a bar and I tried not to get too drunk, but I had on a dress shirt and was sweating through it so badly that I kept having to go to the bathroom to dry it out, which was driving me nuts.

Then, I went to the bathroom to pee, but there were so many people around that I couldn't go. I eventually had to say that I forgot something in the car, then drove to a fast food joint to pee. When I drank, I had a bladder like a three-year-old, so not even fifteen minutes later, I had to go pee again. The bouncers started looking strangely at me. By the time I got back, Noah and the two girls were wondering if I was alright. I said, "Yeah, why?" Meanwhile, the entire back of my shirt was soaked with perspiration and somebody behind me loudly said, "Oh, that is disgusting!" and I was sure they were talking about my shirt. I tried to make up an excuse, but it sounded stupid. I knew my only solution to this anxiety problem was to drink as much as possible as quickly as possible. I went to the side bar and started doing shots of 151 Bacardi rum.

When I got back, the girl asked me to please come dance with her. I never learned to dance and wasn't nearly drunk enough try. I told her to ask someone else. I went to the bar and started doing more shots. By the time I saw the girl again, she and this guy were basically making out on the dance floor. I thought to myself, I just can't make it off opiates like a normal person, which is the last thing I remember.

Apparently, all the shots of Bacardi had kicked in and I made a complete ass of myself. I threw up and fell asleep in the back of a car. I felt so awful in the morning that I decided to drive to the bad part of Charlotte and try to buy heroin. It was the only solution that popped into my mind.

I drove to the worst part of Charlotte I could find and pulled up to this little corner store and waited. All these people started looking at me like they were wondering what the hell a white boy was doing there. Then, a guy came up to my car and said, "I can see what you're looking for, you're dope sick." I wasn't dope sick, but I told him I was. He said, "How many do you need?" I asked, "How much are they?" He said that they cost twenty dollars a bag. He also wanted me to give him the money upfront, then he would leave and come back with the heroin about ten minutes later.

Under normal circumstances in the drug world, you never give anyone your money and hope they come back because ninety-nine percent of the time, they won't! But I knew no one in the area, so this was my only hope of getting high. I told him, "If you take my money and don't come back, you will never see me again, but if you come back, I will come to you all the time and you will make a lot more money." I gave him twenty dollars and waited.

To my surprise, he left and hurried back. When he approached my car, he handed me a piece of rolling paper that was used to roll a cigarette, but it had heroin inside of it. I unwrapped it and sniffed half of the heroin inside, after I realized it was good, I gave the guy twenty more dollars for getting me the heroin and got his phone number.

About five minutes later, the heroin kicked in, which immediately chased away my hangover. The embarrassment about the night before faded away as well, as did the anxiety, depression, and lack of endorphins that had plagued me for the last six months. When I got back to Noah's, I was a different person. I was happy, energetic, and couldn't care less about making an ass of myself. I cleaned the whole house and washed my clothes and my car.

That night, we went out and I picked up two girls in five minutes. I hooked up with one of the girls right in the bar. Noah told me that I was myself again and kept asking, "Where the hell did this Andrew go?"

I promised myself that this was a one-time thing. For this night only, I just wanted to feel good in my own skin, then it was back to misery. I kept my promise for eight hours. The next day I went back and bought more heroin and again promised myself that this was the last time I would buy heroin.

As always, I started doing heroin every day. This lasted for about a month until one day I was out of money and pawned some of Noah's things. I was sure I would get them back as soon as the money I had coming arrived, which was just like with Scott's computer. I just needed to make sure Noah didn't see that his things were missing.

As it always happens in these situations, it never works out like it's supposed to! Despite all my good intentions, the money did not arrive on time and Noah noticed his stuff was missing and the shit hit the fan. I felt so bad!. Noah wasn't an angel, but I should not have been stealing from him! He asked me to leave and told me that he was going to tell my parents what was happening. I asked him to wait to tell them until the day after Christmas, so that it didn't ruin Christmas for everyone.

So, I drove home and acted like everything was fine and told them that I planned to go back to Noah's after Christmas. My real plan was to take whatever money my parents would give me after Christmas, then go buy enough drugs to overdose with. I wanted to have one last Christmas at home and then it would be 'goodbye.' By this point, I had given up. I didn't want to go through the whole "Andrew relapsed again" thing and hear how awful I was, or that I was never allowed back, and that I did this to them, so they would again be kicking me out of the house as well as the 300th will. For the last twenty years, all of this was getting very old by now and I had had enough.

I had tried to stay sober, but it didn't work. My anxiety made being sober a living nightmare. I had done so much damage to my brain that life was unbearable if I didn't have some chemical in my system. This was the God's honest truth and, in my mind, I had given it my best shot and decided I could not go on like this.

Everyday had been a struggle. I did not have one day where I was happy and at peace being sober. Had it not been for my horrible imagination and the unimaginable suffering I believed I was sure to face had I committed suicide; I would have killed myself a long time ago. Living in my skin wasn't living at all, it was just surviving. I never woke up and said, "Wow, this is going to be a great day!" All I could think about was how I was going to suffer the least that day. I don't care who you are or how strong of a person you think you are, if you live like this for long enough and nothing gets better, dying starts to seem like the best option.

GIVING UP

THE DAY AFTER Christmas, I woke up early and told my parents I was going back to North Carolina. I said my goodbyes believing this was the last time I would ever see them and took off to buy drugs in Atlantic City.

On the way there, Noah started calling me. I just threw the phone out the window. I felt bad about the way things ended with Noah, but the idea that he was calling my parents seemed a little hypocritical, especially because it was about drugs. I didn't even care enough to argue with him. I just wanted this nightmare to end.

I got some awful hotel room and bought a bunch of heroin. At first, I decided to enjoy the high once more before I died. I did a couple of bags and let a couple of hours pass. The problem was I really didn't want to die, I just wanted to stop suffering.

The next morning, I woke up and put sixteen bags of heroin into a syringe, then shot it into my arm. I was not even scared after I shot it, I just blacked out. I woke up a few hours later scared because I had not died and did not have enough money left to kill myself with heroin. For some strange reason, the city of Camden came to my mind.

CAMDEN/HELL ON EARTH

I NOW HAD two problems: I was alive, and I was out of money. All out of options, I thought I'd give Camden a try. I had a dream when I was a child that I ended up on the streets of Camden and, strangely enough, it was looking like it might just come true.

During the drive to Camden, I was drug sick and hoping for a miracle. I had no idea exactly where to get drugs in Camden, but I had always heard that the best heroin in the world was there. If you were broke and needed to get high, it was the place to be. If you wanted to kill yourself, Camden dope was the strongest and would easily get the job done.

When I got there, I took an exit and drove around until I found a place that looked like the people there were selling drugs. Out of pure luck, I drove into the most popular spot in North Camden and dealers were selling heroin right on the street.

It was about ten o'clock on a freezing cold night. I had a Ralph Lauren leather jacket that cost five hundred dollars and my plan was to try to sell it to a drug dealer for heroin. I pulled over onto the street and could see there were all these people getting out of their cars and going up and buying drugs, then jumping back into their cars. In fact, there was a girl who only looked young selling drugs. I thought she was my best chance of getting someone to buy this jacket, so I asked her.

When I approached her, she said, "How many you need, nigga?" I said, "I need ten, but I want to make a deal. I have this leather jacket for sale." She angrily replied, "Nigga, dis ain't no department store! You got cash or keep it moving." So, I walked back to my car.

As I was getting in, she came up to me and said, "But if you want to rent this car out, we got a deal." At first, I said 'no,' but then she said, "I just need it to pick something up and I will even let you wait at my house with my family." Under normal circumstances this would have never even crossed my mind, but this was far from being a normal situation, so I told her 'yes.'

She took me to her "house," which was across the street. She gave me five bags of heroin. They were white and looked different from the blue ones she was selling on the street. She did this right in front of these two older ladies who I thought were her parents and then said, "You are going to stay here wit deez niggas, my moms." I thought maybe she had two mothers.

I sniffed the bags right on the kitchen table and found out they really were not that potent. I waited with her "moms" for my car to get back. The problem was these people barely spoke English and this row home was crazy. Their kids were walking everywhere while the adults were drinking, smoking weed, and staring at me. I kept thinking, "Where the hell am I?"

Then, one lady said, "I don't know how long she said you could stay here, but you have to leave in five minutes because we are leaving." I said, "But, she isn't back yet. I'm waiting for her to get back with my car right here," and she said, "No, you ain't, nigga," and pulled a gun on me.

Shocked, I turned around and saw a ten-year-old boy standing right behind me with his mom who was also pointing a gun at me. She said, "You leavin' dead or alive, but you leavin'." I was almost as shocked that she could speak English as I was by the fact that she had a gun pointed at me. The whole time I was there, all they spoke was Spanish.

I moved to the side worried that this crazy woman was going to hit the child, but he stayed behind me as I moved. I had no choice but to leave. Death didn't really scare me at this point and I even thought about asking her to shoot me, but I worried about this little kid getting shot because of me, and I couldn't live with myself if that happened. I certainly didn't need that on top of everything else wrong in my life.

I left their house at gunpoint. She slammed the door behind me, then all the lights went out. I thought I heard one hundred different locks latching behind me. It was literally about five degrees outside and all I had on was this thin jacket. I had no phone and nowhere to go. I walked out onto the streets of North Camden at midnight hoping by some miracle this thug girl would come back.

At midnight, it was like the whole neighborhood of North Camden turned into an eerie ghost town. I eventually gave up and knocked on a door. When they answered, I asked to use the phone, but they wouldn't let me in. In fact, no one would let me in until finally I knocked on the twenty-first door and a drunk guy let me inside. He called the police and said, "Yo, yo! Dis nigga just got his ride jacked and ya'll niggas better get down here, word?" I couldn't understand why everyone here called me "nigga." I waited outside shivering and a police officer showed up about thirty minutes later.

I said, "Officer, my car got stolen," and he didn't even get out of his car. He just looked at me and said, "Well, what the fuck are you doing out here?" I made up some story that I had to find a friend who was lost. I thought he bought it, but he angrily replied, "Bullshit! You were buying drugs out here like all you fucking junkies do!" I said, "Even if I was, my car got stolen and that is why you're here, right?"

He flipped out and started yelling, "Fuck you, junkie! You come here and get around all these animals in Camden, then cry to us for help!" He said, "You are the reason all these bad people are here in the first place." I replied, "Considering this is the first time I've ever been in Camden, I doubt I'm the reason for anything here." He laughed, "Bullshit, I see you every day here buying drugs and have arrested you before, you fucking junkie!"

The officer was an asshole. He had clearly confused me with some-one else. When he ran my name and realized this, I thought he was going to apologize, especially when he saw that I had never been arrested here before. But he just offered me a ride to the bus station after he reported my car stolen. When he dropped me off, he said, "Stay the fuck out of Camden or you're going to get murdered." I said nothing as I got out of his car and stepped into the bitter cold night.

I couldn't believe how stupid I was for letting this girl take my car. Now, I had nowhere to go, no money, and no car. It was five degrees outside, and I was in one of the worst cities in the world. It seemed the only place that was semi-warm was the bus station because I noticed homeless people huddled in there trying to keep warm. It was now about two o'clock in the morning, so I decided to sit down with them in the station because I was freezing.

This young girl was there who looked about eighteen years old and was very pretty. She offered to share her blanket with me. She said, "I haven't seen you out here. You have to be new," then introduced herself as Michelle. I thought it was really nice of her to let me have some of her blanket. She said, "Make sure you don't shut your eyes or lay down because the police will go nuts."

Lying next to her, our bodies were barely keeping each other warm enough, and we couldn't stop shivering because the sliding doors were jammed wide open. I asked her why in God's name were the doors open. She said, "The transit cops put them that way to freeze us." I refused to believe that was true.

It was so cold and windy that a person would have to be evil to purposely prop open these doors. I seriously doubted a police officer who was supposed to "protect and serve" and who I admired my whole life would ever do such a thing. After a little bit, I couldn't take it anymore and went over to shut the wide-open doors by dislodging this plastic thing that was stuck in them.

A second later, a Port Authority police officer came running out of the back office and immediately yelled at me, "What the fuck do you think you are doing?" I said, "I am closing the doors because some idiot jammed them open and we are freezing in here." He said, "That was me and they were going to stay open." I said, "Not only are you freezing human beings, but the energy bill must be going through the roof with the doors open." He then turned to me and said, "The mayor said we can't kick you out, which is fine, but you bums are not going to have one minute of comfort on my watch!" He then told me he had to get back in his warm office because it was too cold out there and suggested that I keep the doors open if I wanted to keep my teeth.

I had no idea what he was talking about with the mayor, but I could not believe this was happening. Another human being and, even worse, a police officer (who I have always looked up to and stuck up for when anyone said bad things about them), could watch a whole room of people suffering in the bitter cold and did not have the heart to shut the doors to keep them from freezing. There were old people and women, for God's sake!

About thirty minutes later, I dozed for a second before I was startled by a sharp kick to my calf. I looked up expecting to see some gang member trying to kill me, but it was another police officer. He had come out of the back room to kick me because my eyes had closed. I couldn't believe how hard he kicked me. If I had kicked another person like that I would have been charged with a crime. He growled, "Don't make me come out of that back office into this cold again, or else!" I had not been in Camden for twenty-four hours and the police had already physically assaulted me, verbally assaulted me, and threatened me. It was a completely backwards world here, so far.

The sweet girl next to me said she was sorry. If she had noticed I was sleeping, she would have woken me up. She said, "All the cops were like this to the homeless people and drug addicts." At first, I was going to say, "But I'm not a homeless person or a drug addict," but I suddenly realized I was both! Although I had not been homeless for twenty-four hours yet, I was without a place to live and I damn sure was an addict. I guess I was just too ashamed to admit it even to another homeless addict in a bus station in Camden, which made no sense.

I had always been a supporter of the police, but coming to the worst city in the country, I realized the police here were just as nasty as the people. I always thought the police were there to take care of people who couldn't take care of themselves and stick-up for them. These homeless people and drug addicts were made up of women, old people, and others who I saw as those who could not stick up for themselves, and it was the most cowardly act to pick on them.

I was also amazed that this was normal to this girl. The same girl, this homeless drug addict who was helping me stay warm by giving up part of her own blanket and some of her warmth in the process. While the police officer who was supposed to be this pillar of the community, there to protect and serve, was purposely getting his kicks watching a group of already suffering people freeze. I know there is a special place in Hell waiting for those cops, and they know exactly who they are!

I asked this girl how the hell did she end up here, and she told me that she was sexually abused by a neighbor for years. As a result, she developed a terrible anxiety problem and started taking Percocet when she was young. Eventually, they got too expensive for her, so she went to heroin. When she was seventeen, her parents had kicked her out when they discovered she was using heroin. She ended up living on the streets and became a prostitute to support her habit. She told me it was very hard for her as a prostitute because she wasn't promiscuous at all before. Sadly, she was raped and beaten up multiple times in Camden while prostituting. I wanted to help her but I couldn't even help myself.

I told her about my car being stolen and she truly seemed sad to hear this. She said that early in the morning she was going to turn a "trick," and if she did, she promised to "get me off E," which was a term that everyone in Camden used to refer to the first shot of heroin for that day that gets you un-sick. Most addicts wake up sick and when they get the first shot of dope in them, they say they, "Got of E."

I was blown away by the actions of this total stranger. Here she was in a horrible situation and was going to sell her body, then use the proceeds to help me from feeling the withdrawal effects of heroin. As I would soon learn, addicts are some of the most giving people in the world. They will share their last dollar to help out another addict. People always look at the negative because it is a lot easier to do, but there are also a lot of positives about addicts that no one speaks about. They are some of the kindest, big-hearted, friendly, caring, and loyal people I have ever met. A small minority of them give all the rest of us a horrible name.

The next morning, she got up and told me she would be back. I never expected to see her again but waited just in case. The cold was really starting to get to me now. The heroin from the night before had worn off and I was starting to feel sick. I went into a Dunkin Donuts to get warm for a minute but was quickly told to buy something or leave.

Just as I was about to give up, I see this girl coming around the corner with a smile on her face. She came up to me and said, "Let's go get well, sexy." I followed her to this abandoned house. I met a guy named Rob there, who knew her, too. Immediately he started asking her for some and offered to shoot me up. He said people called him "the doctor" because he was so good at it. She told him that she had copped "The Source." The Source was the name of the most popular and strongest Heroin in Camden. Twenty thousand bags of it were sold daily on their drug set.

Rob went to shoot me up, and it took him all of two seconds to find a vein and hit me. Then, I got the best rush I had ever had with heroin up until this point and I started to realize why everyone said Camden's dope was the best. Instantly, I went from freezing cold to feeling warm and comfortable. All my worries, which included being homeless and not having my car, were gone. I even thought for a second how cool it was to be hanging out with other people who were just like me. This would all change once the dope wore off, but for now everything was fine.

Michelle left after that and told me to meet up with her tonight at the Walter Rand Transportation Center. Rob said I could tag along with him. He was waiting for this guy named Scott to come back to Camden with money he made stealing things and he was going to get him high. I decided to tag along with Rob even though I could tell in two seconds that he was a complete slimeball. He looked and acted like a used car salesman and insisted on teaching me what he thought I needed to know about surviving on the streets of Camden.

Rob asked me what my hustle was, but I had no idea what he was talking about. He said, "If you are going to live out here with us, you have to get a hustle." He explained that some people steal from stores, then sold the stuff in Camden as a hustle, while some people sold their bodies, some people pan handled, some people sold needles, and others were runners.

Runners would wait around at the Transportation Center for people to get off trains or buses and walk them in to buy drugs. I wondered why anyone would want someone to come with them to buy drugs, but I soon found out why.

"Running" was a very common and lucrative means of getting high for homeless people in Camden. Runners would find out which drug sets had the best drugs of the day. When I say the best drugs, I mean which were the strongest. The strength and purity of heroin changed daily, and runners had the most updated information about it.

If I was coming off a bus ready to spend $300 on heroin and wanted to make sure I got good stuff, I would take a runner with me. For a bag or two ($10 or $20), I got good drugs instead of risking getting $300 worth of crap!

Hiring a runner is a very smart thing to do if you have a decent amount of money to spend. The difference in heroin purity could vary so much from day to day on different drug sets that it was impossible to guess which one was good or not.

In Camden, they have areas that only sell one brand of heroin called a 'Stamp.' For instance, a block from 7th and York to 8th and York Street sold a brand name heroin called "The Source". A block away, they would have a different name.

The block or sets would have about twenty people working on it. The first people you saw were lookouts who cruised around on bikes or on foot and watched out for cops. The next people you came across would tell you where the actual dealers were on the block, like in an alley or an abandoned house. They had security people watching after dealers and making sure no one robbed them. Past the security people, you finally reached the dealers who gave you the drugs and did the hand-to-hand transactions. Lastly, there were the "Case Managers." They watched over everything that was going on. At certain times there were up to twelve different drug sets selling in a six by six block area of North Camden.

Besides heroin they also sold powder cocaine and crack cocaine. The runners knew the sets very well and the people at the sets got to know the runners. The runners also helped prevent you from getting robbed. It's not that they were physically imposing or even good fighters, it was just that it was always best not to travel alone in Camden because this lessens your chances of getting robbed or shot.

Lastly, the runners helped insure you didn't get arrested. How they did this was, the police would get used to their faces and knew they were drug addicts. After stopping a person in Camden so many times, the police would just stop bothering them as much. If you were "walking while white" and the police didn't know you, you had a much better chance of being stopped than if you were not with a runner.

Rob was a runner, or at least he was trying to be. The only problem was that he had a lot of competition. He was trying to feel me out on whether I was able to get money for him or could possibly be his competition.

When Scott, the guy he was waiting for, showed up I could tell that the only reason Rob was concerned about Scott was because it was easy to get money from him. They both couldn't believe my story about my car. We even saw a guy driving it around Camden but could not catch him.

GETTING MY CAR BACK

I HAD BEEN living on the streets of Camden for three days and was walking in front of a Dunkin Donuts when my car with two girls in it pulled up to a light. I immediately jumped in the back. The driver was the girl who had originally taken it and she had another girl with her.

After I jumped in the back, I said, "Pull the fucking car over right now or I will hit you in the face." The girl in the passenger seat jumped out. I was worried about punching this girl because I didn't want her to crash. She kept saying she would pull over, but she never did. Finally, we came to a stop light and I reached for the keys in the ignition. The girl jumped out of the car with the keys as she tried to lock the doors and run away. I caught her in about five seconds. She started yelling, "This is my car now, nigga! You ain't gettin' this shit back." I grabbed her and told her to shut up. She started screaming, "He's hurting me! Help!"

These security guards ran over to us and she said, "This crazy fool is trying to rape me." I laughed and said, "This little troll stole my car." She argued, "Nope, he sold it to me for drugs." Then, they got suspicious of her and said, "Let's get the cops here and see whose name is on it." She started yelling, "Naw, niggas, dis is my shit! Dis is my shit!" As soon as they started calling the cops, she ran.

They then apologized and said they were sorry because all they heard was a girl screaming and just wanted to help. They said, "She was so ugly, we knew something was up. Especially when she cried 'rape.' Damn! I mean, I thought she was an ugly man." We laughed for a second, then they told me to be careful with these "fake ass gangster wannabe bitches." They were two black guys from Camden, and they could tell what she was in a second, but they also said, "Damn drugs, bro. You don't look like an addict!"

DRIVING BOOSTERS

Now THAT I had my car back, I picked up Scott and Rob. Scott had money and so long as I had the car, they told me I would have an endless supply of money and drugs. They told me about this group of people in Camden called "boosters." They were very good at robbing stores and all they needed was a ride to nice towns like Moorestown that had CVS or Rite Aid type stores.

They would steal Prilosec, Rogaine, and Mach 3 razor blades. They would have you drive them to about five different stores and fill your car up with stolen things. You could then drive back to Camden and sell it for cash at the bodegas. With that cash, you bought drugs. The problem was that it seemed to me like it was too much work to get high. But after a while I started to realize that to stay high in Camden, I needed to do something like this.

The first booster I took out was this fat guy who claimed to be the best booster in Camden. He looked completely disheveled and would be easy to pick out in a store as someone who was there to steal. When I took him to the first CVS, I wasn't sure what to expect and was nervous as hell. He told me to relax and that no one would even know he was stealing because he was so good at it.

After about two minutes in the store he came running out yelling, "Start the engine!" While boxes were falling out of his shirt. I opened his door, he jumped in, and we sped off with people chasing us and the whole parking lot staring in awe. He turned to me and said, "That never happens! I have been doing this for five years and that never happens." I absolutely believed him until we went to the next place twenty minutes later.

He went in and the exact same thing happened! He wasn't in there one minute this time and I was amazed at how many things he had in his arms while rushing out the door with employees on his tail. It was like a scene out of a funny movie. After he got in the car, I said, "We have enough stuff and we're going back to get high now." He said, "What the hell are you talking about? We just started!"

The way I looked at it, it was just a matter of time before we got arrested. We already had about $300 worth of stuff and I was not feeling well. We compromised. We would drive back to Camden to cash the stuff in, get high, then go back out and boost some more.

We drove to this store in North Camden and he went in with all the stolen stuff. The owner took him to the back and gave him cash for the items. I never knew exactly how much he got, but I had to take his word for it. Rob was tagging along with us and I felt bad because Paul (fat booster guy) told him that this time he would only give him a bag of dope for introducing me to him. I also gave Rob a bag a dope out of my cut, but after that, Paul wasn't giving him shit.

This really upset Rob, but I couldn't figure out why. Rob didn't drive or even come with us, he didn't steal, or need to worry about getting arrested. He just introduced me to Paul and then would wait for us to come back to Camden to buy him drugs. I cut Rob off, too, which really made him angry. He said, "I'm going to tell all the boosters not to go with you and I'm going to tell all the other drivers not to go with Paul." Paul laughed and said, "Go ahead, Rob, no one's going to listen to you anyway, but I would love to see you try!" Then, Paul snatched away the bag of heroin he had given Rob. Rob had already promised someone one bag, so this meant he was shit out of luck now and he started going crazy.

Rob turned out to be a complete low-life scumbag, even among the lowest of the low. He was the kind of person who would steal from you, then help you look for it. Eventually, word spread around about Rob and he was almost killed by someone else he had spread rumors about. Apparently, he got mad at someone and decided to spread a rumor about the guy being gay, which for some reason Rob loved to do. Well, this guy got really upset about it and I heard he found Rob in a dark alley and stabbed him. He came really close to dying. Then a gang he stole from found him and stabbed him again, he barely survived.

Paul and I continued to boost for about a week, then he finally got arrested, which wasn't a shock to me at all. We went to one final store after being out all day. Paul always wanted to go to one more while I just wanted to get back and get high. It was like he enjoyed stealing, like it was also a high for him. But this last store ended up being a big mistake.

When we pulled into the parking lot, it was very crowded. I dropped him off up front and went to get a parking spot. Literally, one minute after I dropped him off, I saw a police car pulled up to the front door. This made me nervous, but it wasn't until I saw two more pull in that I knew they were there for Paul. The store had been robbed by Paul many times before and they knew his face very well. As soon as he walked in, they called the police who were close by. All the police did was wait for him to come charging outside like a bull and then they arrested him.

Once I saw the third cop car, I left the parking lot, but felt for sure I was going to be pulled over and arrested as I was leaving. It wasn't until I made it back to Camden that I felt safe, but I had a carload of stolen goods and no way to sell them. The bodegas had been getting shut down by the police for buying stolen goods because of the pressure stores were putting on them. Unless they knew you, they wouldn't buy stolen goods from you. Eventually I found a guy who was about fifty-five years old named Israel who could cash in the stolen goods.

ISRAEL

ISRAEL LIVED IN Camden and was a bad heroin addict. He had prison tattoos and could look like a person to be feared one day, then someone's grandfather the next. He told me that he was the best booster ever, like everyone else I met. He also told me that if I took him out boosting, I would not have to deal with the bullshit the other boosters did and that he made at least $600 a day. He told me that every morning I came to pick him up to go boosting, he would start the day off by buying me two bags of heroin. This way, we could focus on getting money. That was all I needed to hear, and I was in.

Israel was a character and he loved my car. He could not stop telling me that if he had a car, he would be retired by now considering all the stores he would have ripped off. He too seemed to love stealing, just like Paul did. On the first day I took him to go boosting, I was absolutely amazed, humored, and horrified at how he did it.

Israel came walking to my car dressed up like Mr. Rogers and push-ing, of all things, a freaking baby carriage! Which was a nightmare to try and fit into my car. I started laughing when I realized that he was going to rob stores with it and couldn't stop laughing the whole way there.

The first place we went to was Sears. Where Paul was the smash-and-grab type of guy, Israel would take thirty minutes in a store. I would be outside in the parking lot nervous as hell and he would come strolling out pushing a baby carriage like he was out for a Sunday walk.

Once he got to my car, he would start pulling boxes of DVD players, video games, and things like that out of the carriage. People seeing this in the parking lot would look at us in astonishment because it looked like Israel was my grandfather and we had a grandbaby with us. I can only imagine what the hell they were thinking when they saw what came out of that carriage.

This was much better than being with someone like Paul, so this became my routine. I would pick up Israel in the morning at Mc-Donald's in Camden. Next, we would drive to The Source drug set to buy heroin, then go shoot up. Afterwards, we would drive around the surrounding towns robbing stores. After we had enough merchandise, we would head back to Camden to cash-in. After that, we got high with the money, then started hitting the stores again. Sometimes we would go up to five times a day back and forth.

Israel had this one problem. When he gets high, he would act absolutely insane for about thirty minutes. After he injected heroin, he would start yelling as loudly as he could and speaking some alien language. It was the craziest thing, especially if you didn't know it was coming. It didn't matter where he was or who he was around. The better the heroin was, the more of a scene he would make.

Most of the time we would get high in a parking lot on the waterfront as we tried to be as inconspicuous as possible. We would even duck down, so people would not see us. The first time Israel went crazy, I had no idea what was happening, which made for an awful experience.

We had pulled into this crowded parking lot on the waterfront. Israel was very nervous that someone would see us and call the police. He kept telling me to park in a different spot. When we finally found a spot he liked, he still kept saying, "Keep the drugs down while you mix them," and, "Don't look suspicious… talk quietly."

He was so nervous that I started to become twice as nervous. Once I finally mixed up, I injected as inconspicuous as possible. I was feeling this amazing rush and, out of nowhere, Israel started screaming. I didn't know what the hell had happened. He was yelling so loudly, it sounded like he was a banshee being stuck with a cattle prod. At first, I thought the drugs were bad, or something bad was coming after us. I started the car and was looking around thinking the cops had us surrounded, Godzilla was behind us, or the world was ending. I remember saying to myself, "Oh, God. This is it." Then, Israel flung the door open and got out in the middle of this crowded parking lot and, of all things, started dancing around like an Indian while screaming and yelling like a sheep. He was yelling, "BAH, BAH, BAH!!!!" at the top of his lungs. To top it off, he started to take his pants off.

I jumped out of the car, grabbed him, and threw him back into the car. I locked the door and demanded, "Stay here and shut up." A crowd had gathered by now, so I drove away as fast as I could. So much for not drawing attention to ourselves.

For the next twenty minutes he, "Bah, bah-ed," at any car that pulled up alongside us, even a police officer. I told the officer that he was retarded, and he just yelled, "Get him home now! We don't want that out on the street." I was sure he was going to arrest us but found it humorous that he had called Israel a "that." Had this been any city other than Camden, the officer probably would have arrested us, but they see stranger things on a daily basis. This was normal in Camden.

I thought this was a freak occurrence with Israel, but it turned out to be a normal thing with him. The only way to make sure this would not happen was to only let him have two bags or less of heroin. However, the other way to prevent his outbursts was to mix the heroin with cocaine. I later started doing this, too, which is called speedballing, and it's awful in a very awesome way!

SPEEDBALLING

Speedballing is when you inject heroin and cocaine at the same time by mixing them together beforehand. It is such an intense feeling and truly the best of both worlds in terms of drug highs. Cocaine is an upper and floods your brain with dopamine, which is a great feeling, but this only lasts for about a minute, then the fear, anxiety, and craving for more takes over. That "more" can never be satisfied no matter how hard you try. There always comes a point where you will want more. The solution to the negative aspects of cocaine is to mix it with heroin.

Heroin is generally considered to be a downer because it relaxes, calms, and puts you in a euphoric state, which is different from cocaine's euphoria. Some people also get very sleepy on heroin and nod out, which are the side effects that make it the ideal drug to mix with cocaine to achieve a perfect high. After injecting the two drugs together, you get to enjoy the intense rush of cocaine without the anxiety and horrible craving. You also get the extreme euphoria of heroin without getting knocked out in a nod.

Israel was the first person to recommend this to me. One day, he suggested that we buy some cocaine and add it to the heroin. I was a little nervous to do it, but at that point my life wasn't looking too bright anyway, so I said what the heck. We bought a ten-dollar bag of coke, otherwise known as a dime bag, and put half in my shot of heroin and half in his.

As soon as I injected the speedball, I remember tasting it in my mouth immediately. Then, I got this amazing rush that made me feel like I was falling, but in a good way. My ears started going 'wow-wow-wow' and it was almost too much to handle, but then, thankfully, the heroin took over and slowed everything down. I was left in this amazing euphoric state that I had never experienced before.

After doing my first speedball, I never again wanted to do heroin by itself, I always preferred the heroin and cocaine mixture. It was a great feeling, but it is also incredibly bad for you and can easily become deadly. You are speeding your heart up and slowing it down at the same time. Many people have died from heart attacks after speedballing such as River Phoenix, John Belushi, Chris Farley, and many others.

Besides the great high, I also wanted cocaine for another purpose, which was to keep Israel from having his flip-outs because they were getting unbearable and dangerous. It was just a matter of time before we got arrested or he "BAH, BAH-ED" some gang banger and got us both shot.

LOSING MY CAR AGAIN

Israel would always tell me, "No matter what, don't lose your car because you will always be high and have shelter if you have your car while being homeless in Camden." This was good advice.

At night after I dropped Israel off at his son's apartment, I would drive to this hospital called Our Lady of Lourdes where I parked to fall asleep. Strangely enough, it was the same hospital where my dad used to be the Vice President.

I would pull up not too far from the emergency room entrance and turn the heat up as high as it would go. Right before I would fall asleep, I would shut the engine off so I wouldn't run out of gas, but still had enough warmth to fall asleep in. About three hours later, I would wake up freezing and in pain from sleeping in a car seat, so I would start the engine to warm up again. Then, repeat the cycle all over again. It went this way every night and some were worse than others.

One morning, Israel did not show up and I had no idea what I was going to do. I waited for about three hours, then started to panic because I was getting sick from not having heroin. I drove out to a drug set and asked a guy there for a loan on one bag. He had seen me there every day for the last two months, so I hoped he would help me out, but he said 'no.'

As I was walking back into my car, another guy came up to me and asked if I would rent him my car. He said he would give me a bundle (ten bags of heroin) and cash, too. I told him I had a bad experience once and wasn't interested. He said, "He does it every day with other people and I could always know where to find him." Then, out of nowhere, the dealer who turned me down for a loan came up and handed me a bag and said, "Don't loan your car. Go get well." I couldn't believe he just handed it to me like that. I thanked him profusely and told him I really appreciated it.

For the rest of the day, I still couldn't find Israel. By nightfall, I was sick again. That night, I didn't sleep for even one minute and was freezing the whole night worse than normal because I did not have enough heroin in my system. The next day, I was getting desperate and went looking for that dealer who wanted to rent my car.

Apparently, he was the only white drug dealer in Camden. He wasn't really a dealer as none of the street people selling drugs are; they just work for a dealer. Somehow, he had gotten in with them and worked for one. It was very rare to see a white dealer in Camden.
I finally found him. He was being a complete clown and trying way too hard to fit in. He reminded me of B-Rad from "Malibu's Most Wanted." He sounded like he was speaking a foreign language and was saying things like, "Yo, yo, bee use gots gets me dat doe yo n we gonna ride yo whip yos fo dat cheddar money grip." I needed a freaking translator to understand him.

I walked up to him and said, "So, you'll pay me a bundle of heroin and fifty bucks to rent my car for twenty-four hours?" His word was obviously not good as he gave me six bags and fourteen bucks, but when you are as sick as I was, you don't really have a choice. So, I just said, "Give me the dope and I will meet you here tomorrow."

To my utter amazement, tomorrow came and he returned with the car. He tried to tell me a story, but I was in no mood to listen to anything he said, but he offered me the same deal for another twenty-four hours. Being sick again, I decided to do it even though I promised myself I would not do it again no matter what.

Tomorrow came, but he didn't. Although he hadn't stolen my car, it turns out he crashed it. I found out later that he was driving the car eighty-five miles per hour in a twenty-five mile-per-hour zone and flipped it around a corner because he was drunk. He just left it there. The car was totaled and taken to a scrap yard. He apparently thought it was funny as people said he was laughing about crashing "some white boy's car."

Two months later, he was killed in a drive-by shooting in the exact same spot where he crashed my car! I seriously doubt that it was karma for crashing my car as he had much worse karma coming from the drugs he sold that had actually killed people. Still, it was pretty crazy that he was killed in almost the exact same spot where he totaled my car.

REALLY HOMELESS

Now I HAD no car and nowhere to live. I was officially homeless in Camden, New Jersey with a pretty decent heroin habit to top it all off. It was an awful and scary feeling when you realize the truth of your situation. All the heroin on the planet couldn't numb that out!

After this, I started thinking about jumping off a bridge. Although, I could not get the guts to do it because I was either in withdrawal and too anxious to walk on a bridge let alone jump, or I was too high and when I was high, I didn't want to kill myself. It was like always being the tightrope of life.

The only solution I could come up with was to try to stay high all the time by whatever means necessary and figure out the rest as I went along. The next day, I tried to steal from the CVS in downtown Camden. Stealing from any store in Camden was a big no-no, but I had no way to get out of Camden. I was sick, so I decided to go in and grab whatever I could.

I charged into the CVS, put some razors into my pocket, and tried to walk out of the store. On my way out, I was met by a big black man who flashed a police badge and told me to come in the back. In the back, he had me empty my pockets. I had three Mach 3 razor set ups worth about thirty-three dollars. He then told me the police were coming to take me in. I had never been to jail, but I was sure I would go now.

The police came and took me to the Camden Police Station. The police station was awful. They take you into this building with no windows or carpeting. To get into the booking area, you go through a gated cell door and the police secure their guns in lockers. Then, they bring you into the booking area and handcuff you to a bench. I sat there waiting for about twenty minutes. They finally came over to me, uncuffed me, and gave me a ticket, then let me out the front door. They told me to appear in court the next day.

I was in complete shock that they let me out. At this point, I was not aware of how the police, jail, and the court system worked. In Camden, crime was such a normal occurrence that they had to cut loose those with less serious offenses, or the station and the jail would be jam packed.

It had only been a couple of months and I had lost my car, gotten involved in a crime spree, been arrested, had warrants out for my arrest, and was now living on the streets. Being homeless in Camden was not going well for me so far.

DRUG ADDICT'S DREAM

CAMDEN IS A horrible place for anyone except a drug addict. For an addict, it can be a dream world to live in. After being arrested, the strangest thing happened to me that made me realize I may be able to survive here after all.

I couldn't find Israel, couldn't steal, and had no idea how I was going to make money or get drugs. I was walking from the police station across the street when a bunch of people at McDonalds asked what I had gotten locked up for. I said, "Boosting," like I was some hard-core professional or something. Then, a guy said to me, "Wow! You must be dope sick if you just got out of jail." I told him I was, and he offered to take me with him as he was going to buy drugs. If I took a walk with him, he would "look me out." His name was Dan. Dan said he knew exactly what it felt like to be coming out of the police station in withdrawal with no money.

The rest of the day we spent in North Camden getting high. He had about $500 and shared everything he bought with me. He lived in a town about thirty minutes away and he took the bus to Camden daily to get high.

After that day, he told me that if I could be at the Transportation Center every morning to meet him, he would take me to get high. From then on, getting the most important shot called "the wake-up" was guaranteed so long as I met him. You better believe that no matter what, I made sure I was there every morning.

Through Dan, I met everyone in Camden. Most importantly, I met the people who came to Camden to buy drugs. At the time, there was a constant flow of drug addicts who would get off the train or bus every five minutes at the Transportation Center and go to North Camden to buy heroin. Within a month, I had about six regulars and twelve others who came down every other day or so and I would walk with them to get high.

NORTH CAMDEN

GOING TO NORTH Camden to buy drugs was an adventure. It was fun, scary, exciting, and terrifying all at the same time. I would meet people and we would walk from the Transportation Center to North Camden. To get to North Camden, you could either go under the highway through a tunnel or over a small bridge.

Going through the tunnel could be dangerous. People were often robbed, and the city eventually had to put security cameras all over. The tunnels were littered with needles and empty heroin baggies everywhere. It was impossible to walk through without stepping on both.

Once you made it through the tunnel, you came to a small apartment complex and a walkway that went through it. After passing the apartment complex, you enter the jungle of North Camden.

You walked straight and on the left was the first drug set you would pass. They would start yelling at you to buy drugs there. Less experienced people would often make the mistake of buying from the first place that offered, and they usually had the worst quality drugs.

If you got past them and didn't buy, they would yell things like, "You better not walk past here on your way out because you didn't buy from us."

If you kept walking straight, you would come to State Street. By this point, you would normally pass ten addicts who had already bought drugs. Most of them would ask, "What did you buy? Was it good?" or "Was 'The Source' out?" Meaning were the guys on The Source drug set out there selling drugs. If the cops drove by, the dealers would go away for a few minutes. Other times they would run out and you would have to wait for them to go back to the stash house to get more drugs.

So, I would ask and get a response like, "Yeah, but you better hurry because they said if another cop drives by, they're shutting it down," or, "Yeah, they're out and the dope is fire," meaning it's good. Or even, "They're out, but another set is giving out samples that are better, so go to 4th and York Street." Your heart would race as you crossed State Street and were only a block away from The Source drug set. You had to look for police, people trying to rob you, and people pretending to be dealers and selling fake drugs.

Once you made it to York Street and made a right, you could see if dealers were out selling or not. There would be a bunch of people and someone would yell at you to "hurry up and have your money out!" They would flag you to go between two houses where there would be a line of about twenty people buying drugs. You wait and pray that they don't run out or get a radio call telling them cops were close and run off before you get up to get your drugs.

Finally, you get up to the guy with the drugs and say, "I need five dope and two powder (translation: five bags of heroin and two bags of cocaine), which costs seventy bucks. You hand him the money, then he would give you the drugs. Now that you have the drugs, they tell you to walk out through the back of the alley of the abandoned home and get the hell out of there. I would make one final stop at this abando (abandoned house), which was about a block away and get high. There could also be somewhere around twenty other people in there getting high.

Worst case scenario, you could get robbed, raped, or killed in these abandoned houses. Hopefully you just got high and walked out of North Camden. The walk back was like how you feel after having sex; you were high but also drained from all the excitement.

Another part of North Camden that was great for addicts were the "Samples." The drug sets would give out samples on a daily basis to drum up business. The only set that never gave out samples was The Source. They had more business than all the drug sets in Camden combined and had no need to give out freebies. All the other sets did so on a pretty regular basis.

If you got to North Camden early enough, you could easily get two samples every morning for free. I would get the samples as much as possible, then meet people coming to buy drugs and spend the whole day getting high..

There was always something going on in Camden. You were never bored, ever. You could just go sit at the Transportation Center and see a whole city of people revolving around the drug trade and the excitement it brought with it.

People came up with the craziest schemes imaginable and they were beyond amusing to watch. They would sell fake bus tickets, single cigarettes for fifty cents apiece, food stamps, and so on and so forth. Everyone seemed to be looking to get over on someone.

Selling pills was the big thing at the "Transpo" as the Transportation Center was called. It was the main hub for prescription drugs in Camden. People would sell real pills, fake pills, and semi-real pills. They sold Xanax, Percocet, Oxycontin, Valium, Klonopin, Fentanyl, Dilaudid, Opana, Ativan, Lortabs, Loracets, Vicodin, Subutex, and Suboxone.

You just had to stand outside the Transpo for five minutes and you would have ten different people approach you trying to sell you pills. It was fun to watch all the action surrounding these pills while you were high. People were always getting arrested, fighting, or running away with someone's money. Prostitutes looking for dates and selling pills created a nonstop live soap opera. The cast of characters grew daily.

WHERE TO SLEEP IN CAMDEN

IN THE WINTER when it got below thirty-two degrees outside, we were allowed to sleep on the floor of a government building because of Code Blue. Code Blue meant it was so cold outside that people could die sleeping on the street. They knew people were on the street, but only cared if they froze to death because that looked bad for the city of Camden. The churches and volunteers were the only people who really cared about the homeless.

The Code Blue building was a mix of drug addicts and homeless people who were truly crazy. No one in their right mind would choose to live like this. The crazy people were the typical ones you would see and say, "There goes a homeless person." The drug addicts were not the typical homeless people who came to mind. They weren't as rough-looking and were usually younger. Some looked truly out of place there.

Staying in Code Blue was unpleasant at best. You would enter the building at around ten o'clock at night and they would let you find a place to sleep on the floor. If you were not careful, people would steal everything from you. Most people smelled bad and some smelled rancid! There were times when you could be sleeping right next to a homeless person's bare feet on one side and another person snoring inches from your face on the other. People would claim spots and want to fight over them. Some made noises like wild animals and others stayed up all night talking to themselves.

The drug addicts would group together for the most part. They would give each other food and blankets. They were also mostly not from Camden, and surprisingly, many were young females. You could tell the females had been through hell.

The security guards would wake you up by blasting horrible music at an ungodly hour. They would kick you out at four-fifty in the morning when it was still ridiculously cold out with nowhere to go to escape it. So, there would be this huge group of about ninety people huddled in the freezing cold surrounded by big empty buildings that had heat.

GETTIG ROBBED AND ALMOST KILLED

ONE DAY, I had forty dollars given to me by an addict who saw I was sick and wanted to help. A lot of addicts who lived at home and came to Camden to buy drugs felt bad for us addicts who were living on the street. Some would even invite us to their houses for a night. Sadly, most of them would end up right where we were eventually.

When he gave me the money, I went to North Camden as fast as I could. Earlier that week, someone warned me that a group of guys were robbing drug addicts who were going into North Camden. They had a gun and had even smashed a pregnant girl's face with a basketball. The dealers didn't like this because if the addicts didn't feel safe coming to North Camden, they would go somewhere else in Camden or even Philadelphia. If there was one group of people you didn't want to steal from, it was the dealers. When you robbed addicts, they looked at it as if you were stealing from them.

That morning I wasn't thinking about the robberies, only about getting well. As soon as I came through the tunnel into North Camden, I ran into another addict named Harry who told me that he was very sick and had been trying to get high all morning. He asked if I could help him out. I told him I had forty bucks on me and would give him some of my heroin, so he wouldn't be sick. He was very grateful and then started walking with me.

As we came to the first set of apartments past the tunnel, these two younger guys approached us and asked if we wanted samples. I had never bought nor had I ever known anyone to buy from those apartments, so this should have been a huge red flag, but Harry insisted that we at least check it out. I reluctantly agreed.

They said we had to walk around the corner and try it in front of them because they wanted to see if their "dope and coke was good." Dealers had done this same thing before, so it wasn't like they were asking something that no one else ever did, but it still didn't feel right.

As soon as we turned the corner, we were surrounded by about nine guys, seven black and two Spanish. One said, "If this shit's good, you are going to buy, right? You got money?" Harry then blurted out, "Yeah, he does," and pointed at me. As if on cue, I felt something hard smack me on the back of the head and I fell to the ground. As I was trying to stand up and wondering what had just happened, I opened my eyes to see something metal coming toward me, then it immediately hit me square across my nose, which exploded in blood all over my face. Out of the corner of my eye, I saw Harry running away.

The next thing I saw was a guy putting a gun in my face. He pulled back the slide to cock it and said, "Give me all your money!" Being dope sick (in heroin withdrawal), I was not going to give up my forty bucks because of a small thing like being shot in the face. Even though their goal was to rob me, they took their time getting there because they would not stop hitting me from every direction. It was like they turned into a group of wild dogs when they saw blood. I was hit with a gun, a metal pipe, and fists. It became more of an attack than a robbery.

I decided my only option was to just start fighting back and hopefully get away. Luckily I was able to slip away and run when I somehow connected a punch to one of the thugs, but I could not see which one as blood was covering both eyes. I just threw a punch and prayed. Thankfully, I was able to escape and run to the North Gate Towers about two blocks away as fast as I could. When I got there, someone screamed, "Call the police! He's been shot!" There was so much blood coming from my nose and my head that I was covered head to toe, like I was in a horror movie. But that didn't concern me as much as being drug sick. As soon as I heard an ambulance coming, I ran away. I was more scared of ending up in the hospital dope sick than dying. There was no way I was going to the hospital in withdrawal. I ran to the corner of 7th and York Street to go buy heroin.

When we got to the drug set, a dealer said, "What the fuck happened to you?" No one could believe that I was buying drugs covered in blood. I told him that these guys tried to rob me. He said, "You show me where those fuckers are and they will all be dead when the boss finds out." He said to another guy, "Yo, this nigga's a big spender and they are not gonna rob him." I wasn't a big spender, they just saw me a lot.

I didn't have time to get involved in that though. The blood was pouring out of my head and if I passed out, I would not get well. So, I went to the abandoned house and got high as fast as I could. When I came out of the house, there was this black Cadillac Escalade waiting out front. My first thought was that it was the guys who attacked me, and I remember saying to myself, "Damn, these guys really want that forty bucks!"

Then, a guy rolled down the tinted window and said, "Get in. I don't care if you're covered in blood!" He was a huge fat Spanish guy and he drove like a maniac. He had these huge gold rings on the fingers of both hands and all these big religious symbols in the car. He said, "I own the house you guys get high in." I started to say I was sorry, but he interrupted me by saying, "No, I don't care about that at all. Tell me who robbed you. Did they know you were coming to buy drugs?" I said, "I am white and going into North Camden, of course they knew I was going to buy drugs. My stupid friend even told them I had money on me." He listened very seriously, then dropped me off at Cooper hospital. He gave me $400 and told me, "This will never happen again!"

Still to this day, I have no idea if he was the boss or who in the hell he was. I heard later that the guys doing the robberies and attacking people were "taken care of." How much of that is true I don't know, but I never heard of any group of people robbing people again after that.

Even though I looked like the woman in the movie "The Shining" in the scene where she was covered in blood, I still walked into the hospital high and happy because of the $400, which is like forty thousand when your homeless. The doctors gave me an IV and stapled my head back together while I was awake. My nose was broken in a bunch of places, but besides giving me Percocet, there wasn't much they could do about it. I left the hospital as soon as possible, so I could go spend that money. Within one day, it was all gone.

PARADISE TO HELL

AFTER THE ATTEMPTED robbery, things kept getting worse. I started getting more tickets from the police for loitering, and I was averaging one per week. Basically, they would stop you if you were "Walking While White," then run you for warrants. If you don't have any, they will give you $1000 Lottering in a Drug Zone ticket and let you go. Since the whole town of Camden is basically a drug zone, it was a pretty easy ticket for them to write and they add up quickly.

As soon as the temperature gets above freezing, they shut down Code Blue and I had to find another place to sleep. I tried staying in a tent and it was awful. Not only was it freezing in there at night, but we would get soaked whenever it rained. Being wet and cold is a horrible way to live. Also, there were people coming in and out of the tent all night long. The guy who lived in the tent smoked crack, too. As soon as he took a hit, he would spend the next three hours searching the tent for things.

I just wanted to sleep, and this nut job would be going through the tent nonstop for hours looking for something that didn't exist. He would get all paranoid and wake me up asking, "Did you see [whatever]?" He would ask me if I stole his crack pipe, and other times he was too paranoid to even talk and would just stare at me for hours. I lasted a couple nights there, then realized I couldn't take it anymore.

I started asking other people where they stayed. Most were very guarded about where they would spend the night, but this one guy named Frank told me that he had an abandoned house where he slept and said I could sleep there, too, if I wanted. Apparently, no one knew about this place. I thought it was a little strange that he extended this offer so easily, but I accepted as I really had no other choice.

What would happen is that people who once lived in these homes abandoned them for whatever reason, the town would come in and board them up. Drug addicts and thieves would break in to steal the copper or anything of value, then use it to get high or live in. Sometimes they believed that this made them the rightful owner, like Frank.

Frank was a nutty older man who started to believe the abandoned house was his. He even thought that I should pay him rent for staying there. On the third night he went off for hours about how he expected me to pay him rent for being such a "good landlord!" All I wanted to do was sleep and did not need this hassle. The idea of paying him rent was ridiculous considering the circumstances.

I think because he saw me run around all day with a lot of people that he thought I must have a lot of money or drugs. He would start begging me for drugs the minute I got there. Being that most of the time I never had any come nightfall, he would become angry and say, "Don't fall asleep or I will stab you through your neck." He was an older man and I easily could have beaten him up, but if I was asleep, there wasn't much I could do. I found out later that he had done twenty years in prison for murder. So, here I am in this abandoned house in Camden with a convicted murderer threatening to kill me in the middle of the night. The next day, I ended up in CCJ for the first time.

JAIL

THE THOUGHT OF going to jail had always frightened me as I am sure it would most anyone, but everyone who is homeless in Camden ends up in jail at one time or another. I knew it was just a matter of time before I did, too, and any preconceived notions I had of jail from movies made it look like a scary and awful place, which it absolutely is.

That day, I was in an abandoned house with two other people about to do my first shot of heroin when a Camden police officer surprised us by pointing his gun at us. He yelled at us to come out with our hands up, which we did. He asked us what the hell we were doing, and we told him we were getting high. He said he was going to run us for warrants and so long as we didn't have any, he would just give us a loitering ticket and let us go.

I heard him report my name and information into his radio and the dispatcher came back a couple of minutes later and said the worst possible words I could have heard, "He is positive for two warrants for missing court in the amount of five hundred dollars." Five hundred dollars or more meant that the judge wanted to see you. If you did not have the five hundred to pay for bail, you were going to sit in the county jail until you saw the judge. Upon learning of my warrants, he handcuffed and took me to the station.

I was back at the Camden Police Station, but this time I wasn't walking out the front door. After about five hours of being handcuffed to this cold steel bench, they transported me in the back of the most uncomfortable van in the whole world to the county jail. It was about two blocks away. The whole time I was in opiate withdrawal as I was not able to do my first shot when the cops showed up. This made my experience even worse!

I was nervous as hell about going to jail, but not about getting beaten up or raped. I was nervous for two reasons. The first was withdrawal. The thought of getting dope sick in a jail cell was scarier than any prison rape or beating could ever be. Second, I could not pee in a stall if there was another man in the bathroom, so how in the hell was I going to pee in a jail cell with another man?

When they bring you into the county jail, they take you to this shower room where they strip you naked and search you. Then, they put you in a small cell with about twenty other guys sitting on a cement floor. You waited on that floor for five hours until your name was called. You then talk to an officer who asks you questions, then puts you in the next cell over with just as many men and you're back on the floor again.

You are crammed next to someone the whole time. I was in withdrawal but could not move anywhere, which is like having a horrible itch but not being able to scratch it for hours. It was hot as hell, stunk to high heaven, and is about as uncomfortable as it gets.

After another six hours, you finally see a nurse, then they move you to the last cell, which looks the same as the first two. You wait until you go upstairs to a "two-man cell." People want to get upstairs so they can lay down on something besides concrete. I was in complete agony from the withdrawal and couldn't care less about a bed or laying down somewhere comfortable.

They brought us upstairs after about twenty-two hours on the cement floor to a space that was originally designed to be a one-man cell. Eventually, they added bunk beds, so it became a two-man cell. Then, because of overcrowding, they had to put one bed on the floor to make it a three-man cell. If the jail became even more overcrowded, they put two on the floor and it became a four-man cell. When I arrived in the cellblock, each cell had become five-man cells and I was that fifth person, right next to the horrible smelling metal toilet.

The whole time I was there, I had not been able to go pee. On top of the withdrawal, I was in excruciating pain from my bladder, too. There was absolutely no way I could pee in front of four other guys in this small cell. After a while, I was sure my bladder was going to explode. I laid there rocking back and forth in pain and started praying for help. Soon, they started calling all our names for video court. We lined up and waited three hours in line for video court to begin.

The area I was being held in is called seven-day lock down. When you first come into Camden County Jail you go there for seven days and are not allowed out of your cell. It is an absolute nightmare, especially for someone like me. I am claustrophobic and this was like being locked in a closet for seven days with four other men. They only let you out to go to court, which is in a little room with a TV about twenty feet away from your cell.

The seven-day area is in a "POD" where there are two floors of one hundred cells. There are fifty upstairs and fifty downstairs set in a U shape. There are other PODs in the jail all aligned in a big circle with the guard station in the middle, so that they can view every POD from there.

The PODs were dark and depressing. Everything is hard, there is no softness anywhere in the building. Even the mats they give you to sleep on are hard. They have small windows in the cells, but you can't see out of them. The cell doors are heavy and slammed hard and loud. There is never any peace and quiet in jail. There are people always banging on cell doors and yelling, which echoes horribly. Opiate withdrawal amplified all these things.

I finally got to see the judge on a small TV screen. He just asked me how I plead to the charges of loitering in a drug zone? I lived in Camden so I wasn't guilty of loitering, but if I pleaded not guilty, I would've had to stay in jail because I couldn't afford to bail out. So, I said I was guilty. He gave me a $1000 fine for each ticket, which in my current situation might as well have been a million. Then, he said I was ROR, which meant Released on my Own Recognizance. This made me happy because as soon as they finished the paperwork, I would be set free. At this point, I would have pleaded guilty to the Kennedy assassination to get out of jail.

They processed the paperwork and let me out about six hours later. Losing your freedom is an awful feeling and it felt great to be out. The only problem I was concerned with was finding somewhere to urinate, then I could focus on finding heroin to get well. I was so sick now that I could barely walk to North Camden. Worst of all, it was eleven o'clock at night and I had no money.

I finally did make it to North Camden and, by the grace of God, found two people who were getting high in an abandoned home by candlelight and asked them to help me out. They did give me a little, which went a long way considering the condition I was in!

ASSAULT ON A POLICE OFFICER

Now BACK ON the streets of Camden, my life continued on until one day I was arrested again. I ran into a few guys I knew at McDonalds. They told me they were going to North Camden, but they wanted to ditch this annoying guy they had with them.

When I saw who they were talking about, I recognized him as the guy who had ripped me off a while back. He had not recognized me because it had been a while since I last saw him. I met him when I was in North Camden one day. I was buying drugs and he had come up to me saying how sick he was, like Harry had the day I was beaten up. I offered to help him out. When we went to an abandoned house to get high, he ran off with all my drugs as soon as I turned around.

After telling the guys this story, they said we should get him back. We came up with a plan and decided to act like we were heading into North Camden to buy heroin. When we went through the woods on the way there, we would take all his drugs that he kept bragging about. He thought we were going to buy cocaine to mix with his heroin to do speedballs.

We started walking toward North Camden and took the bridge instead of the tunnel. Right after the bridge, we went to this wooded area and I confronted him. I said, "Remember me?" and grabbed him. He motioned like he was going to hit me and I ducked and hit him back. He fell to the ground, and Kevin started going through his pockets saying, "give us the drugs you owe him", but all he had was one bag of heroin. He was lying to us about having all this heroin and was probably planning to rob us or give us fake drugs to mix with the cocaine, so that he could get some of ours.

People did this as a way of getting drugs for free. They would claim they had either heroin or cocaine, but only wanted to do a speedball. Then would find a person who only had even money to buy one or the other but still wanted to do a speedball. They would buy coke or heroin and he would claim to add the other from his "stash" to the mixture and get high for free while adding nothing. Surprisingly, some people made this their hustle and got pretty high on a daily basis by doing this.

When we tried to get the bag from him, he started screaming this high pitched wail. I grabbed the bag anyway and we took off. He tried to follow, but Kevin, who was one of the guys with me, turned around and started punching him, saying, "Addicts don't rip each other off! You're getting what you deserve for leaving him sick." Then, we left.

We walked to a drug set and bought cocaine. As we were walking out of North Camden, I noticed these car headlights pulling up slowly behind us. For a moment I thought we were about to be shot in a drive-by, but all these police lights started flashing and cops were yelling at us to get down on the pavement.

The second I laid flat on the street, I felt a hand slap my leg and heard someone say, "Ouch!" When I got down on the ground the cap to my needle in my pocket had flung off. The exposed needle stuck the police officer in the hand. When he realized it was a needle, he started beating the shit out of me as I was defenseless lying there in handcuffs. I would always tell police I had a needle on me to avoid this exact situation, but this time I didn't have the opportunity because it happened so quickly.

The reason they were arresting us was because after we left the screaming guy, he flagged a squad car down and told them he had just been robbed by three men at gunpoint. He said, we stole all his money, his phone, and his jewelry, which were all lies. He gave them our description as a way to get back at us.

The police arrested us and took us down to the station. I was in serious trouble and knew it was just a matter of time before something like this happened to me in Camden. When they got us down to the station, they figured out quickly that not only did we not have a gun, but that this guy's whole story was a complete lie. They let the two guys I was with go but kept me with a serious charge of assault on a police officer. They took me to Camden County Jail with a $50,000 bail. I was completely expecting to be in jail for a long time, but then something amazing happened.

The next day, I saw a judge on the video camera just like before and he just read me my charges and said, "Bail is set at $50,000," then they took me back to a cell. I had been sitting in the cell for a few hours when they called my name to "roll-up." I was completely in shock and, still to this day, I think they made a mistake. I didn't pay the bail and the judge never ROR'd me, but they still released me, so I certainly wasn't arguing!

An angel must have been looking out for me that night, but where the hell was this angel when all this stuff happened in the first place? Either way, I still like to look at this as someone was watching out for me.

ABANDO

AFTER I LEFT jail, I started staying in an abandoned house I'd dis-covered in the middle of North Camden, right in the worst spot possible. No one else was staying there, so I thought that was lucky, but one night I had a really frightening experience.

I was laying on the couch when I started hearing these noises in the dark, which woke me up. I tried to stay as quiet as possible thinking it might be the police, but then I saw a shadow walking around. The abandoned house was all boarded up so there wasn't any light to see. There was just enough to make out a male figure and then I saw a knife in his hand. Behind him, another guy was looking around. I got off the couch as quietly as possible and hid underneath it. They didn't hear or see me. Then, one of them took his knife and stabbed it into the couch like he was going to kill anyone in it. Had I not woken up, I have been stabbed! They stabbed every chair, every couch, and even the walls.

They were both high on something and speaking Spanish. I had heard these awful stories about people being murdered in these abandos at night alone and thought this could become my reality now. Just my luck, these two clowns come and lay on the couch right above me. I thought they knew I was under there. I had to sit there for hours thinking I was going to have to fight for my life. When morning came, they finally left and I was able to leave.

After that I started sleeping in the basement of the house, which I knew no one would ever enter. The basement was full of dirt, paint cans, broken bottles, needles, and trash everywhere. It was literally like a dumpster. Every night rats would run all around me. I took this blanket I found and covered my face, so they wouldn't bite me.

The first night I slept down there, there was a shooting right outside of the house. The cops came and searched the whole abandoned house. They started coming down to the basement, but after shining their lights around they were like, "Okay, we've seen enough. We aren't walking down there." After a few months of crashing there, the city came by and re-boarded the house, so I had to find a new abando to live in.

GIVING A GIRL NARCAN

ONE DAY, A guy who used to come to Camden and have me walk with him to get heroin asked me if I wanted to come back to his place for a night to get a shower and get off the streets. He said he would get me high all I wanted.

After living on the streets, you never take things for granted anymore. People don't realize how great things like heat, hot water, clean clothes, and so on are when you have had them your whole life. It was so nice to get a shower after being on the streets and lay down feeling safe and warm without gunshots and crazy people keeping me up all night.

The next morning, the guy's girlfriend showed up and wanted to get high with us. She went in the other room and her boyfriend shot her up because he had to take her clothes off. Not long after, she turned blue and collapsed.

Her boyfriend freaked out and froze. I told him to call 911 immediately, he said, "I can't! We both have warrants." He had told me he had Narcan, so I asked him where it was, and he pointed to the bathroom. I ran and grabbed it. I had never given anyone Narcan and had no idea what the hell I was doing, but this guy could not move. He completely froze.

There were two needles. I somehow figured it out and injected it into her butt cheek, but it wasn't working immediately since I gave it intramuscularly rather than through a vein. She was still completely blue and not breathing. I grabbed the other needle and miraculously must have hit a vein because within seconds all the color rushed back into her face and she came alive.

She immediately started crying and screaming. He grabbed her and they both held each other and were thanking me. He gave me some money and drugs and I left to catch a bus back to Camden.

OJAS

I MET A guy from India named Ojas one day as he was in the North Gate Towers parking lot. People would park there to get high after getting their drugs. I would see Ojas driving this nice Audi TT convertible and knew he was getting high because he looked so out of place in Camden. One day, he saw me and asked if I would look out for him. He told me that he would save me some heroin for doing so. I did and after that we talked for a while and soon became friends.

Ojas lived in Cherry Hill with his parents. He was going to medical school to become a doctor and we got along very well. He had these great ideas about how to cure cancer. We immediately became friends.

After that day, he would come to Camden sometimes three and four times a day. He would always give me some of his drugs. He even brought me back to his house a few times and let me take a shower. He had this great German Shepherd that he loved very much. I always loved dogs and having the chance to play with him was a nice break for me. He was like a big teddy bear.

He had these strange neighbors who were devout Muslims. They hated Ojas' family and the dog. One day, they started yelling that they were going to do this and that to the dog when he was in the backyard. This was right after we had just shot cocaine and I lost it. I said, "I would love to see you try to hurt his dog!" They started yelling to Ojas, "What's the matter? Do you need a white boy to fight your battles for you?" Then, I yelled something back and we went back and forth for a while. A week later, those same guys I was yelling at went to Fort Dix Army Base pretending to be pizza delivery guys and tried to kill a bunch of soldiers. It was on the national news and was a very big deal. The next day the FBI was at Ojas' house accompanied by news vans. At first, he thought it was about him and buying drugs. He thought they were really going overboard for one guy using drugs, to say the least

I truly valued and appreciated Ojas' friendship and he sure helped me a lot. Sadly, a couple years after I met Ojas, I called him, and his wife answered the phone crying. They were having a baby girl in three days and I wanted to wish him the best. Ojas had gotten clean for a while and wanted to get high one last time before his daughter was born. He didn't want her to see him high ever, even as a baby. His last time getting high, he overdosed in his bathroom. His family found him later when his dad broke the door down and there he was, on the floor dead!

THE TRUCK

THE NEXT DAY, Ojas dropped me off and I met another person that I really didn't like named Dominic. He seemed like such a slimeball in everything he did. Being that he offered to get me high, I decided to hang out with him. He had the IQ of a rock, but he wasn't stupid and innocent. He was stupid and evil, which is a horrible combination. You just got the feeling that something terrible was going to happen around him all the time.

One morning, he came to North Camden to buy drugs in this old pickup truck. He told me to jump in with him and get high. I said fine and we started driving outside of Camden. He drove to this Rite Aid pharmacy in the town of Cherry Hill. He said, "Look, I'm going to get you high, but first I need you to go in and steal all this stuff from Rite Aid." I told him that I wished he would have just told me this first or I never would have come with him, to which he replied, "So, you ain't gonna do it?" I said, "I am not good at stealing," then told him to drop me off.

The next thing I know, this idiot angrily pulls out of the parking spot and hits a car behind him. Then, he speeds off telling me he has warrants for his arrest and can't stop. I couldn't believe what I had gotten myself into with this clown. I told him to take me back to Camden. He said he needed to stop at his girlfriend's first and would drop me off afterward. He drove to his girlfriend's and told me to wait a minute. He parked around the corner because he said her dad didn't like him and couldn't see if his car was there. So, I never even saw him go into a home.

After an hour, there was no sign of him, and I was getting angry. Next thing I know, a police officer pulls up. He told me to put my hands on the dash, then informed me that I was in a stolen vehicle. I couldn't believe my luck. I knew this guy was bad news and the drugs caused me to make these incredibly stupid decisions. The police took me to the station and they never found Dominic. They gave me a ticket for receiving stolen property and released me because I did not have a record. I walked all the way back to Camden.

TERRIBLE WINTER

THAT WINTER CAME and so did the horrible weather with lots of snow and ice. I was sleeping in an abandoned house without any heat and got so cold that I came down with a horrible case of pneumonia and almost died.

One night, I was in the abando when it dipped down to zero degrees. I put this frozen mattress over me. I tried to use my breath as warmth, but it was just too cold. My breathing started to become difficult. It was too cold to go anywhere because of the wind I probably would have frozen to death before I got there

Around four in the morning, I started to panic. I had never been so cold in my life. The only way to survive that kind of cold was to use your own breath to heat the blanket you were under, but that wasn't even keeping me warm anymore. I was freezing to death.

The wind and snow were rustling through this abandoned house at a furious pace and I was shaking so uncontrollably that I thought I was chipping away at my teeth. I tried everything to stay warm, but nothing was working. I could feel myself starting to lose consciousness and I knew if I didn't start moving, I would die. I went down the broken stairs, which were covered in snow and stumbled out onto the street.

Now it felt like a race against time as I had to get warm before I froze to death. There was no one in North Camden who would let me into their home. There were no stores open to take shelter or anywhere else to get warm. My only hope was to walk to the nearest hospital and hope they let me in.

The nearest hospital was called Copper Hospital. The problem was that I truly looked homeless by now. I went to their emergency room waiting area a week ago to get warm and a guard came and kicked me out. I was also there when my head was smashed open and they ushered me out the minute I was patched up.

I was really concerned that when they saw me again, I would not be allowed in. Plus, my breathing was almost impossible right now and my lungs felt like they were starting to freeze. When I finally got there, the thing I think saved me was that I went into the bathroom and ran hot water over my arm until I could inject heroin. Afterwards, I was still shaking, but I could finally breathe. The ER people did not think my condition was that serious until they checked my oxygen level. It was so low they could hardly believe it. My body temperature was also incredibly low. They rushed me into the ER, and I collapsed just like in the movies.

I woke up a couple of days later in a hospital bed and was told that I had hypothermia and serious pneumonia. They said they had admitted me to the hospital and needed me to stay at least a week to get healthy. I immediately asked to see the doctor because I needed something for my heroin addiction. They told me they were giving me methadone already. I wasn't in full withdrawal but was definitely not feeling well, so I did not believe them. I kept saying that I am really not feeling well and needed to see the doctor. For some reason, medical professionals for the most part are very unsympathetic.

I met a nurse in rehab who said she was mean toward addicts until she herself became one and realized what they were going through. After that, she felt so awful for how she had treated them.

I finally saw the doctor and asked him how much methadone he was giving me. He said they were giving me ten milligrams a day. Ten milligrams was nothing for me. It was like putting a bandaid on a broken bone. So, I asked if he could raise it to forty milligrams twice a day. I really needed double that, but I knew there was no use asking. He said there was "nothing else he could do" and would not up the dosage. He said I was lucky I was even getting ten milligrams. I then asked him for my discharge papers. He told me I would die if I left. Again, I told him I needed at least forty milligrams of methadone or I would take my chances.

The crazy part was that if I had come in and lied to this man by saying I was in serious pain, he would have given me something much more powerful than ten milligrams of methadone. Being that I was an addict and in reality, more pain than any physical injury could even come close to, he would not budge.

This was a horrible miscalculation and misjudgment on the part of a medical professional, and this happens way too often. If they feel that it is perfectly fine to let a person suffer because they "did this to themselves," I wonder what they think of someone who smokes and gets cancer or eats too much and ends up with heart disease? Would a doctor not give them the medicine they need because "they did this to themselves?" I bet more than half the things doctors see in hospitals are due to someone "doing it to themselves." This is an awful consequence of the War on Drugs and the vilification of drug addicts!

Knowing what I know now, if you deny an addict in withdrawal enough medication, you are causing an unbelievable amount of needless suffering. In an ignorant attempt to make sure a person doesn't get high and feel good, you are causing harm and that is against everything a doctor swears to uphold when they take their oath. The War on Drugs has turned drug addicts into the enemy.

The nurse said she would tell the doctor to up the dosage. She was a really nice lady who didn't want me to leave. She was not very pretty, but apparently, I told her she looked beautiful on my second day there. She must have not been told that a lot and she thought it was so nice that she went to bat for me. She tried hard, but the doctor said he was not going to give me something just so that I could "feel good."

I was blown away by how awful people can be to each other. I wasn't trying to get high. I just wanted to get out of misery. All that the doctor had to do was increase the dosage by thirty milligrams and I would have stayed. It was more important that I did not "feel high" from this drug even if that meant my death. So, I left the hospital and went back to the freezing cold streets of Camden with full blown pneumonia.

Whoever that poor nurse was who tried to help, thank you. I am sure God has a special place in Heaven for you. You tried everything you could to help me and it meant the world to me. I noticed she was so sad when I left, and I felt bad for her. She called after me, "Come back if you need to. Please don't die." I never came back, but I didn't die either.

DEAD BODIES/I ALMOST BECOME ONE

EVENTUALLY, THE PNEUMONIA went away as did the cold weather. That spring when things started to warm up, I ran into two dead bodies from overdoses. The first one was in an abandoned house right behind The Source drug set. I also almost robbed their stash house, which is a sure way to get killed.

I was sleeping in the "bedroom" upstairs of this abandoned house. I came down in the morning and noticed a guy sitting on a bucket hunched over. I went up to ask him if he was okay and I was shocked to see he was cold and dead. He must have come there and died while I was sleeping. He had been there the whole night as I slept above him. I also noticed his jail ID. He had just gotten out of jail that day and came right here to get high.

A lot of people would come out of jail, get high and die because their tolerance was so low being that they had been clean for a while. A bag of Camden dope could easily kill someone without a tolerance. I also noticed that his name was Andrew, like mine and I felt bad for his family. I decided to run back upstairs to grab my bag, then go find someone and tell them to come get the dead guy.

While I was upstairs, I heard voices entering the house, so I went to the top of the stairs where I could see them, but they couldn't see me. At first, I was sure it was two drug addicts coming to get high, but then realized it was something that could easily get me killed. The dealers were using this place as a stash house.

Amazingly, they just walked over the dead guy like doing so was completely normal. Then, I saw them stand up on a milk crate and remove a ceiling tile before reaching up and pulling out about one hundred bundles, which are ten-bag increments, from out of a much larger bag. Then, they left.

When the dealers set up for the day, a set like The Source would sell about five thousand bundles in a day. They would use a stash house to store heroin and cocaine in case of a robbery or police raid. They would bring a hundred bundles out at a time. When they ran out, a runner would go to the stash house to retrieve another hundred bundles.

Just being caught in one of these stash houses was enough to get you killed or beaten up at the very least. If you robbed one, they would cut off your hands, torture you, and then kill you.

We would notice how people in Camden you saw often would suddenly vanish and never be seen or heard from again. Then, it would get around that the person robbed a stash house and got caught, so they killed him. They found one of the guys I knew in the river with his hands cut off. He had robbed a stash house.

So, I was in a bad situation to say the least. If they heard me, they would never believe I wasn't trying to rob them. They all carried guns and did not hesitate to shoot each other, so I doubt they would think very hard about shooting me.

After they stepped over the dead guy again as they left, all sorts of thoughts immediately started running through my mind. I could grab the whole thing and take off, then I'd be set for a long time. Or I could grab the whole thing and get caught, killed, and tortured. Or I could grab a couple of bundles and maybe no one would notice. My thoughts were racing the same if not faster than my heart was.

Eventually, I decided to at least go up and look into the ceiling to see how many drugs were in there. First, I waited to make sure they didn't come back right away. Then, I tiptoed right to the spot they were and put the milk crate up and stood on it. I slid the little opening over and looked in at one of the most beautiful sites I had ever seen.

There were thousands of bundles of the best heroin Camden had to offer. There were hundreds of dime bags ($10 bags) of powder cocaine and hundreds of bags of crack cocaine and about maybe $10,000 in cash. Just as I saw it, I heard multiple voices coming back and my heart dropped.

The runners must went out and told the case worker that there was a dead body in the stash house. He told them to go back and remove the stash before someone found the body, called the cops, and the house was sealed off.

I was not sure if this was good luck or not. I slid the tile back over the opening and rushed upstairs before they came in. The problem was I left so quickly that I forgot to move the crate back. I thought they were going to start searching the house and I would have to fight for my life, but thankfully they just grabbed the drugs and the cash and took off.

The second dead body I saw came not too long after this situation. I went to a drug set early in the morning to get a sample. After getting it, I went behind this fence alongside a popular trail in the woods where people went to get high.

I moved back pretty far so no one could see me and came upon a bike leaning against the fence. I saw another person laying hunched over. I grabbed him on the shoulder and pulled him over and was shocked at what I saw. His face was so purple it was unbelievable. Shockingly, I knew who he was. I would see him come down to Camden and get drugs with another runner almost every day.

I guess he came down by himself this time and overdosed alone. It was another advantage to having a runner with you. Most addicts, at the very least, would call you an ambulance if you overdosed. Luckily the governor of New Jersey changed the law that said if you called the police for an overdose and stayed to help the person, you wouldn't get charged with a crime.

Having someone arrested for calling to get help was one of those useless laws that they claim saves lives, but they only hurt people. Laws like the one the governor passed actually do save lives. Sadly, it was too late for many people already. I will never know if someone left him there because they didn't want to go to jail, but it would not be completely unreasonable to think that this is exactly what they had done.

Another sad part besides him dying was that his phone was ringing nonstop and when I looked, it said his dad was calling. His dad must have called it two hundred times hoping his son would pick up. I think some parents have a sixth sense about these types of things and his dad knew something was horribly wrong. But I couldn't answer it and tell him his son was dead. I wasn't even high yet. I just dialed 911 on the phone and left the area and never looked back.

GLOUCESTER COUNTY JAIL

THAT SPRING, I went to jail again and had no way of getting out this time. The day I went, I was walking with someone into North Camden to get drugs and got stopped by a police officer. He ran us for warrants and here I am expecting a negative on warrants, but the call came back over the radio that I have a No Bail Fugitive warrant. I was completely blown away by that and thought it was a mistake.

Apparently, the ticket they gave me for receiving stolen property with the truck was a Superior Court charge. I had never had a Superior Court charge before and didn't understand how they worked. If you miss Superior Court, they put out a "No Bail Warrant" for you and, even if you have a million dollars, you cannot get out of jail. People who commit murder can get out of jail easier than someone who misses court.

The only way you can get out is if you see the judge and they set bail for you. The problem is that it pisses a judge off when you miss court, so they make you sit in county jail for at least thirty days before seeing you.

Before this, I had never been out of seven-day lock down and most of the time I had spent there was twenty-four hours. Now, I had no chance of getting out for at least thirty days and when I found this out, fear set in. I would be forced to go through an excruciating withdrawal in a jail cell. I also could not pee in front of people, let alone in a confined space. This was going to be a huge problem, and essentially sheer torture for me! While this may not sound like a big problem, try holding your pee for six hours and feel the pain. Now, imagine thirty days straight of that pain and not being able to do anything about it.

The first real thought that came to my mind was suicide. When you arrive and they find out you are coming off heroin, the first thing they do is put you on suicide watch. Suicide watch means they put you in a green "turtle suit" completely butt naked and throw you in a glass cell with about twenty other people. You stay on a cold floor and you are observed twenty-four hours a day. If you were not suicidal before being in the turtle suit, you would be very shortly thereafter.

The room smells awful and there is throw-up on the floor and human feces on the walls. A crazy guy next to me kept sticking his feet in the metal toilet that people were using, then walking over everyone. The room was cold and dark, and I was shaking nonstop. I waited until three in the morning when everyone finally went to sleep to try to pee and it took me three hours of trying to finally get relief. I made the decision not to drink water after that. Eventually, I had to drink a little because I became way too thirsty.

I also had not pooped since I got there. Pooping in front of twenty guys who were just inches away is one of the most uncomfortable experiences imaginable. I was in withdrawal now and it was coming out whether I wanted it to or not.

I went to sit on the toilet, and everyone started yelling things like, "Oh, no! Don't shit," and, "that better not smell!" as though it was a choice. The heroin makes you constipated, so when you haven't gone regularly, it comes out like a log and the pain is awful.

So, I was on the toilet trying to push this painful log out of my body with these crazy people yelling at me. I pushed so hard that it literally ripped my insides causing the toilet to fill with blood, but the log came out. We had no toilet paper and I banged on the window and asked the CO (Corrections Officer) for some, but he told me if I wanted toilet paper, I shouldn't have come to jail.

Some of the Correction officers in Gloucester County are some of the most horrible human beings I have ever encountered. If the public knew the things they did, they would be in jail with us. I understand they are dealing with some real scumbags, but I was still shocked at what I saw.

There was this huge black CO named Cora and the rumor was that he had killed two inmates. I personally saw him stomp on the chest of an old man in handcuffs so hard that I thought he had killed him. I couldn't believe that the people who called themselves officers acted like this. The inmates were not much better.

The jail separated municipal and superior charges in different areas of the jail. My charge was the lowest possible superior charge but was still serious enough that I got put with the people who were facing serious charges like murder.

There were two different types of people in the jail. There were the "real criminals" who sometimes used drugs and the drug addicts who commit crimes to support their drug habits. The difference was that before drugs, drug addicts didn't commit crimes. The real criminals committed crimes whether they did drugs or not.

Most real criminals had been in some sort of lock-up as juveniles before arriving at an adult jail. They were used to the jail system and the prison lifestyle. Most of them had been to prison many times and lived a certain predator and prey lifestyle. They all had these prison tattoos that were some of the most dumbest things ever. They had misspelled words and things like "I'm a badass," which automatically meant the opposite.

They all played poker and gambled to pass the time. They loved to pick on new people or people who didn't know anything about jail. Some had "hustles" they would do in jail, like selling commissary items. They all acted happy to be in jail, which I never understood. It was like this was where they belonged. They got free food and could sleep all day and that was more than enough for them. It was really a sad thing to see.

In jail, they have a set way of living. They get really crazy about "respect," like people reaching over people's food and stuff like that. You learn the jail rules very quickly through trial and error. No one comes up to you and tells you what you should or shouldn't do.

People sell drugs in jail, too. Not a lot of street drugs, but everyone cheeks their pills, then sells them to other people. They found all kinds of ways to get other drugs into jail, but just not on a regular basis.

Some people in jail were funny characters, which made things a little interesting at times considering how unbelievably boring jail is and the hours just creep by. I had been so sick during the first two weeks that I gave away all my food, but after a while I started eating everything I could. I was starving all the time in jail. They don't feed you near enough, which means everyone is starving. I did not think it was ever possible, but when in jail you will be hungrier after you eat. The only thing to look forward to is mealtimes and that isn't saying much.

The medications in jail were the only way to get a buzz. When I finally saw a psychiatrist in jail, I told him I was schizophrenic, so he would give me a strong medicine to knock me out for as long as possible. I also told him I needed Wellbutrin for depression. All the guys in jail would crush it and sniff it in their cells for a cocaine-like buzz.

After the physical withdrawal from heroin went away, I was so depressed and bored from the post-acute withdrawal that anything I could take to change the way I felt was very welcome. I even convinced the doctor to give it to me twice a day. I also asked for Thorazine to quiet the "voices" in my head. I never had any voices in my head, but if I took enough Thorazine I could sleep at night, wake up, eat, then sniff Wellbutrin, take the Thorazine and then go back to sleep. I'd do the whole thing all over again the next day. Thorazine was a blessing because there was no way possible that I would have been able to sleep at all without it.

The third week I was there, a guy hung himself in his cell with a sheet. He had gone to his cell while everyone had been let out to roam and said he needed some privacy to use the toilet. Then he hung himself in his cell from his bed with a sheet. After they found him dead, I was amazed at the lack of compassion or caring among the inmates and the guards. It was literally like it was just more of an annoyance than anything else to them.

I must admit that I was thinking about doing the same thing, especially knowing that I wasn't going to get out for over a month. The jail made you get a verified address before you can leave. If you didn't have one, they kept you there until you could get one even if the judge released you. I had no hope of my family verifying anything, but I decided to call them anyway. To accept a call from jail, they had to use a credit card. They did accept my call, but only to tell me to never call them again.

I had to deal with the urination problem the best way I could. The only way I was able to go was if I sat in the shower for an hour. There was something about the water that helped me go. I didn't want to pee in the shower, but I had no other choice. I took about six showers a day. One time, it got so bad that I went to the clinic and they tried to catheterize me. What they didn't understand was that this wasn't a physical problem, it was a mental one. It was so bad that if someone had told me that if I peed, I could leave jail and get a million dollars, I still couldn't have made it happen. Having this problem as bad as I did was an absolute nightmare in jail, and it was driving me nuts.

Even after I would finally pee in the shower, I was immediately thinking about when and how I was going to pee again and worried that my bladder would explode if we ever got locked down for an extended period of time and I could not use the showers. At night when we were locked in the cell, I would wake up at three o'clock and stay awake waiting in pain for morning to come, so I could take a shower and pee. This was on my mind every day, all day, so when I went to see the judge, I would have pleaded guilty to anything, so I could get out of jail.

The public defender asked if I could bail out and fight this. He told me this would easily get dropped to a misdemeanor or completely thrown out if I could just bail out. He flat out told me no prose-cutor would dare fight it in court with a trial. I told him about the situation with my family and he just shook his head in disbelief. He said the judge would lower my bail to a hundred dollars if I could just convince my parents to bail me out, then this felony would be dropped. I told him my parents wouldn't bail me out no matter what. He said, "The only way to get out of jail is to plead guilty and then they would let me go." I said fine and immediately asked, "Where do I sign?"

After that, he said I just needed to stay clean and avoid trouble for a year and this would fall off my record. I said, "Great, no problem," knowing there was no way that was happening. I just wanted out and signed everything without reading it, and said I was guilty to whatever they wanted.

I didn't realize the impact of that decision but try holding your urine for twenty-four hours a day for over thirty days, then someone tells you that you can leave if you say you're guilty, and you will say you're guilty! Before I knew it, they called me to "roll-up," and I was back in Camden. The temperature was now much warmer, and I couldn't wait to get high to forget what I had just gone through.

OVERDOSE

As soon as my feet touched ground in Camden, I started walking toward North Camden. On my way there, I ran into a guy I knew named Tommy who was going to cop (buy drugs). As soon as I told him I had just gotten out of jail, he said, "Come with me and I'll buy you a bag. I'm sure you need it."

He told me about this new drug set that had just opened that had really strong heroin, so we decided to try there first. It wasn't organized well like The Source set was because it was too new. As soon as we got there this guy ran up to us and asked how many we needed. Tommy said, "Twenty-four dope." The guy told us he would be right back, but that we needed to quickly exit the same way we came once he gave us the drugs because the cops were very close. He looked panicked, so we believed him. He came running back over and handed us the bags, then ran back as fast as he came. The one thing he forgot to do was ask for the money. We both noticed, so we started walking away as quickly as possible without looking too obvious, expecting someone to yell, "Hey, get back here!" Eventually, we were far enough away and in the clear.

Because of what had just happened, we decided not to get high in North Camden. Tommy said he always went into the bathroom at Rutgers College to get high because everyone just thought he was a student. So, we decided to go there. We took stalls next to each other and started mixing up our heroin. I noticed the heroin was super dark. Tommy had given me two bags, but it looked like I had mixed six. I found a vein instantly and pushed the plunger in, then everything went dark.

The next thing I knew, I was laying in the back of a parked ambulance. The doors were open, and I was surrounded by emergency workers staring at me. I had seen movies where a person woke up from this type of situation and would freak out. I always thought they were idiots and that I would never do such a thing. Sure enough, I freaked out. For some reason, I just started running from them as fast as I could and didn't know why.

After a couple of blocks, I noticed I had a horrible pain in my right foot. I just kept going despite the pain, trying to catch up with Tommy. Not only did we get free drugs, but he also had $250 on him and said we were going to do speedballs with that money. I couldn't care less about that overdose. I wanted to do the speedballs and thought about them every day in jail. That day it never happened because I never caught up with Tommy.

It turns out that I overdosed in the bathroom of Rutgers Campus. Tommy dragged me outside and called an ambulance. He took off because he didn't want to go to jail. While I was lying there on the sidewalk, a car ran over my foot and broke it in three places. Then, the ambulance showed up and gave me Narcan. When it hit me, I awoke confused, so the first thing that came to my mind was that I was in trouble and going back to jail, so I ran.

I ended up at the North Gate Towers hoping to find Tommy walking back into North Camden to get cocaine. While I was waiting and trying to figure out exactly what had happened, a car pulled out of the underground garage. This young black guy was running behind it with a gun and started shooting at the car. It was broad daylight and he let off about ten shots, then ran back into the building. Immediately after, people went about their day as though this was normal. It occurred to me that getting back into this life was not the best decision.

BACK TO CCG

As I MENTIONED before, I had a horrible pain in my left foot that would not go away ever since I woke up from the overdose. For a couple of weeks, I just walked around Camden with a limp. My broken foot also led me back to jail, which may have been a blessing now that I look back on it.

Being that I was homeless and never went to probation, the judge put out another No Bail warrant for my arrest very shortly after I had left jail. Going back to that place was something I absolutely dreaded, but once that warrant was put into motion, I didn't have a choice and knew I would have to go back.

One day I was walking with this girl in the woods going to a place where everyone went to get high. She was afraid of being robbed, so I agreed to escort her because she said she would get me high. I knew the guys who were robbing people in the woods and they knew me. They always used a fake gun, but kids from the suburbs would almost always give up their drugs and money to these clowns.

As we were walking, these guys approached this girl and I with masks covering their faces and demanded, "Give us the drugs!" They even claimed to be "police," which was ridiculous. Once they realized it was me, they backed off and said, "Oh, man! Why didn't you say it was you?" Like I should have been wearing a sign in Camden saying, "You probably know me, so don't rob me." Apparently, these fools had just robbed about five different groups of people and one of them decided to call the police. So, a minute after they arrived trying to rob us, the cops showed up behind them.

This girl must have thought she picked the worst guy possible to walk with her. She wasn't with me for five minutes and we had an attempted robbery and now the police are here. Of course, they ran my name even though they were just looking for the two morons and saw that I had a No Bail warrant. So, I ended up back in Gloucester County Jail once again. This time, it was practically the exact same experience as the first time, except now because I did not go to probation the felony would stick and be on my record for life. The punishment I got from the judge was probation until I paid a fine of $600.

Nothing about the jail had changed. The people were all the same, only the names were different. They were playing cards, working out, doing hustles, and waiting for prison.
For a guy like me whose life is an absolute hell, I was starting to realize that no matter what I did, if it involved getting high, this was how I would end up. I didn't want to go to my parents for help, but I did not have any other alternatives. I also started praying to God to help me out of this mess.

The day I was released from Gloucester County Jail, they transported me to Camden County Jail because of warrants that were issued for the loitering tickets. I pleaded guilty and they released me with a $1000 fine for each one. As soon as I got to Camden, a strange feeling came over me. I decided not to get high until I called my parents. I said to myself, "If they agree to come get me, I won't get high." I knew if I got high even one time, I would be right back where I started and never go with my parents.

I called and asked my dad to please come get me. Amazingly, he told me they would be there in two hours and to wait somewhere safe. It was like God was helping me because I was doing the right thing. I waited for them and never got high. They came and got me.

HURRICANE SANDY

HURRICANE SANDY STRUCK shortly after my parents had picked me up from Camden, and their house was destroyed. Before the hurricane, things were going well between us. I was staying clean and for the most part we got along.

After we realized that their house was destroyed, friends of ours were nice enough to let us stay in one of their beach houses in Avalon, New Jersey. At first, things went great. I started seeing a probation officer and finally realized exactly what I had pleaded guilty to. After speaking to the officer, he said I was not the typical guy he saw. His name was Glenn and I liked him. He told me I had to go to NA meetings in the area and, most importantly, stay out of trouble, which also meant I could not use drugs.

At night, I started going to these NA/AA meetings and even started enjoying some of them, especially because of a few of the pretty girls who attended these meetings. One girl named Samantha especially caught my eye. One night, I drove her and her girlfriend to a late-night meeting in Ocean City.

SAM

ON THE WAY home from the meeting, Samantha and I ended up making out. We were kissing for a while and then she told me her whole life story. At first, it seemed like I had met the perfect girl. She explained that she had one long-term boyfriend and had lost her virginity at nineteen. She said she had no kids, owned her own home, and had basically taken too much Percocet and that was why she was sent to rehab. She made it clear that she wasn't a typical girl in the meetings. She said she never slept around and was the most loyal girlfriend a guy could ask for. She told me that she was the most honest girl I would ever meet, especially in NA as all those girls were, as she put it, "damaged goods."

The next night, we had sex at my house and a few things she said kind of threw me off guard. The things she said were strange for such an inexperienced girl. It made me think of the song "Things that make you go hmmm." I just blew it off as nerves because she was inexperienced, but in the back of my mind, I couldn't help but think the worst.

For the next month, things went well between us. I was starting to like Sam and almost considered her to be my girlfriend. Until one night, we went to a meeting and things got crazy. Sam called me beforehand and said, "Let's go out afterwards and spend some time together." I was in the meeting waiting for her when a random girl came in and took a seat next to me.

The next thing I know, Sam walks in, sees this, and flips out. She stormed outside furiously and I followed her. We got into my car and started driving away. She was so angry and started screaming at me. I asked her, "What the hell is wrong?" She replied, "That bitch sat next to you, of course." I turned onto the highway while still trying to understand what the hell she was mad about. I soon responded, "Girls sit next to me all the time. What's the problem?" After I said this, she decided to jump out of my car as we were traveling down the highway at about sixty miles an hour.

As she was jumping out, I jammed on the brakes and tried to hold her in. Had I not gotten a grip on her arm she probably would really hurt herself. I almost got rear ended by five cars and caused a major pile up, too. She ran to the side of the highway screaming at me that "I didn't love her!" then ran into the woods. I had no choice but to drive away.

The next day, she came over to apologize. Her idea of an apology was to bring me a bag of heroin and asked me to do it with her. She told me that she had been doing it for a while now and claimed that most people in the meetings were getting high. I turned her down and kicked her out. This perfect girl was turning into a nightmare. I was also pissed because she knew my whole situation and that I was on probation, but I was especially irate because she knew how bad my addiction was, yet she still decided to offer me heroin. It was a shitty thing to do. One thing I can say about myself is that I never once brought anyone else down with me. If I relapsed, it was only by myself. I have never encouraged a clean addict to get high, ever!

The next night, she called me. I decided to talk to her because, frankly, I missed her. She said she was sorry and wanted to come over to talk about things. When she arrived, she again had heroin with her. Instead of asking me to do it with her, she did it in front of me and told me how great it was. I did not use that night, but it did get my mind thinking.

The next night, I gave in and did some with her. When I did it, I felt bad, It felt dirty, and wrong. Gone was the carefree attitude I enjoyed upon getting high. Going to AA/NA meetings ruined the joy I felt when getting high, to a point. Either way, my addiction still had a grip on me, and that one time sent me off to the races with heroin again.

From then on, it was a downward spiral. Eventually, I found out that Samantha was lying to me about everything. She was so pretty that people gave her the benefit of the doubt. Not only was she lying to me about being sober, she was one of those people who came to meetings high, then got people to relapse with her. Sam is the "misery loves company" type of addict.

People tried to warn me about her, but I blew them off. Even my NA sponsor told me to be careful around her. She would use her looks to meet a sober guy and hook up with him, then get him to become her using partner. I was the fourth guy in the last six months she had victimized in this way. Sam was a pretender who was many miles away from what she claimed to be.

I found out she was the exact opposite of a prude. She had slept around with a ton of guys before me and also had four kids with three different guys. She lived with her parents and didn't have a job. I am not sure why I believed everything she told me, but I guess I didn't expect a woman to lie to my face so many times and so boldly. I knew that my guy friends would lie to women to make themselves look better in the hopes that they would sleep with them, but this was the first time I had ever heard of a woman doing this.

Once I started using with her, I didn't stop. Things got progressively worse as time passed, like always. I started having to lie and then make up lies to cover up those lies. Eventually, it all came out as it always does, and I was kicked out and sent to some crazy rehab in Kentucky.

KENTUCKY

HERE IS SOME solid advice: Never go to a Christian rehab run by a Jewish man in Kentucky who promises a miracle addiction cure through a Walkman and Jesus.

The rehab I went to in Kentucky was about the worst possible rehab center on planet Earth. You have a better chance of getting sober while living homeless in Camden than in this place. Your daily schedule Monday through Friday was brutal and never changed. You started the day by reading the Bible from 5am to 9am, then built wooden crates for nine hours a day, so the owner could make a profit, and breakfast, lunch, and dinner consisted of donated doughnuts that were always stale. After dinner, you read the Bible until bedtime. Weekends involved more slave labor and Bible readings.

They had no medical staff and the head "counselor" was a client they hired because he had slept with the owner's daughter and got her pregnant. They let a client run the whole place and he was the last person who should have been running a rehab. It was literally like letting Ted Bundy or Charles Manson run death row.

On Friday night, they took you to either a college football stadium or a professional sports stadium to clean the parking lot. After the game, you cleaned the whole stadium and underneath all 90,000 seats. It took about fifteen hours. You made zero dollars while the owner got paid eighteen dollars an hour for your backbreaking work. Then on Saturday, you did it again and worked until Sunday morning.

Ninety-five percent of the people there were forced to stay for eighteen months or had to go to prison for ten years, so they really didn't have a choice. The other five percent were tricked into going there by the promise of a fake miracle addiction cure based on lies.

They had pictures on their website that were completely fake. From horseback riding to swimming, it was all a big lie set up to make money in the name of Jesus. To this day, it is one of the most evil places I have ever been. You could feel the evil, especially because they were conducting their business in the name of Jesus to get donations.

They claimed that the recordings you listened to with the Walkman would reset your brain chemicals to normal levels, but this was also a complete scam. They preyed upon suffering people by promising them peace and wellness but delivered none of either.

Their Walkman treatment was a scam. Basically, they took people in full opiate withdrawal and connected them to a Walkman with little wires, which were taped to them behind their ears. They said the Walkman would send impulses to your brain that would reset the chemicals to normal levels, but it literally did nothing except make you even more uncomfortable wearing this stupid thing around your head.

I should have seen the bright red flag when they call your family once you get there. They would say, "If your loved one calls you and tells you bad things about this place, don't believe them. We know what we are doing, and addicts are liars." This was the first thing they said to families and it is also explained on their website.

While this may sound dramatic, I actually had to escape from this place, like I was escaping from prison. I did it with another "prisoner" there. I first told the "counselor" that I wanted to leave, but he said that this was not possible because my parents were paying for me to be there and wanted me to get well. The truth was that the owners of the facility just wanted my parents' money and did not want to lose one of their slaves.

They told me if I ran, they would call the police and have me brought back. They told all of us that they had an agreement with the local police to arrest anyone who left their property. They also threatened to keep our belongings and IDs and would not let us use the phone. The closest bus station was well over twenty miles away. We were stuck there, and they knew it.

After a couple of days had passed, I finally hatched an escape plan with a guy named Scott, then we executed it. Scott sneaked into an office by climbing through the ceiling, then used the phone to call his mom and told her to come get us. With this part of the plan complete, we knew our next challenge was to run through a door that had an alarm. Once alerted, they would be chasing us on foot and in their vans, so we had to make it to his mother before they found us. It's ironic how I came to this place voluntarily and was now running for my life from these "deliverance" people.

Once we ran off the property, we hugged the side of the road as we made our way to where his mom was supposed to meet us, which was about a mile away. By the time his mom showed up, the place had almost gotten me back. Scott's mom was petrified by what he was telling her about the place, so she called them on her way to pick us up. We had already escaped, so they told her that not only had Scott made up all these lies, but he had taken a person who was legally supposed to be there, which was another complete lie. I was not court ordered to be there, but Scott's mom believed them and refused to take me with her. Eventually, the sweet hippie side of her gave in, thankfully.

After that, I stayed with Scott's parents who were a very nice couple. His mother was especially sweet. They let me stay at their house for a couple of days. Scott was a horrible addict and had robbed his parents blind, but they still loved him and wanted to help, which amazed me.

His mother tried calling my mom, but she hung up on her. This woman couldn't believe my mother wouldn't answer the phone. I heard her say to her husband, "The phone must be broken." Then, she said to me, "Your mother must be so worried! I have to talk to her," but I knew that my mom couldn't care less about my well-being. She was angry that I had left the place because she was paying for it. I am sure she thought the best way to get back at me was to not answer the phone. The facility had called my parents to tell them not to help me and to make sure I came back. I am sure my mother believed everything they said and decided that no matter what I said, I was going back there.

After about a week, Scott's mom got me a bus ticket to Philadelphia, and I headed back to Camden. She told me how sorry she was that my family was upset and that I was always welcome in their home. I thought that was nice of them, but I had had enough of Kentucky. One day while I was there, Scott took me to his friend's place where they were making their own meth.

They made it in a bathtub, and it was one of the most depressing and horrible things I have ever seen. The smell from the meth was incredibly strong and could literally make paint peel off the walls. The people that used it looked awful. They all looked much older than their actual ages and they talked constant nonsense, which made them unbearable to be around. I was very glad to leave Kentucky.

BACK IN CMD

THE FIRST DAY I got back to Camden, I was high after being there for only fifteen minutes. I had been in Kentucky for three weeks and felt awful the entire time. It was such a relief to finally be high. Had I been high at that hellish facility in Kentucky, it would still have been unbearable, but being sick made it that much worse.

After getting high, I remember thinking back to Kentucky and believing that this was it for me. I was just going to use till I died, then this nightmare that was my life would be over for good. I wanted to stop fighting! I was tired of being sick, tired of being anxious, tired of being depressed, tired of being used by these rehabs to make a profit, tired of being blamed for everyone else's problems, and tired of living a life that seemed as though it was nothing but a vicious cycle of pain and suffering.

The only thing that gave me any peace was the one thing that everyone got angry at me for doing. So many people judged me for using drugs without even walking a minute in my shoes. I thought to myself, "I dare someone to walk in my shoes for one week let alone years! I bet they would end up using drugs, too."

Back in Camden, I ended up living in a tent city. It was a horrible place to live. Everything was wet and dirty. It seemed like nobody had anyone's back as people were always fighting over something or arguing about nothing.

The tents were supposed to be a homeless community, but there isn't much community when drugs are involved. People were always stealing from each other, lying, and doing other shady things. You never felt safe going to sleep and you could never trust anyone completely.

In a tent next to mine was this guy named "Scumbag Mike." He wasn't called a "scumbag" because he was a decent person. He had done thirty years in prison for a double murder and was one of the worst human beings I have ever met. He had this story about killing two guys who raped his "old lady." There were two big problems I had with this story. First was I really doubted a female would be near this guy ever and second, the story sounded too good and heroic. If you were defending your girl from two rapists and happened to kill them, I doubt you would get charged with first degree murder and sentenced to twenty-five years in prison.

Scumbag Mike was constantly causing problems in Tent City. He would beg people for drugs nonstop and go crazy if you didn't give him some of yours, but he never shared his with anyone. If you were sharing your drugs with him, but refused him one time, he'd run around telling everyone you were greedy. It was like being around someone you could never win with. He was not happy unless he was getting over on someone or causing problems between people. Not all homeless addicts were like Scumbag Mike though.

CHRIS/BEAR MACE STORY

I THANKED GOD that I met Chris. Chris was a guy around my age from Florida. I didn't like him at first and we didn't get along for a while, but eventually we started working together to get drugs and helping each other out. If one of us had drugs, we would help the other one out and vice versa. It was nice to have a friend who you could trust in Camden.

Chris had a rental car when he first arrived in Camden, but it got shot up one night. It was three in the morning when Chris and another guy were looking for an open drug set in Camden. The only one they could find was in South Camden. While they were waiting for the guy to come back with the drugs, some guy walked up behind his car and started shooting at it with a .357 Magnum. Somehow, he missed them both.

Chris was now driving around Camden in a rented Toyota Camry with bullet holes riddling its rear end. It was just a matter of time before the police stopped him and impounded it, but before they did, he was able to spray bear mace at a girl in North Camden with the help of the rental car.

Chris had been hanging out with this girl for a while and they were getting high together. One day, they were stopped by the police while Chris was trying to steal stuff to sell for drugs and Chris was arrested. She promised to look after his stuff while he was in jail. He even took the arrest partly for her, so she at least owed him enough to take care of his things. When he got out of jail, it took him forever to track the car down. When he finally found it, all his stuff was gone. She sold it for drugs and then disappeared. She had been driving his rental car around the whole time and now it had no hubcaps and looked like it had been through a war. He did not see or hear anything from her. He just took his rental car from the place it was stashed.

One day about a month after getting the car back, we were driving to North Camden to buy drugs with these two girls from the tents. It was funny because one of the girls was just complementing Chris about how nicely he treated women. She said how most guys in the tents were verbally abusive toward them, but she could tell that Chris truly respected women. No sooner had she finished complimenting him about how he "respected women," Chris looked across the street, then got out of the car without saying a word and carrying something in his hand. He walked across the street and tapped a girl on the shoulder who was standing at the corner waiting for the light to change. When she turned around with a big smile, he unloaded a can of Super Bear Mace right into her face. It exploded from the can like a firehose and her face went from white to completely red in under a second. She then started screeching and howling. The sounds coming from this girl were horror movie–type vocalizations that echoed off the dilapidated buildings and alleyways in North Camden. I am sure she could be heard for miles.

I could not believe what I had just witnessed. Chris was the last person you would think would ever do something like that. He didn't think he just acted, and it was hilarious. The girl in the back seat immediately said, "Well, so much for respecting women." We all busted out laughing. Chris got back into the car and sped off without saying a word, which made it even funnier. As we drove away, a guy across the street yelled, "Yes!" like he had just seen the best thing in his life and the people around him were laughing, too. Meanwhile, this poor girl was in agony with Super Bear Spray covering her face. In any other town in the country, this would have been a shocking thing to see with people running to her aid, but to the people of Camden, this was great entertainment!

Unfortunately, making people laugh by spraying other people in the face with bear mace was not going to make us any money, so Chris and I found many other ways to make money. One of which was looking as homeless as possible and standing on the off-ramp of an exit for Camden with a sign that read, "homeless and hungry." I never thought I would stoop this low, but I was at the point where didn't give two shits. Chris and I started to have fun with it and made quite a bit of money. We also met a lot of people this way who really tried to help us by driving to Camden just to give us money, food, or warm clothes. However, being out on the street like that in Camden also made you visible to the cops, which gave them a reason to harass you.

MY DAD DIES WHILE I AM IN JAIL

ONE OF PEOPLE'S biggest fears when getting locked up in jail is having a loved one die while you are in there. Sadly, I got to experience that.

I was picked up by a police officer for a warrant in Camden for all these loitering in a drug zone tickets I had received. When I got in front of the judge via video court, I had racked up seventeen citations. He said, "I can see what is going on here." He was an old man named Judge Thomas. I was sure he was just going to have me plead guilty and ROR me. Previously, when I had a female visiting judge in Camden who was the sweetest judge ever, she dismissed twenty-one of these same types of tickets and just gave me a noise violation. That didn't happen this time.

Judge Thomas said, "I am sentencing you to ninety days in the county jail," and still gave me fines. My heart dropped. Three months in the Camden County Jail felt like three unbearable years to me. There was nothing I could do though. He had made up his mind and that was that. I am sure he thought he was helping me, but ninety days seemed a little excessive for walking around the place where I lived.

Regardless, I had to accept my fate and try to get through it the best way possible. I expected it to be awful and it was.

After about two months into my sentence, my mom started writing to me, which was a sign that something was wrong. Two weeks had passed when I got a letter from her that said, "A sad thing happened," then she sent another one that said, "Everything is going okay except your father died." I couldn't believe how the letter was written. I wasn't sure if I really believed it at first but knew better. It crossed my mind that maybe this was a joke, but my mom never joked around. Period.

I had always wondered how I would react to my father passing. The fact that he had lived as long as he did was amazing in itself. He had diabetes and gorged himself during every meal. He gobbled down unhealthy food and he was already way overweight. He had lost his eyesight, had heart failure, and his feet and limbs were literally eating away at themselves, so I knew it was just a matter of time. The crazy part is that I didn't feel anything when I learned he had died.

I had truly become numb to everything by this point. It was almost like everyone in my life was already dead and gone. I now know that when a child is sexually abused, especially by a parent, they lose that normal sympathy and caring that humans have for each other. I was really upset that I wasn't more upset, but it was hard to feel love for anyone because I had never been shown love. It was easier for me to love an animal than a person because animals had shown me love. I would have felt more heartbroken if my dog had died and that made me feel like I was a bad person, but considering all I had been through, I was incapable of showing love by this point.

My father wasn't a bad man, he just had no idea how to be a good father. He had a horrible anger problem and self-destructive nature that made it unbearable to be around him. But he was the closest thing I had to a loving parent and I still thought I should be more upset. I finished my final month in jail with the knowledge that my father had passed away.

After I completed my jail sentence, I was let right back out onto the streets of Camden, which was like putting a gambling addict in the middle of Las Vegas. It wasn't long before I had a needle in my arm. As bad as Camden was, there were good things that happened there occasionally. Mainly because of people who I like to think of as angels. If it wasn't for some of these good people, I would not have survived.

PAUL, JOHN, JOE RIPA, PATTY THE NURSE & OTHER ANGELS

AFTER EVERYTHING I had dealt with, I guess it would be easy for a person like me to hate everyone and everything. Surprisingly, being in Camden also showed me the best in people. Some of these people I consider angels did some of the nicest, most selfless acts I could ever have imagined and helped me keep my faith in humanity. No matter how bad things got, it always seemed like there was one bright spot shining through.

An angel that really stuck out to me was a man named Paul. Paul was this seventy-year-old very rich gay man who used to drive to New Jersey every day to go out to lunch with a young man he knew. Paul owned a bunch of local supermarkets.

One day, Paul was at a stop light in his fancy new BMW. When he pulled up beside me, he gave me money. From then on, he started to stop and give me money every time he saw me, and we started having conversations. After getting to know me, he would show up almost every day with food, money, and clothes. Paul wasn't looking for sex or recognition, he was doing it out of the kindness of his heart. Not only was he rich, he even knew President George Bush personally. He was even nominated to oversee some huge area of the government during Bush's presidency.

Paul would sometimes show up twice a day once it got cold and even came looking for me during a snowstorm to bring me gloves and a hat. He would always ask where the hell my parents were and offered to help me find a job and get a place to live if I ever got clean. He would always say that I didn't belong out here and was too nice for Camden.

I just couldn't believe that this old man was out driving in a snowstorm to make sure I had money, food, and warm clothes. There were days when I was so drug sick that I felt like giving up and killing myself, but Paul would show up right on time like he was sent from God. I know people will say, "Well, he wasn't that good of a person if he was giving you money to buy drugs," but they don't understand. I was a homeless heroin addict and being broke didn't stop me from using. Paul showed me the best that humanity has to offer. Because of his friendship, not only did I not end my own life, I never committed some horrible crime out of desperation or got shot trying to rob a drug dealer.

Another man named John also started to come see me and is the main reason I got off the street and lived to tell about it. John was a teacher at a local school. He had a big family. He wouldn't give me money, but would bring me food and clothes, then did everything in his power to get me off the street.

John was a great man. He volunteered his time at the homeless shelter and expected nothing in return. He also introduced me to Joe Ripa, the father of Kelly Ripa, the TV show host.

Joe Ripa was a local politician who also tried to help me. He was friends with John and donated his time serving the homeless people food in a soup kitchen. John told him all about me and they tried to do everything possible to get me help.

Joe called Social Services to get me Medicaid and called rehabs and friends trying to find a place for me to stay. Eventually, I got off the streets of Camden and my life was saved because of John and Joe. These were two men who didn't know me from anyone else but were willing to try to do everything possible they could to help me. These are the type of people that make our world a better place to live in.

There was a sweet nurse named Patty who came by to see me every day and gave me five dollars each time. You could see she had a kind heart just by looking at her. She wore a big cross around her neck, and you could also tell that she was a real Christian. She lived according to the Bible's instructions. Being a homeless guy on the streets of Camden, I didn't scare her one bit. One day she stopped and spoke to me as if God was sending me a message through her. The following account is one hundred percent factual...

Patty pulled her car over to speak to me one day in Camden. She said, "Andrew, I went through all kinds of horrible things as a child. I know what you have been through. My father molested me. I was a suicidal alcoholic and know what you are dealing with, but you must forgive those who hurt you. It is the only way. God wants you to be happy and have a good life" After telling me that God loves me, she gave me twenty dollars and drove off. I just sat there stunned. I had never told this lady anything about me, yet she somehow knew what to say. I still to this day don't know how she knew what she did, but it was amazing.

Another time, a young black guy pulled over and literally stopped traffic to give me money. He even yelled at another driver for only giving me a dollar, then somehow got all these other people to start giving me money.

There was a Mexican family who were obviously illegal immigrants and could not speak English, yet they pulled up in their dilapidated car to give me as much money as they could. You could tell they didn't have much, but they said, "We are in a much better situation than you and are happy to help."

Another time, this sweet black woman drove up and told me that she couldn't find her cash, but she was going to drive twenty minutes to her house, then come back to give me money. She had just gotten off work and would be driving at least forty minutes out of her way because she was so determined to help me. Amazingly, she did come back to give me money, but she also planted a big kiss on me and told me that she loved me.

I will never forget the day that a car full of young black gang members pulled up to me. I thought they were going to call me a drug addict and say horrible things to me, but they rolled down their windows and gave me money, then offered some words of advice: "Player, stay up."

I even had a police officer help me. He stopped and put me in the back of his car, then took me to get food and gave me money. Even his own partner said, "He is normally such an asshole and hates people, but there is something about you that got to him." It made her cry seeing him be nice to me. He wouldn't shake my hand or really look at me as he said 'goodbye,' but I could tell he cared.

Eventually, John the teacher took me to a methadone clinic and even paid the $100 admission fee, so that I could get in. After being at the clinic, it allowed me enough freedom that I planned to go into rehab. The methadone clinic helped me get into rehab and gave me the strength to leave Camden. Without John's care and generosity, I never would have left Camden and would probably have been trapped there for life. Again, John was just a stranger who decided to stop and help me one day for no reason other than he felt it was the right thing to do.

John is an amazing man and I am very grateful to him for everything he and all these other angels did for me. They were people from all different walks of life who had no reason to help me but did out of the kindness of their hearts. It was as if I had to hit rock bottom before I was able to see the best in all these people, which helped me believe that there truly are caring and loving people in the world.

PHILADELPHIA ANARCHISTS

I WENT TO Philadelphia with three other homeless addicts. We were on a mission to get money, so we could buy drugs. My friend Jim was getting a Western Union from his mom, but had no ID, so we had to get the money from a Western Union branch in Philadelphia for some reason.

When we arrived, this group of people gathered in protest against the government. When they saw us, they tried to rope us into their cause, but we weren't having any of it. We were trying to survive and did not have the luxury of protesting. We also saw the hypocrisy in these people right away.

Someone yelled through a loud microphone, "See these four guys here? They can relate to the struggle caused by this capitalist society and the horrible jail system." I guess they could tell we were homeless drug addicts and thought we would join their cause without a doubt.

The problem was they were protesting jail conditions, but none of them had probably ever been to jail. They were protesting this horrible capitalist society, but none of them had ever been homeless nor had they spent the night in an abando where they almost froze to death They were protesting bad health care, but none of them had ever been thrown out of a hospital or denied medicine while they were suffering. They were protesting the police, but none of them had ever been beaten by the cops or charged with a crime they didn't commit or been kicked by an officer because they'd closed their eyes.

They claimed that their parents were evil for things like pushing "their religion" on them, but they had never truly been hated by their parents or had a parent sexually abuse them for their own pleasure. The women with them said they were protesting the evil treatment of women by men in society, but they had never seen the real horrors women were facing on the streets of Camden. They were not being raped and forced to sell their bodies every day. Hearing these women cry "abuse" because their husband expected them to stay at home was literally like hearing a billionaire complain that the seats in his private jet were not comfortable enough! Maybe they were but to us this was small potatoes.

They were protesting things that they themselves had never gone through or experienced. If anyone should have been protesting, it should have been us and those girls on the streets of Camden. Not these spoiled little brats that pretended to be victims of society when they had never experienced the worst it had to offer. We wanted nothing to do with their cause.
They were playing the victim card while surrounded by people who were real victims, and this pissed us all off. It got to the point that I punched a woman in the face after she hit me, which was something I swore I would never do.

A bunch of them came up to us and said they wanted us to join their cause. They wanted us to go up on stage and speak about the evil white male Republicans and how they were the reason we were in the situation we were in. This pushy woman with them said that my friends and I were going to speak in ten minutes. Meanwhile, they offered us no help or formally introduced themselves. When she said, "Republican," my first thought was of Paul, the old man who brought me money and food daily. I remembered that he was a Republican and he didn't seem too evil to me. So I told we told this lady we were not interested in speaking.

When we told her to get lost, she went crazy. She expected us to do whatever she wanted. I explained to her that she was wrong about what she was saying. Things were not black and white. I told her, "Sure, there are bad cops, but there were also good ones who had fed me and let me go when they could have arrested me." I continued, "Yes, health care and hospitals aren't perfect and have kicked me out, but they also saved my life. I told her that capitalism has nothing to do with me being on the streets. It was a combination of my own choices and the things that happened to me when I was a child that led to my current predicament." She just stared at me, so I told her, "You said white male Republicans are evil, but one was coming down to see me on a daily basis to bring me food and money."

She started to get angry as people gathered around and listened to what I was saying. I asked her what she had done to help the home-less. She said nothing, but what she was doing right now would help them. I laughed and said, "Lady, you have no idea what you are talking about. You're probably too scared to set foot in Camden, but this "evil white Republican man" would come there every day to help me. Tell me again why I should support your cause?" People around me started to agree, then told her to stop interrupting and listen to me. This made her even angrier.

I finally asked her to tell me where she lived, and she said in Lower Merion, which is one of the richest towns in the area. I said, "You are a spoiled little brat that doesn't know the first thing about suf-fering or helping people. You claim to be helping women, but the women who really need your help are not at this protest, they are in the streets of Camden. Will you go help them?" She said nothing and flew into a crazy rage. As I turned my back to walk away, she swung her fist and punched me with all her might. Without thinking, I turned around and punched back. I hit her square in the face. The force lifted her off the ground and laid her out cold. Her boyfriend ran up and stammered, "Wh-why did you attack her?" I was sure I was going to have to beat up this loudmouth, but he did nothing, which surprised me more than anything else! It was sad and pathetic. He just yelled for the police. The same police he was just bad mouthing!

I helped her up and she looked completely shocked and confused. I said to her, "In the real world, things are very different than in mommy and daddy's basement or on the internet. If you hit people, expect to get hit back." She just stared at me without saying anything. It was like she was so stunned that she was at a complete loss for words, which had probably never once happened in her life. In her mind, she felt that she could hit anyone who disagreed with her and assumed I couldn't hit back because I was a man! Normally that would be the case, but this was different.

When the police showed up and dispersed us all, we left the area. We managed to get Jim's Western Union money and bought a boat load of cocaine in Philadelphia before going back to Camden.

CAMDEM COMES TO AN END

THANKFULLY, BECAUSE JOHN and Joe Ripa had gotten me in the methadone clinic, it gave me some freedom and mental clarity. After I got to a high enough dose, I didn't have to think about heroin all day or where I was getting my next bag. This gave me some time to try to find a rehab that would take me. The methadone clinic helped with this as well.

One night, a female cop stopped me and ran me for warrants. I ended up having a warrant and she took me to jail for the night. While I was in jail, the booking sergeant, who was a black woman, pulled me out of the twenty-man cell and said she wanted to talk to me. I had no idea exactly what was going on.

She told me I wasn't in trouble, but she needed to ask me a question. She was dying to know what had happened. She had seen the photo from my driver's license and the mugshot from when I was first arrested and said, "You were a nice looking man! What happened?"

It hurt to hear this, but she was right. I looked terrible. I hadn't showered in weeks. My hair was a mess. I was about sixty pounds underweight, my skin looked awful from the heroin, and I basically looked like death. I told her it was drugs and she said, "You really need to get help." I knew she was right about that, too.

After I got out of that jail with another $1000 fine, I seriously wanted to change my life. The counselor at the methadone clinic was a nice woman who was helpful and seemed to care. I was also taking Xanax now as well as methadone, heroin, and cocaine on a daily basis. When my routine drug test at the clinic kept coming back dirty, she said I needed a detox, then a long-term rehab. She was going to find me one, but I had to keep attending group at the clinic if I wanted to go.

The problem with attending group is that most of the people in the clinic had gotten their lives together and had a place to stay. If they took methadone, they didn't steal or use other drugs, so their family let them back in. I was still on the street and smelled horrible. Being in a little room with a group of people was embarrassing and I felt bad for them having to smell me. Surprisingly, most of the people felt bad for me and tried to help instead of complaining.

Addicts understand and sympathize with the suffering other addicts face and they can be very caring toward each other. After three weeks of going to group, my counselor came to me and said she had great news. She had gotten me into a detox in Paterson, New Jersey called Turning Point and I was leaving in two days.

Had it not been for John and Joe Ripa getting me on methadone, I never would have been able to go there. Luckily, Paul gave me enough money to survive and get enough Xanax to make the trip. I know homeless people who could not get enough drugs to be well enough to make the trip to rehab, so they just never went. This has happened hundreds of times. No addict was going to take a two-hour trip to rehab while sick.

I knew once I got to the detox that I would have to kick Xanax and methadone, which would be extremely difficult, but I was prepared to do so. I was also ready to get off the horrible streets of Camden for good. I was either going to end up dead or in jail by being out there, or worse—I would survive and just keep on suffering.

STRAIGHT & NARROW

STRAIGHT & NARROW was in Paterson, New Jersey. The detox had males and females. You basically sat around and watched movies as you came off drugs. This is really the best way to detox as you don't have the energy for much else.

When I got there, they were concerned about me having seizures coming off the Xanax because they were not giving me another benzodiazepine like Valium to wean off the Xanax. They were giving me something called phenobarbital. Also, they would not just stop the methadone. They had tried to bring people off methadone before, but because coming off methadone was so hard, they would only let you detox if you were below thirty milligrams, which was fine with me. I wanted to do one detox at a time and get myself stable first. So, they started a slow taper of methadone by reducing my dose by five milligrams a week.

Most people complained about being in the detox, but for me, it was nice to have a bed, heat, food, hot showers, and a TV to relax in front of instead of running around like a chicken with my head cut off trying to get money. My first three days there, I slept like I never slept before in my life. I literally didn't open my eyes for more than five minutes.

In Camden, I had been in a constant state of fear and stress for so long that it was great to just relax. I was grateful no matter how shitty I felt from the withdrawal. I started eating as much as I could to put weight back on. A guy named Calvin came with me from the clinic in Camden and was withdrawing from Xanax and methadone as well. We bonded pretty well as did the other people in there. There is a common bond among people who are suffering together, like how I imagine soldiers will bond during war.

People came into the detox to hold NA/AA meetings. They wanted us to see that people got their lives together and it was possible to stay clean. They all shared the same basic story. They had a really messed up childhoods and ended up drinking and smoking weed very young. All had anxiety and depression problems and just about everyone started with prescription painkillers before turning to heroin.

After that, they lost everything, stole from everyone they knew, went to jail, and almost died. When all hope seemed lost, they somehow made it to rehab, got involved with other addicts and stayed clean. It got to the point where I could almost know a person's story before they even started speaking. The only problem was that I was trying to think about staying clean but was more concerned with where in the hell I was going next.

I had been on the streets for so long and in the few days of being in this warm, clean detox, the last thing I wanted to do was go back out on the streets again. Thinking about it scared the hell out of me because I was in a bad position with no money, no ID, no clothes, and no health insurance. All I had were the clothes on my back. I had no idea how the hell I was going to get into a rehab or, if I did, what would I do afterward. I started thinking that there was no way this could work, but I really didn't want to go back to the way I was living.

I started praying because that is what someone told me to do. So, every day and night I started praying to God to help me out and, amazingly, he did. Not exactly how I wanted him to, but he still came through for me.

INTEGRITY HOUSE

THERE WAS THIS young girl who worker at Straight & Narrow named McKayla who was an awesome intake worker. In some of the places I have been, workers didn't give a damn what happened to you after detox, but this girl worked her butt off to get me and Calvin into Integrity House. She is another person I consider an Angel in my life.

I have no idea how she got us funding, but as it turned out, she got us into a short-term program at Integrity. This was the best thing that could have happened to me. I heard rumors that Integrity was this horrible place. I heard they gave "haircuts" and all these other concepts that never worked for addicts. "Haircuts" are when a bunch of people scream in your face. Things like that never helped anyone with an addiction problem. These were TC concepts.

"TC" stands for therapeutic community. Basically, they make it like a bootcamp in a TC. They yell and scream at people and let other clients become the leaders. This is one of the dumbest treatment models ever, in my opinion. This treats addiction as if it's just people behaving badly, which is over-simplifying the problem to put it mildly. TCs would tell you that you all have an incurable disease and then treat it like it was a moral deficiency. Also, letting addicts who are new in their sobriety be in charge of other addicts who are also new is a bad idea. TCs had the lowest success rate of any treatment modality. Normal treatment centers have a three to five percent success rate after a year. TCs had a one to three percent success rate after a year. If any other business on the planet had a three percent success rate, they would have been shut down years ago.

So, I went to a short-term program at Integrity House and really got something out of it. It wasn't anything like they said it would be and could not have been further from TC. It was co-ed and a nice place to be. There were a lot of employees that really cared for their clients and wanted to help. I ended up having a great counselor who seemed to want the best for me. The schedule of the day kept us busy but also allowed us time to reflect and interact with others. The only bad part was this drug court situation.

Drug court was a good idea but had terrible execution. They went about things the trial and error way and people abused it. Drug court was a separate court for drug addicts, but drug dealers and criminals used it to get out of jail. In doing so, they made the rehabs uncomfortable for anyone serious about getting help. They turned rehabs into their personal hunting grounds to prey on vulnerable people.

Criminals and dealers would tell the drug court people that they had an addiction and immediately they were admitted to drug court. Then, they would get to go to rehab instead of jail. The dealers would brag about how they were just drug dealers and laugh during the groups. They would stay in their rooms and refuse to help with chores or anything else we did. They would blast music in their rooms during groups and fight with the staff. If they were forced to sit through a group, they would laugh or sleep and snore. Their whole mentality would bring everyone down. I saw people leave the place because of how the "drug dealers" made the atmosphere.

They also went after women like they had never been around girls before. There were forty-year-old men passing notes like sixth graders. They also claimed to be these rich drug dealers but did not have money to even buy cigarettes. They were begging these people they were calling "fiends" for cigarettes and anything else. They would even go as far as trying to set up drug sales to the people in rehab.

Had they not been there, the place would have been great. Even though the dealers tried to make it as miserable as possible, I still got a lot out of Integrity. Integrity was the first place that I really accepted that I was an addict and had no way of beating this addiction on my own. Integrity also gave me hope for the future. They would try to make sure you had a support system and an aftercare plan set up before you left. They would also call courts and try to reschedule court dates and have warrants removed. They even helped me get an ID I needed so badly. It was the first treatment center that actually did things that would help addicts stay sober, not just get sober in the short term.

After short-term treatment, I entered long-term, which was only composed of men. It wasn't bad either. Long-term was like short-term because we went to groups all day, but it didn't have the distraction of the dealers trying to sleep with the girls all day and causing problems. They were there, but to a much lesser extent.

There were a couple of people I became close with while there. One was named Matt. He was a young guy who came from a nice family. We had a lot of late-night conversations and he really wanted to change his life. He told me how much he loved his family. He had a sister named Sydney that he adored. He told me how much she cared about him and how concerned she was about his addiction. I even got to go on a pass to her high school graduation with him. His parents were nice people who seemed in shock about the whole thing, but they supported him. His mother was very loving and concerned about Matt. It was bittersweet to see a family that cared so much for each other. I was happy for Matt but sad that my family was the exact opposite of his.

Matt and I tried to laugh as much as possible. We were part of a group of about six guys who hung out together and helped each other. We snuck in coffee, which was nice because we didn't have any in Integrity. It was great having a good group of guys to laugh with and talk about our experiences with, it really made time fly by.

Sadly, while writing this book, I found out that Matt had died of a drug overdose. I felt especially bad because I saw him while on a business trip to Philadelphia at a train station. We had planned to meet up, but we never did. I sometimes think that if I would have met up with him, maybe I could have talked him out of getting high.

After long-term, I went to Integrity's halfway house, which was also located in Secaucus in the same huge building as the long-term rehab. I ended up getting a job working for an energy company in Jersey City. Things were going well until around the second week I was working there, and reality gave me a slap in the face.

I went to a company party and drank alcohol. I did not realize how hard it would be to follow the rules of the halfway house and my new sober life until I was out in society. Being new in this company, I did not want to look strange as our boss put shots in our hands and I didn't want to be the only person turning him down. But drinking was against the halfway house rules and if they caught me, I would be asked to leave with nowhere to go. So, this was a huge risk for me. Even though I never considered myself an alcoholic, alcohol was not a good thing for a person in recovery to be doing. It lowers your inhibitions and could make it much more likely that you decide to use drugs while under the influence. Many addicts have relapsed by just having one drink.

My mother also started talking to me around this time. She had written letters back to me after I wrote home because John from

Camden had contacted her. I am sure he expected her to immediately talk to me when she found out I was getting help. John probably couldn't understand why she was not talking to me in the first place. I think the fact that he and Joe Ripa were helping me made her feel like she had to contact me. It was also important that I had someone sending me things. I needed things like money, cigarettes, and clothes. Sadly, that is how I looked at my parental relationship, kind of like an ATM. I wanted a normal loving relationship, but every time I tried, it just led to a letdown.

While I was in the halfway house, I ended up meeting a girl in New York City. We kissed the first day we spent together. After that, we got into a semi-relationship. She said she was falling for me faster than any man she'd met before. She jokingly said, "You are fun, sexy, confident, and smart, so there has to be something wrong with you?" I felt bad after she said that, and my conscience started going wild.

I felt I had to be honest with her. She wasn't aware of where I lived and didn't know about my past addiction problems. I know that people never tell all their secrets to someone they just met, but being an addict was something I felt she should know before falling for me. It is just a hard thing for people to understand and I feel that some people will never even give you a chance given the stigma surrounding addiction.

A couple days before New Year's Eve decided to tell her everything. I told her the truth about where I lived, my struggle with addiction, and my whole past. Amazingly, she said she was glad I told her the truth and that she was fine with everything.

At first, I felt good about being honest with someone, until New Year's Eve came. We had plans to spend the night together until she called me and said she did not want to see me anymore a couple hours before with no explanation. It hurt and I started to think honestly that it might be impossible to find a girl in my situation, which was upsetting.

After our breakup, some guys at the house noticed I was down and invited me out to dinner in Hoboken. During the meal, one of them suggested I try a website called Tinder. I didn't know what Tinder was, but he said he used it to meet girls all the time. It sounded good, but I had little faith in a dating app. We talked and laughed about his funny experiences with it throughout dinner.

I asked what they would tell girls to explain the halfway house situation and they all said, "Lie, you idiot!" They explained how they would make up what they did and everything, he said, "Come on, dude. This is just to meet women. Being all noble and honest is great in the movies, but in the real world, the truth will get you nowhere." Considering what had just happened to me, they had a point.

After that, one of them said to me, "You're smart. You should just tell chicks that you're a doctor. It's a great explanation for why you can't drink and have to leave at night. Just say you are working at the hospital." He grabbed my phone and set up a Tinder profile with my occupation as a doctor. I didn't take the whole thing too seriously and didn't even check it for over a week.

Not long after, I started getting matches with girls and one especially stuck out to me. Her name was Karen. I thought she looked very pretty and sweet. I texted her to say 'hello' and we started talking via messages at first. Eventually, we had our first phone conversation, which was hard because I was in the halfway house and people were always around, so I didn't know how to explain this.

KAREN: MY FINAL ANGEL

FROM OUR FIRST conversation, I felt bad about lying to Karen. She sounded so sweet on the phone. Of course, one of the first things she said to me was that she was in the medical profession, too, and worked in a doctor's office. I couldn't believe my luck! I did everything possible to change the subject whenever the topic of work came up.

From the start, I could tell she was very open and honest. She told me her husband had cheated on her, then left her with two kids to take care of in a bad situation. He had also not been paying their mortgage and she was losing her home. A friend had also scammed her out of most of her life savings, plus ran up thousands of dollars on her credit. She said she had not slept in three days and wasn't eating because of the stress she was going through.

After we talked for the first time, I felt it went really well and she told me it had been so long since she had smiled, laughed, or felt happy, and thanked me. I kind of felt the same way she did. There was this instant connection between us, and our conversation just flowed so naturally it was like we had known each other our whole lives.

The more we talked, the worse I felt about lying to her. I remember saying to myself, "What if she turns out to be the one and I blow it with this crazy doctor story?" I thought that maybe I should tell her, but I was sure that if I did, any chance of getting to know her was out the door. I said to myself, "After we meet, I will tell her."

I had some bad experiences with women by this point and figured they were all going to be the same. I said to myself, "She is probably lying to me, too. She probably is sleeping with a bunch of people from Tinder and just making up the story about her husband cheating on her." I believed that every woman I met would eventually hurt me because this is what my life experiences had taught me.

Finally, Karen and I met. The crazy thing was that I got caught up at the halfway house and could not leave to meet her when I said I would. This made her think that I must have been a "catfish," which is when someone uses online dating to scam people. This had happened to her before, but she didn't give up when I told her I would be late. Finally, we made it to dinner at Houlihan's in Secaucus, New Jersey.

When she showed up, she looked beautiful and I was as nervous as ever, especially because I was going to tell her that I had lied to her. I ordered a drink, then kept drinking. As the night went on, I started to like this girl even more.

Then, she started telling me about this guy she met on Tinder who lied about everything. It was a really funny story and we laughed about it, this guy made up everything. He said he was a millionaire and all this other crazy stuff. He sent her pictures of Lamborghinis and fancy houses and told her on their first date that he was going to bring piles of cash in a Louis Vuitton bag for her. But he also told her crazy things like he was really married, and his wife made him wear a dog collar and she would beat him.

After hearing about this clown who called himself "Cash Cow

Mike," I decided I would keep my secrets a little longer. If I told her I was lying about something right after talking about "CCM" as we called him, this would have made things very uncomfortable and I didn't want to be associated with CCM in any way. I just figured when she finally disappointed me as all women eventually did, it wouldn't matter anyway, which is what I thought to myself for reassurance.

Before she left, we kissed, and I really liked kissing her. She had this shy way about her, but when I looked into her eyes, I just saw goodness. There was something very special about Karen and I knew it from our first date.

After that date, we spoke every morning, afternoon, and night. As time went on, things became more stressful as we became more attached. I had to make up lies about why my car wasn't there, when I had to go to work, and where I lived. I had to lie about who the people were in the background and why she could never see my place. I also had to lie to the people at the halfway house about who I was going out with, where I was, and about drinking. The whole thing became incredibly stressful.

I kept expecting to find out that she was cheating on me or something else horrible about her, but it never came. The more I started to like her, the harder it became to tell her the truth. Especially when she started doing some of the sweetest things anyone has ever done for me.

She would bring me gifts and cards telling me how much she cared for me. One night we rented a hotel room and finally slept together. Afterwards, we stayed in each other's arms and I started to feel that I had feelings for her, which was completely foreign to me because I had never felt for another human being before.

For the first time in my life, I felt like another human being may really care for me. Eventually, we even said 'I love you' to each other.

I was very conflicted about this now and started hating myself for lying to her. I knew eventually she was going to find out that I wasn't a freaking doctor (in the medical sense of the word anyway) and I wasn't going to a hospital to work at night. I knew this would happen and the closer I got to her, the more stressed I felt.

I knew I could be very convincing when I needed to be. All my life experiences had taught me how to be an actor and I probably could have been a very good actor if someone had given me the chance. Karen had trusted me because she was a good person and had no other reason not to.

I started drinking more to calm the bad feelings I was having. That started causing more problems at the halfway house. Some people smelled it on me one night when I came home. This made things very uncomfortable there. People started spreading rumors about me drinking and such.

I was being at least three different people a day again. At the halfway house, I pretended to be an addict who was serious about my recovery. At work, I pretended to be a normal guy just doing his thing. With Karen, I was a doctor. None of the three knew about the other two. Being three different people was exhausting and having to remember all the lies was extremely difficult as usual. It was just like I was using drugs again.

One night, I decided to start a fight with Karen as a means of ending our relationship. I felt this was the best way for her to be able to move on. I forgot what it was about, but I made a big deal out of nothing and tried to end it. To my surprise, she started crying and I felt sadness and sympathy for another human being that I had never felt before, with Karen, this was a complete breakthrough for me. Humans always hurt me, and Karen didn't.

She told me that I had changed her whole life for the better. She said that when she first talked to me, she was a complete mess, but after we talked, she actually felt hopeful about her life. I knew I couldn't just leave her, but I didn't have the guts to tell her I was lying about so many aspects of my life.

After our conversation, I went into the halfway house and flipped out on the guy who told me to start this lie in the first place. I called him some horrible names and we almost got into a fist fight. I came close to getting kicked out that night.

I was really mad at myself, but I told him, "Thanks a lot for creating that Tinder profile and getting me into this situation that I can't get out of without hurting someone who doesn't deserve it." I also said some mean stuff like, "You're the reason people hate addicts."

I felt bad after saying these things. The whole situation was simply unbelievable. After all, who could ever imagine that I would meet someone like Karen on a dating app? And one that I thought was just for people who were trying to hook up. I understood why most of the guys at the place went on it and it wasn't to find love. I was sure that all the women on Tinder must be easy. While this was the wrong thing to think, I certainly never expected to meet a woman like Karen.

Back at the halfway house, things were not getting better. I didn't want to be there.

We had this one counselor named Jen who was very overweight and had never been a drug addict. She was not the best counselor. Even though she had degrees, she knew very little about addiction other than what is written in books.

She fell for the drug court guys' lies every time. She would applaud them and tell us all to be like them. Most of them never worked and would sit around the house all day. When the guys came home from work, we would love to point out things like how their chores weren't done or that they didn't make it to a meeting that day.

So, having a counselor that knew very little about addiction did not give me any incentive to talk with her about anything. Surprisingly, when a pee test came back positive for alcohol, I was able to convince her that it was because I accidentally drank cologne. I have no idea how that worked, but it did.

I will always be grateful to Integrity House for helping me, and the fact that I had to deal with some drug-dealers, fake-gangsters, and a bad counselors won't change my opinion of the place.

After dealing with Jen and the fake gangsters, I knew I wanted to leave the Half-Way House. Although, at this point, I just didn't have a place to go or enough money saved yet.

NIGHTMARE MIKE

EVENTUALLY, BECAUSE OF my drinking on the weekends, the staff finally had enough and asked me to leave. A friend named Mike who I had gotten close with while at Integrity House had left already and he offered to let me stay with him because I had helped his family buy food before. I went there but it turned into a complete nightmare.

Mike was literally smoking crack in the car when he pulled in to pick me up at Integrity House. Before we left the parking lot, he offered me a hit. He relapsed an hour after leaving Integrity. He lived with his wife and six kids in a horrible section of Jersey City.

I was feeling so down at this point that I took the hit he offered me, and it immediately set me off. Crack was never my thing because it made me too anxious. Right before Mike came to pick me up, my mother and I had been talking and I think she felt bad somewhere deep down. She started sending me money regularly. I didn't tell her why I was really leaving the halfway house. I just told her that I was ready to leave, and she offered to send money to help me find a place. Having her extra money and now smoking crack was a very bad combo.

Two things happened after I took that hit. One, I started having a terrible panic attack and two, I wanted more. Mike said we could stop and get more before we got to his house. I also asked him to stop at the liquor store as I needed some hard liquor to stop this anxiety from the crack. When I told him why I wanted the booze, he said he had a whole bottle of Xanax bars for sale. He had stolen them and would sell them to me for cheap, so I bought them and started taking them, too.

That first night, Mike and I smoked crack, drank beer, took shots of liquor, ate Xanax bars, and used heroin. The worst part is that he did this in his kitchen with his family right upstairs. They were completely broke because Mike had stolen everything. His wife Sue had a good job, but Mike convinced her to quit so that she could get this $100,000 buyout offer.

Mike had run through all that money and lost his job, too. They had lost their home and their life savings and were now living on welfare in this Section 8 house in a horrible section of Jersey City. They had almost no food and the kids were running around all crazy and out of control.

Mike had only been using drugs for less than two years, which made the amount of damage he had caused amazing. After an accident, his doctor put him on Oxycontin, and it turned him into a monster. One day, he got so desperate that he robbed a convenience store around the corner from his house while using a knife.

After getting arrested for first degree armed robbery, his older brother had paid over $100,000 to a lawyer who got Mike into drug court, which is why he was in Integrity House. He was there with me for about six months before leaving to go home. He was now on a destructive path like I had never seen before. He was facing eleven years in prison if he didn't complete drug court and even the thought of this didn't stop him.

Their family friends had started a Go–Fund me account to get Mike's wife Sue a minivan so she could take the kids to school. Mike had sold their last car for drugs. They got her this nice Honda Odyssey minivan with the donation money, and Mike basically destroyed it while driving high to buy drugs. He was driving it around on a flat tire for so long that it was on the rim now. There were sparks flying around everywhere he went. He drove it that way to the courthouse for a drug court appearance and almost got arrested again.

While at the courthouse, he spotted another minivan and decided to steal a wheel off it. While he was doing that, a woman ran out and yelled at him, so he drove off like a bat out of hell. He drove away so fast that he hit three cars trying to get away. He left the crashed minivan in the woods after that and it was eventually impounded.

This stuff obviously took its toll on Sue. She looked like she had been through a war. For some reason, she couldn't say 'no' to Mike. She was nice and sweet, but this situation made her so angry that she would yell at the kids like a tyrant. She had been through so much that she was very angry and you could see the effect this had on her.

The first night I slept there, I woke up to her yelling at the kids to get ready for school. She was literally screaming at the top of her lungs at the kids but they looked numb to it all. This became a daily occurrence, which began at 6am and lasted at least an hour and a half until the kids left for school.

After a few days of staying there and using drugs every day and night with Mike, I realized that I could not live there and keep my sanity much longer. The kids were out of control, Sue was sad and angry, and Mike was an insane addict. It was like living in an insane asylum. Mike just wanted to get high all day. He stole anything of value and was getting me into trouble. I knew this was going to end badly. It was so depressing, especially because it was getting close to Christmas. Thankfully, Karen invited me to come over and spend the holiday with her.

KAREN MY ANGEL CONTINUED

I PACKED A bag and took the train to Karen's house. I really liked her two boys. She had two adorable dogs named Lola and Tucker, two cats named Nitro and Reeses, and two turtles. I love animals and they were perfect for me. Karen had adopted all of these animals. She was an amazing mother to the boys and the animals. Once I got to Karen's, I never wanted to go back to Mike's place.

The problem was that I had been using drugs for a few weeks in a row, which meant I was dependent on the drugs now. Plus, adding Xanax to the mix took things to a different level. Xanax makes you do and say things you normally never would. It is like the crazy cousin of Klonopin.

In Kentucky at that crazy rehab, I met a guy who was in law school. One night, he went out drinking with friends drinking and they all took Xanax bars. In the morning, he woke up in a jail cell and could not remember anything. Apparently, he drove to a cell phone store and broke in, then took all the phones and filled his car up. Then, he just fell asleep in his car directly in front of the store he had just robbed. Things like this happen whether you want them to or not while on Xanax.

While at Karen's, I quickly ran out of Xanax and had to start taking more and more to help me deal with the stress of her eventually discovering my lies and everything. Eventually, things went downhill. I started to steal from Karen, and she was catching on. I felt so bad about stealing from this woman who was so great to me that I started to think about committing suicide after I got a life insurance plan and made her the benefactor.

Eventually, I had to tell her that I had a drug problem, but her response was not what I expected, she wanted to help me. She wasn't happy, but she didn't kick me out either.

My whole life, the reason I never told anyone I was in trouble with drugs was because I expected the same response I always got from my mom, which was always to get angry and tell me I was out of her life forever. Karen was the first person I have ever felt I could be honest with and she might not do that.

I still had this big problem of all the lies I told her. I was sure that when she found out everything, she would not only hate me for lying, but would end our relationship permanently. After trying unsuccessfully to stop using, I finally decided to go to detox.
This time, I wanted to go. I knew I could not keep hurting this woman by lying and stealing from her. I felt so low every day because I was hurting the woman who not only cared for me, but with whom I was in love with.

The more I got to know Karen, the more I liked her and the worse I felt. She was a great mother. She was loyal. She wasn't someone who slept around with every guy she met. She was honest, caring, kind, thoughtful, and everything else I had been looking for in a partner, but never found—until now.

I decided to go to detox and then rehab afterward. In the detox, I

had a bad withdrawal, but felt this awful depression especially because I had hurt Karen. I honestly thought that I deserved the pain
I was feeling.

Every day, I expected to hear from Karen telling me that she was
leaving and to never talk to her again. I knew she was speaking
to my mother and that was never a good thing. Karen didn't yet
know what happened and wasn't aware of the reality of my mother's
personality. She just thought she was a loving mother concerned
about her son.

I told Karen to lie to my mom about my relapse. I am sure that
Karen could not understand why I would lie. In her mind, she
probably expected that my mom would be upset that I had relapsed
but would be happy I was getting help. I knew different, but Karen
could not lie to my mom, she was an honest person.

After a few days in detox, I started to sober up and made up my
mind that I was going to tell Karen the truth. I really thought that
she was going to leave, which meant that I would have no one in my
life, but I had to tell her everything. She deserved that much at least.

I planned to do it the day I got out of the detox. With how I was
feeling, it would be the worst possible time, but this was killing me.
Karen had been so good to me and it was time to tell her the truth
and deal with the consequences.

The day I left the detox, I called Karen early that morning and asked
her to come pick me up and give me a ride to rehab. I said that I
wanted to see her and tell her something. She showed up on her
way to work and I got into her car. When she saw me, she said I
looked awful. I was so depressed from the withdrawal that I started
to tear up. I said I needed to tell her the truth and that is that I was
lying about everything. She said, "Everything?" To which I replied,
"Pretty much." Then she said something that shocked me. She said
that she already knew.

Apparently, Karen had told my mother that I had relapsed on drugs. My mother was furious and decided that because I had done this to her again, she would tell Karen every awful thing I had ever done, and I am sure she left her own contribution out of the equation. I even later found out she had told Karen that she had to leave me. Karen told my mom she would not leave and then my mom said that if she didn't leave me, that she would have to stop talking to her. My mother claimed it would be "too hard" to keep talking to Karen.

That is how my "loving mother" decided to get back at me. She was not doing this out of love, she was doing it out of hate. She was so angry that Karen wouldn't leave me that she told her it was too hard on her to speak to her anymore. She knew that would hurt me and that is the only reason she did it.

Karen would not give up on me even after everything I did. I had lied, stolen, and not been a good partner by being high all the time. Amazingly, Karen was willing to forgive me. By Karen not giving up on me, I actually started to not give up on myself. She said the most important thing to her was that I get better. My whole life people's love for me had always been conditional. My parents would love me so long as I was good. My mom would love me so long as she could abuse me. No one had ever loved me for me until Karen.

I thought Karen only loved me because she thought I was a doctor and could provide financial support. I was sure when she found out that I wasn't, that her unconditional love would be extinguished. But to my amazement, it wasn't. She really was a good person and I could tell that her love was real.

Karen started writing me letters of support and telling me how much she loved me. This must have angered my mother something fierce because she even decided to send one of her famous letters telling me how awful I was and how I was never to talk to her for three years or more. But she did one last evil thing. She sent the letter to Karen first because she knew Karen would be put in a horrible situation of having to give it to me. My mom probably hoped she would read it and change her mind and end our relationship.

My mom would never stand for another woman loving me after she told her not too and she tried hard to make sure that didn't happen. The letter really upset Karen and she was torn on whether she should even give it to me. In the end, she did.

After talking to a counselor who told me she had been in the addiction field for thirty years, she said that she had "never seen or heard of a mother writing something so awful to a son who was getting help!" I decided not to read it, which took away the power my mother had over me.

My mother's horrible letter was the greatest gift she could have given me. I was quiet about the abuse I endured from her throughout the years because it was just too shameful for me to ever talk about. Had she never written that letter, I doubt I would ever have been able to talk about it. But I did, and that letter kind of set me free. My mother's abuse was killing me and keeping me sick. Writing about it in this book and talking about it was the best thing I could have ever done to heal myself.

Karen continued to visit me every week. She brought me clothes, candy, food, and anything else I needed. She wrote me a letter every day, so I would get one every time they had mail call. It was so nice having something to look forward to everyday. She got me a bracelet with our initials crossing paths. She also bought me a necklace inscribed with the longitude and latitude of where we first met. I thought it was such a sweet thing to do and a nice reminder that I had someone who truly cared about me. She also got me this box which had 100 different things she loved about me in it.

The things she wrote to me in her letters were the nicest, sweetest things anyone has ever said to me in my whole life. There was nothing for her to gain by doing this. She knew the whole truth about me and still loved me. For the first time in my entire forty years, I felt true love from another person. All the meetings, groups, counselors, doctors, medications, drugs, and everything else were never as healing as that love.

That may not be a huge thing to some people who are used to love, but when you have never been shown love and you don't know what it is, there is this huge hole that is missing from you. You try to fill it with drugs, but it never quite works. You try to fill it with anything at all such as food, lies, gambling, sex, money, whatever, but nothing fills the place like love.

Without love, the world is a cold, dark, and decrepit place where happiness is fleeting. Love opens doors that you never thought possible just like it made the impossible for me possible, which was to get off drugs and stay off them, so I could finally be content in my own skin. The more Karen's love grew, the more I started to heal and the stronger I felt. It was like this amazing switch for me was turned on. Once I realized that someone could love me for me, with all my faults... I started to love myself a little bit more each day.

I ended up leaving rehab early instead of doing the whole six months. When I told my counselor that I was leaving, she was upset. Everyone in the place kept saying, "He's leaving to get high," and warning me, "You will be high the day you leave." None of what they said bothered me though because I knew in my heart that things would be different this time.

The last day I was there, I called Karen and told her to come get me because I was ready to come home.

When she showed up, she didn't judge me or tell me I was stupid for leaving early. She didn't tell me about all the horrible things I had done or the pain I had caused her. She didn't tell me that she would be watching my every movement and that her trust was not going to be regained for years. She didn't threaten to throw me onto the street if I relapsed. She didn't tell me what an embarrassment I was to her friends. She didn't tell me that this was the last chance I had. In fact, she said nothing negative whatsoever.

All she did, besides looking unbelievably beautiful, was give me a big hug and kissed me. Then, she told me that it was glad to have me back, and how proud she was of me, and that she loved me, and I believed her.

A NEW LIFE BEGINS

AFTER I CAME home from Integrity House I felt completely different than I had ever felt leaving a rehab. That first night I took myself to an AA meeting and Karen joined me. She said she wanted to learn everything possible so she could help me. I thought that was really sweet that even though she wasn't an addict she was willing to go to a meeting with me. This was the first time I had ever left a rehab and actually when to a meeting the day I got out.

Being home with Karen, the boys, and the animals was different too. I felt a responsibility to them that I had never felt before. Almost as if they were my own kids. I also wanted to help Karen, she had been left in a terrible situation financially and had no one to help her.

The animals were all rescues and I started to see how animals and humans are very similar and can benefit each other. There was something very healing to me about being around animals and taking care of them.

Karen and I even went to a shelter and adopted a kitten we named Ash. One thing about that shelter that stood out to me was how everyone who was looking at the animals were happy and smiling. That is when I realized that animals could help addicts. Most addicts I know love animals and I believe animals could become so healing for addicts in recovery. The love they show is unconditional and non-judgemental, addicts need this.

The second day I was home I went back to my old job and apologized to my boss for leaving. I asked him for my job back which he gave to me right away. It started to seem that as long as I had good intentions and did the right things, good things were going to happen in my life.

I also connected with a few guys that were bringing meetings into Integrity and asked them if I could go with them to meetings. I even started sharing my story in front of people at rehabs and in meetings.

My relationship with Karen became the strongest it's ever been. She was so happy to get to know the real me. We started laughing and having so much fun together. We went down to see the fireworks in Hoboken and had an amazing time. Then I took Karen out to Gettysburg, PA and we had a great time. I showed her all the battlefields and the people there were so nice there. I thought it would make a perfect spot for my rehab. We enjoyed each other's company and were like best friends as well as lovers.

I also started writing this book. While I was In Integrity House I submitted a couple pages of my writing to my counselor. Not long after, she, a worker named Melissa, and the director named Lauren encouraged me to write a book. They said my story needed to be told and that I should do it for myself and others. I will always be very appreciative for their support and encouragement.

The first month I stayed sober was really not that difficult for me. The more I shared my innermost pain the more I started to heal. As I wrote the book and got more of the pain out the better I started to fell. Days staying sober turned into weeks, weeks turned into months and months turned into years.

As I stayed sober and did the next right thing, all those problems in my past started to go away. I held a job, paid my bills, followed the law, told the truth, and helped others. I took care of all my warrants, legal matters, and paid off all my fines. I had to take my drivers license test again, but I got my drivers license back. I have taken care of all my health issues like getting teeth fixed and now have a clean bill of health. I even quit smoking cigarettes which is a miracle in itself.

Karen and I actually got our own place and I paid for it. I will never be able to repay her for all she did for me. 99.9% of people would have given up on me. I have done everything in my power to help her and have even asked her to marry me. She keeps me grounded and I am amazed by her goodness. No one is perfect and I am far from it but Karen is one person that makes me a better person by being in her presence.

I continue to strive towards my goal of helping others. While doing a radio show a man suggested I start a Gofund me page for my rehab and I have also decided to give 50% of the profits from this book to fund it. I am hoping one day a billionaire will read my book and decide to fund my mission. I want to have a rehab/animal shelter in every state. It will be a free rehab that doubles as a no kill animal shelter. The animals help the addicts and the addicts help love and take care of the animals. I will use the things I know that work to heal addicts and end this horrible crisis we have in our country that is being fought all wrong. We need to not only heal the physical drug addiction but that hole that is missing inside of them which caused them to use in the first place.

 I strongly believe there is a purpose for my life and that is to help other addicts recover from addiction. I should have died at least ten times over, but for some reason I did not. I will not stop until I make this rehab/foundation a reality and use it to save as many lives as possible. People have always told me that I could not do things. They said, "I will never get sober", they said, "I will never write a book", and someone told me "I will never start a rehab/foundation". I like it when someone tells me that I will never do something. As I write this I have been clean for multiple years and your are reading a book that I wrote. When I finish this last paragraph I am going to write to my state senator, which is the six hundred and eighth person I have written to see how they could help me start my foundation. Once an addict always an addict!

THE END

AFTERTHOUGHTS

MY LIFE WAS difficult and painful, but that is not what I want people to take from my story. I want my story to be able to help people understand addiction and why addicts are the way they are. I want it to inspire people to speak about themselves and get their suffering out. No one should ever suffer in silence!

Sexual abuse is a huge problem just like drug addiction. The more it is kept in the dark and the more we shy away from talking about it, the more damage it does.

We try to fight addiction the wrong way, in my opinion. This is not a problem that we can arrest ourselves out of. If someone is using drugs regularly, there is probably something they are trying to escape from, something they want to bury deep down. The drugs are not the problem, the thing they are trying to escape from is.

Groups like AA and NA are great and help many people, but if they don't work for you, find something else that does.

To all the good people of this world who are someone's angel, you may not know how much the little things you do means to a person until one day, they write a book and put your name in it. After all, you are the people who make this world a better place.

I see a lot of hate these days based on politics, race, and so on. The world isn't black and white. There are good and bad on all sides and I have seen both. You people I consider to be my angels all helped to save my life and I hope to repay you all someday.

To anyone who did me wrong, I forgive you! Not for you, but for me.

To Karen, you are truly my Angel. Without you, this book or my life would not be possible. I could never say an appropriate 'thank you' in words, but this book is my best attempt. Thank you for saving my life and not giving up on me when you had every reason, and everyone was telling you to. You are my hero, my inspiration, and I love you more than anything in this whole world!

To everyone else, tell someone you love them. Doing so may help save their life!

ACKNOWLEDGMENTS

I WOULD LIKE to thank all of the people that made this book possible. Especially, my Editor Melanie who's hard work and dedication went above and beyond what I expected. I would also like to thank the people who encouraged me to write about my story. They include my Therapist Amanda, My Counselor Natalie, Director of Short Term treatment at Integrity House Lauren, Turning Point Counselor Louise Alexander, Integrity House Counselor Melissa, and the many others that liked my writing and encouraged me to write a book. I would also like to thank others who helped me throughout my journey. They include Dr Edward Baruch, who went above and beyond to help me. Dr. Lawerence Blum who tried his best to help me. Igor Sturm Esquire, a great man and lawyer, who represented me for free and always stuck up for me. Attorney Steven Ames in Columbus, Ohio who saved my life and doesn't even know it. Paul Girdano, a great man who drove to hell everyday to bring me food and money when no one would. John and Joe Ripa for being great men and helping me get into treatment. Edith Palmeri who did everything possible to help me put my life back together.

ABOUT THE AUTHOR

ANDREW MANN LIVES in Bergen County, New Jersey. He lives with his fiancé, two stepchildren, two dogs (Tucker and Lola), and three cats. He is a recovering addict who spends time helping other addicts by going to rehabs and detoxes to speak about his experiences. He is also part owner of a solar company, which helps us deal with our energy crisis. He enjoys surfing, exercises, boxing, MMA, and motorcycles. He also loves to spend as much time at the beach and in the mountains as possible. He is a part-time author and enjoys reading. He hopes to have his own rehab where he can help addicts like himself overcome their addiction.

Made in the USA
Monee, IL
20 April 2022

95104073R00260